The Certainty Illusion

ALLEN LANE
an imprint of Penguin Canada,
a division of Penguin Random House Canada Limited

Canada • USA • UK • Ireland • Australia • New Zealand • India • South Africa • China

First published 2025

www.penguinrandomhouse.ca

LIBRARY AND ARCHIVES CANADA CATALOGUING IN PUBLICATION

Title: The certainty illusion : what you don't know
and why it matters / Timothy Caulfield.
Names: Caulfield, Timothy A., 1963- author.
Description: Includes index.
Identifiers: Canadiana (print) 20240385241 | Canadiana (ebook) 2024038525X |
ISBN 9780735245884 (hardcover) | ISBN 9780735245891 (EPUB)
Subjects: LCSH: Misinformation. | LCSH: Disinformation. |
LCSH: Truthfulness and falsehood. | LCSH: Fake news.
Classification: LCC HM1206 .C38 2025 | DDC 302.23—dc23

Book design by Matthew Flute
Typeset by Daniella Zanchetta
Interior illustrations © ZU_09 / Getty Images
Cover design by Matthew Flute
Cover images: (pawn) © Oleksandr Yashchuk,
(shadow) © vicentesimo, both Adobe Stock

Printed in Canada

10 9 8 7 6 5 4 3 2 1

THE CERTAINTY ILLUSION

WHAT YOU DON'T KNOW AND WHY IT MATTERS

TIMOTHY CAULFIELD

ALLEN
LANE

To science communicators everywhere.
Thank you. It's been rough.

Contents

Part II: The Goodness Illusion

Part III: The Opinion Illusion

Introduction
Adrift in a Storm

In so many ways, this *is* a glorious time for knowledge. Best. Time. Ever.

A time when much of the world has access to rigorously produced, independent, and carefully curated information on everything from our health to details about the black hole at the centre of our galaxy. There are more highly trained researchers than at any time in human history. There are more diverse voices and perspectives in the knowledge-creation mix. There is more research happening on more things. And there are more ways to access and share the knowledge produced by that research and analysis.

This is all good. And it should continue to excite and amaze us. It should give us hope that we can find rational and evidence-informed answers to our problems, both big and small. Both personal and societal.

Hold onto that hope. Hold it like it is a life preserver and you've been thrown into a cold churning sea. And know that there *is* a knowledge-informed lifeline out there. Because, holy cow, that lifeline is getting tougher and tougher to grasp (though I hope this book will help!).

The present reality: our information environment—that space where we seek, contribute to, and interact with the world's knowledge—is completely and truly f*cked. It is a tangle of lies, distortions, and rage-filled rants. This has created a massive paradox: we have more access to more knowledge than ever before and, at the same time, less and less certainty about the issues that matter to us.

Everybody knows this. It is a truism of our time. But it gets worse. The tools we use to navigate through the noise and to find some semblance of certainty—science and academic analysis, expert opinions, representations of consensus, and evidence-informed recommendations—are also being corrupted and twisted, often rendering them near useless. There are, for example, fewer transformative scientific discoveries happening now than in past decades, but research is hyped now more than ever. There are an increasing number of fake and poor-quality scientific journals that pollute both the academic literature and public discourse. It has become the norm to use bad science—and science-y language—to sell us bogus products, procedures, and policy agendas. Fake consumer reviews and ratings exploit our desire for authentic opinion. And even our search for clarity is manipulated by marketers using a manufactured and illusory certainty about what is healthy, needed, and good. We are adrift in a storm of information chaos, and we are tearing down the lighthouses.

This is a knowledge production and distribution crisis. But what if I told you the problem wasn't simply that our information ecosystem isn't providing us with reliable information? What if I told you it has become rigged to promote information chaos? What if I told you it has become incentivized to deceive us? The question is: how did we get here? And much more urgently: how do we get out of this mess?

"Well, why should we trust *you*?!"

The questioner was angry. I mean full of rage. I'd just spent an hour giving a public lecture about the spread of health misinformation. During the talk, I referred to studies published in top journals and to statements by entities like the U.S. National Institutes of Health. In response to this audience member's, um, enthusiastic inquiry, I started to refer to *more* studies to support my ideas. But he wasn't buying it.

"Science is full of shit," he continued.

This exchange happened during the post-talk scrum, so the guy was right in my face. He wasn't intimidating or scary, but his conviction and passion were a bit discombobulating. I was about to retort with even more research and go into my usual spiel about how science is a process and not a list of facts or an institution or an industry, blah, blah. But something in me broke.

"Yeah, it is," I replied wearily.

I think about this moment often. It was before the COVID-19 pandemic, a public health crisis that pushed many into the "science is full of shit" camp and, more broadly, surfaced the fragile nature of our relationship with knowledge and certainty. "Why should we trust . . . well, anyone or anything?" became one of the defining issues of our time. While the pandemic accelerated and heightened people's skepticism, the perverting incentives—clickbait-generating algorithms, hyped and fearmongering headlines, ideologically defined echo chambers, etc.— have long been baked into our knowledge production and information ecosystems. As a result, it is getting more difficult to find an authentic opinion, an uncorrupted data point, or a straightforward recommendation to inform our daily decisions. It is getting more and more difficult for us to be certain about anything, even if it feels like—and this is the illusion part—we have access to the information and opinions that should allow us to be more certain than ever before.

Of course, the search for certainty and actionable, trustworthy knowledge is a thread that runs through human history. At times we've turned to intuition, magic, superstition, religion, and philosophical rationalizing to support our ideas about the world. In 1637 René Descartes was certain in the knowledge that he existed, as summarized in his famous maxim "I think, therefore I am." But in an age where almost all human knowledge is available to anyone with a good Wi-Fi connection, a more apt maxim for this cultural moment might be "I Google, therefore I'm certain."

I've spent my entire career advocating for science and science-informed health policies. And I continue to fight against health misinformation and the ways science gets twisted in service of profit and politics. But I've also spent much of my academic career studying the forces that distort science, including commercial interests and the hype-inducing incentive structures that permeate our research institutions. I've long appreciated that the frameworks that dictate how our science is done and communicated are far from perfect. And in this book, I'll dive deep into what the evidence says—including research I've been involved in—about the profound challenges that exist with *both* the production and dissemination sides of the knowledge creation coin. Still, the process of science, when done well and with humility, remains, as Carl Sagan famously put it, a candle in the darkness—a systematic approach for building our knowledge of the world.

So, right out of the gate, I'm going to put my ways-of-knowing cards on the table: advocating for science-informed strategies or reflecting on what a body of evidence says—about nutrition, fitness, supplements, alternative medicine, mental health, climate change, sustainable agriculture, cancer therapies, vaccines, equitable and just healthcare, etc., etc.—is *still* the sensible path forward. Ask yourself this, if not science, what? Astrology? Tea leaves? Your buddy's hunches?

I am not saying that other factors are not relevant to the myriad decisions, big and small, we make as individuals and as a society. Morality. Spiritual perspectives. Historical reflection. Cultural norms. Considerations of justice and power. Artistic beauty. Relationships. Taste. Whims. Still, when we want to *know* something about our world, we turn to the process of rational and systematic inquiry—or, at least, some approximation of it. We look for evidence. And we look for evidence-informed opinion on how to do the right thing for ourselves and our communities.

This is a critical juncture. Our information environment is becoming increasingly chaotic, spun, polarized, and rage-filled. More and more of us are getting our news and the answers to our questions and concerns from sources—social media, search engines, AI-generated content, influencers—that encourage and profit from the chaos, spin, polarization, and rage. Misinformation has emerged as a global crisis, impacting health, justice issues, mental health, politics, the economy, and our understanding of science. An international survey of almost 25,000 people found that 95 percent categorized the spread of misinformation as either a major (70 percent) or minor (24 percent) threat to humanity, placing it right up there with climate change. In early 2024, the president of the European Union, Ursula von der Leyen, went so far as to suggest that disinformation, misinformation, and polarization were currently the world's most significant threats.

Our sources of information, especially social media platforms, incentivize the spread of misinformation and misleading fearmongering. The information economy is driven not by the profiling of truth but by the accumulation of attention. For example, a 2023 study from Yale University found that one reason misinformation is so endemic is that the reward structures built into social media (likes, shares, follows) "encourages users to form habits of sharing news that engages others and attracts social recognition." For many, obtaining these subtle rewards becomes the dominant motivation for online engagement, superseding truth. Even if you don't spend much time online—and worldwide the average person spends about six and a half hours a day on the internet—it is difficult not to be impacted by these distorting forces. They are in the ether.

To make matters worse, the lens through which we see our information universe has become progressively coloured by ideology and the echo chambers within which we live (and yes, to a greater or lesser extent, we all live in an echo chamber). This means that too often we only see and share information that corresponds to our preconceived beliefs. Of course, ideology has always played a role in how knowledge is created, interpreted, presented, and internalized. When Charles Darwin published the *On the Origin of Species* in 1859, his theory of evolution quickly took on religious, cultural, and ideological dimensions. Some twisted his views to justify everything from racism to imperialistic ambitions. When the life-saving smallpox vaccine was rolled out in the mid-1800s, people protested the legitimacy of the science and the way they felt large-scale vaccination infringed on their personal liberties. (Sound familiar?) More recently, political leanings—right, left, centre—have shaped perspectives on the science surrounding climate change, GMOs, nutrition, gun violence, gender, our built environment, and, yet again, the value of vaccination policies.

In today's fragmented, frenetic, and polarized media landscape, ideologically driven spin happens nearly instantaneously, shaping beliefs and public discourse. A fascinating 2023 study from the University of Pittsburgh, for example, found that political ideology strongly predicts beliefs about the effectiveness of COVID treatments for *both* the public and physicians. The researchers also note that these perspectives are predicted "by preferences for partisan cable news but not by exposure to scientific research." Think about that. Your physician's treatment advice might be more influenced by a fondness for FOX News or CNN than the available scientific evidence. Of course, we should expect—and, I would argue, the professional norms require—physicians' recommendations to be informed by the body of evidence and not the musings of a cable news host.

Despite the grim realities of our current information environment, we shouldn't forget research has consistently shown that most people do value accuracy. Most people are not nefarious bunk mongers with a disregard for the truth. We want accuracy, and we want to be accurate. We want clarity on the issues that matter to us. We want certainty. If you have any doubts about it, take a moment to consider just how much of the internet economy is built around our thirst for information and answers. Of course, having access to reliable and trustworthy information will not—at least necessarily—stop us from falling for lies and distortion, especially if those untruths align with our values and preconceived beliefs. But it seems undeniable that authentic and accurate content is foundational to our effort to cut through the noise in the search for some semblance of the truth.

The value of and need for that candle in the darkness has never been greater. This is a post-truth world. One recent analysis estimated that

20 percent of the content pushed by TikTok—a platform with over two billion users—contains misinformation. Millions of Americans believe lizard people run the government. Over 60 percent of Republicans believe the Big Lie, the falsehood spread by Trump that Biden stole the 2020 election. Twenty-five percent of Americans believe it is "probably" or "definitely" true that the FBI "organized and encouraged" the January 6 attack on the U.S. Capitol. About a quarter of people are open to the idea that the COVID vaccines have microchips in them. And a 2022 study found that 37 percent of Canadians think powerful elites are replacing native-born Canadians with immigrants who agree with their political views. (This is the racist idea known as the great replacement theory.) It isn't just dark in our information universe: it is a hurricane of lies, twisted facts, misleading marketing, and politicized rhetoric. We need something more than a candle. We need bright and trustworthy beacons, blaring sirens, and clear guideposts to see us through the storm.

This book is about those guideposts. It is about the things we turn to when we need answers, clarity, or guidance. It is about our search for certainty. It is about science. It is about our desire to do what is right (what I call goodness). And it is about the search for helpful and authentic opinions that can inform our decisions. Because here's the thing: as the search for certainty becomes an ever-increasing priority in our information-dense world, the guideposts we rely on become more valuable and, as a result, are more likely to be distorted for profit or in the service of a particular agenda. This is an era-defining information conundrum: the more we desire trustworthy information to inform our decisions, the more the information economy is incentivized to spin that information.

Paradoxes abound. As we turn to science as a guide through the dark, the motivation to use science—good, bad, distorted, or fake—as a tool not to inform but to market, persuade, and deceive is heightened, thus reducing the power and, ultimately, social value of science. Put another way: the guideposts are losing their worth—and their ability to reliably guide—precisely because they have become so valued and needed. The more we seek certainty, the harder it becomes to find.

This cynical cycle is happening throughout our knowledge universe, and the incentives built into our information economy are leading to a great flattening of knowledge. Not in the sense that there is more and more equitable access to information—which *is*, in the aggregate, a good thing. And not in that "all knowledge is relative" postmodern sense, because there are and should be some sources of knowledge that, in particular contexts, deserve more weight. (You want an aeronautical engineer designing the wings of aircraft, not a flying carpet salesperson.) It is happening in that "race to the bottom where everything is equally bad and meaningless" sense. We're inching toward a kind of knowledge-degrading Dark Age where real science, worthy goals, and valued opinions are replaced with the illusion of those things.

When someone says, "Science is full of shit," they are, alas, increasingly correct.

Okay, admittedly that is a bleak way to start a book. But I believe we are in not only a misinformation crisis but also a knowledge production crisis. A bit of bleakness-infused urgency is warranted!

Over the past few years, the problem of misinformation, disinformation, and conspiracy theories has, thankfully, started to receive a great deal of serious attention. The World Health Organization, for example, has declared that we are in an infodemic—meaning that harmful misinformation is now spreading like an infectious disease. The current head of the U.S. Food and Drug Administration, Robert Califf, has more than once noted that misinformation is contributing to the erosion of life expectancy in the U.S., which is now at its lowest in twenty-five years. And we are starting to see jurisdictions around the world consider formal policies to address the misinformation challenge.

But much less attention has been paid to what I think is a closely related and perhaps more insidious and far-reaching problem: the systematic degrading and exploitation of the methods and institutions we rely on to produce the knowledge and informed opinion that can counter the misinformation, allow us to climb out of our echo chambers, and give us a constructive path forward. If there are no guideposts we can turn to—guides that are authentic and truly science-informed—then we are left adrift in a storm of misleading noise with no hope of finding a path forward.

There is good news. All is not lost! We have more and more evidence about what is going on and what is needed to rectify the situation. This book is about those things too. Indeed, simply being aware of the ways our knowledge guideposts are twisted and exploited will go a long way to mitigating the harm they can do to us personally, to our friends and families, and to society more broadly. In the pages that follow, I will provide evidence-informed practical advice that will allow you to make the most of the guideposts we have—and, hopefully, see them a bit more clearly through the raging storm that is our information ecosystem. More broadly, I will also provide advice on what needs to be done to fix this situation and how everyone can make a difference—not only for themselves but for society more broadly and, most important, future generations.

This book is structured around three broad topics: science, goodness, and opinion. These themes may seem random. Of course, there are many topics that are relevant to any analysis of our chaotic and polarized information environment, including the state of the legacy media, the delegitimization of expertise, the growing power and influence of social media platforms, and the rise of AI, to name but a few. I'll touch on all that stuff, but I wanted to write this book in a way that mirrors how most people, me included, navigate our information environment when making decisions and forming personal perspectives. We look for scientific evidence, informed opinion, and consider what is viewed as the right thing to do. A 2020 survey from the U.S., for example, found that 81 percent of people say they rely "a lot" on their own research before they make a big decision. For 96 percent of those people, that meant diving into the online information environment.

We'll look at issues you might assume would be in a book that explores the problems with our information ecosystem—such as how science is done and communicated—but also ones that might surprise you, like the twisted facts we are told about pet food, online reviews, ancient aliens, and masculinity. Not only are these latter issues fascinating, but I also hope they will provide unique insight into the breadth and insidious nature of the problems tackled in this book. They touch almost every corner of our lives. Most of my career has been focused on health and science policy issues in the context of public health and biomedical research—so this book often leans heavily, but not exclusively, on topics that fall under the health and well-being umbrella. But know that the conclusions have relevance to almost any topic you can think of, from big challenges like climate change to the ordinary decisions we all make day-to-day.

So, to warm up, here are brief breakdowns of each theme and why they are core to the problems facing our chaotic information environment and our search for certainty.

The Science Illusion

If you are feeling nervy, walk out on the street and ask several strangers this question: do you trust science?

I appreciate that this is a less than clear question. What do I mean by *science*? What do I mean by *trust*? But give it a try. Most will get the gist of what you are asking and most—I'm guessing seven or eight out of ten—will quickly say yes. Some will say it enthusiastically. Some may equivocate after their affirmative response, noting that they don't trust Big Pharma or Big Food or elitist academics. Or some may say they trust science but not *scientists*. Some may add that there are other more spiritual forces at play too. And a few will say no. But even within the no group, I bet many of them really mean they don't like some specific science-informed conclusion about vaccines, GMOs, climate change, or another contentious topic—or maybe they don't like the people who have embraced the particular conclusion, be it a politician, a particular industry, or their annoying relative. It's not that they are rejecting the process of science outright. They are, rightly or not, mad about something or someone, and "science" got in the way.

In terms of *branding*, the Enlightenment won. Yes, as I've already noted, many people believe and pontificate about a host of evidence-free things—including the absurd notion that science doesn't work. There are people, like that audience member at my public talk, who are rightly frustrated with how science is being *represented* in the public sphere. And there are popular trends that are far from being rooted in rationality. Twenty-seven percent of Americans believe in astrology. The popularity of unproven alternative therapies continues to grow. And there are far too many high-profile political figures around the world who embrace hate-filled conspiracy theories. (There are enumerable examples of this depressing phenomenon, but let's land on U.S. congresswoman Marjorie Taylor Greene blaming Jewish space lasers for the 2021 Californian wildfires.) So, from an *operational* perspective, it feels like Enlightenment principles—that is, the embrace of reason and critical thinking—are on very shaky and rapidly eroding ground.

But, and this is key, few overtly reject the value or paramountcy of science as a way of knowing or as an explanatory narrative. (It was Jewish space *lasers*, not a Jewish Thor throwing lightning bolts that Greene blamed.) Alternative medicine works, or so it is claimed, *because* of something science-y—quantum physics, the manipulation of the microbiome, regeneration—not because of, say, the action of winged pixies. Is anyone selling a consumer product that proudly declares that it was produced using *less* science? Even those who are aware of and frustrated with the poor quality of some of the science that finds its way into public discourse aren't suggesting that we revert to a medieval knowledge base.

A 2022 international survey found that, worldwide, 90 percent of the public state that they trust science and, despite all the contentious rhetoric during the pandemic, that trust has increased over the past five years. Ninety-one percent of Canadians say "science is important to their everyday life." Other studies have the level of trust somewhat lower, but almost without exception, stated trust in science remains relatively high. Even in the hyper-polarized United States, where trust in scientists and scientific institutions has slipped, a strong majority of the public still has a favourable view. A 2023 Pew Research survey, for example, found that 73 percent have a great deal or fair amount of confidence in scientists to act in the best interest of the public. Yes, trust in scientific institutions is slipping—for the very reasons we'll explore in this book—but the reality is that few people proudly think of themselves as anti-science, even if they are increasingly concerned about the impact of science and scientific institutions.

This has made science—that candle in the darkness—a target of manipulation. Scientific verbiage permeates pop culture. It is used to market unproven and harmful products and ideas, something I call scienceploitation. There are stem-cell-infused skin creams and microbiome-enhancing weight-loss supplements. Science-y sounding but science-less fearmongering is everywhere. We're told to worry about the harms of toxins, 5G waves, chemicals, and gene-altering vaccines. Increasingly, what comes across our radar—via social media, marketing, influencers, politicians, and the popular press—isn't real science. It is the illusion of science. And studies have shown that, alas, the strategy works. Science-y language injects a veneer of credibility and believability. Too often, our public discourse is driven not by evidence but by this upside-down version of evidence.

As we'll see in the pages that follow, the problem of illusory science extends far beyond deceptive marketing and political posturing. The frameworks, norms, and incentives built into our research institutions and academic publishing practices are fuelling the growth of a vast fake science industry. Predatory academic journals filled with useless and, too often, fraudulent research pollute the scientific literature and the news media. Overhyped research, which is often a by-product of the pressure to perform scientists feel from their institutions, can lead to distortions that take decades to rectify. In reality, science is hard and messy and with only a few striking exceptions moves forward slowly and iteratively because of the work of thousands of academics grinding out data that informs pieces of a complex puzzle. For example, successful animal studies almost never translate into successful clinical trials. And it is rare for an intervention that has made it to the stage of a clinical trial to become a widely used healthcare intervention. The next time you hear about an exciting biomedical study in the media, remember that only about 10 percent of clinical trials will result in a clinical application—and its efficacy will likely be much less impressive than originally promised. Still, it feels like almost every new scientific discovery is presented to the public as a revolutionizing, paradigm-shifting breakthrough. The reality: it's not.

Using both obvious and unexpected illustrations, I will start by making the case that we urgently need to address the predatory practices and incentives structures that allow illusory science to not only spread but to thrive. The growing attention on the problem of misinformation and the potential erosion of public trust should be viewed as an opportunity. Let's get this right. So much is at stake. Well done and trustworthy science is the essential guidepost for our chaotic information ecosystem. Without it, we are lost.

The Goodness Illusion

Our information environment is noisy. Insanely noisy. It has been estimated that by 2025, 463 exabytes of data will be created each day. That is a monstrously huge number, roughly equal to 212,765,957 DVDs. Approximately 4.8 billion people are on social media. Approximately two million academic articles are published every year. There are 8.5 billion Google searches and thousands of news articles published every day. Over five hundred hours of content is uploaded to YouTube every minute. And many of us check our phones hundreds of times each day.

We are bombarded with information through our smartphones, tablets, TV shows, and internet searches. It has been estimated that humans process about seventy-four gigabytes of information every single day.

Neuroscientists Sabine Heim and Andreas Keil have noted that just five hundred years ago, "74 GB of information would be what a highly educated person consumed in a lifetime, through books and stories."

It would be impossible, obviously, to pay attention to and meaningfully engage with all the information that we encounter every day. And being constantly faced with information-rich choices can be stressful. It makes feeling certain about anything difficult. In such an environment, guideposts that promise a shortcut to decision-making—a path past the information chaos—can be tremendously alluring and influential, especially if they play to our desire to do what is right for ourselves, our community, and the world. Enter what I call the goodness illusion.

We all have our own definition of what is good, and I will make no attempt in this book to tell you what that ought to be, because I can't, shouldn't, and that isn't the point. The point is that the version of good being promised by, for example, entities marketing products, influencers creating brands, or commentators and politicians pushing agendas is often misleading or, worse, an outright lie. Deceptive goodness-sounding slogans are rolled out to exploit our desire to do good and to feel certain that we've made the right choice. I recognize that *goodness* is a loaded word, touching on virtue, social norms, and morality. But I think it captures much of what is going on in our information environment. The goodness illusion is a messaging strategy designed to make us think (but don't think *too much*, please) that a particular choice fits with what is viewed as the right thing. In a narrow sense, it can be applied to choices we make about individual health; in a broader sense, it can be applied to choices we make that are related to, say, the environment or constructive social change. The goodness illusion offers the seductive promise of a clear, certain, and allegedly evidence-informed way through our chaotic information environment.

To be clear, I'm not talking about the closely related ideas of conspicuous consumption and virtue signalling. There is a large and interesting literature that illustrates how people (all of us) make choices in part because we want the world to see us in a certain way, including as someone who is and does good. A classic economic study on this point, published in 2011, found that consumers were willing to pay thousands more for an ugly Prius—yup, the first version of which certainly wasn't going to win any beauty contests—simply to signal, through an act the authors called conspicuous conservation, their environmental bona fides. This particular form of conspicuous consumption came to be known as the "Prius effect." Virtue signalling—which, rightly or not, is now viewed by most as an insult meant to highlight performative posturing—is also about representing yourself to others. While these concepts are relevant to the goodness illusion phenomenon I'm exploring here, I'm more interested in a straightforward critique of the claims behind the goodness slogans.

The best and most obvious example of the goodness illusion, and the one I'll start with in this section of the book, is the growing use of health halos. Terms like *natural, organic, non-GMO,* and *locally grown* are meant to be shorthand for "this is good and virtuous." But, as we will see, the available science often paints a more nuanced and complex picture. The truisms behind the slogans are, it turns out, not so true. An exploration of the goodness illusion is also an opportunity to see how a strong desire for a particular outcome—that is, doing what is perceived as good—can skew the conduct and representation of the relevant research. When people believe science is being done in service of a righteous goal, like allowing people to live a healthier life, misleading biases and distortions can creep into the work itself, how it is published, and how it's represented in pop culture.

Not only is goodness-illusion-filled messaging—about GMOs, organic food, chemical-free products, etc., etc.—deceptive and exploitive, but it also has an adverse impact on the very health and social concerns that the claims purport to address. They aren't making us healthier. They probably aren't helping the environment. And they are likely hurting public discourse and distracting us from taking science-informed actions that can make a genuine difference. Goodness? Not so much.

The Opinion Illusion

Somewhere in my house is a first edition of the 1977 edition of *The Book of Lists*. It was a gift from Santa, I believe. I've read it cover to cover, many times. And I have all the pre-internet updates. I have always been obsessed with lists, especially a best of. Most iconic NCAA football stadiums. Top hundred albums of all time. The core *Star Wars* movies ranked (correct answer: 5, 4, 7, 8, 6, 3, 9, 2, 1). The popular movie review website IMDb has a constantly updated chart with the top 250 movies of all time as rated by viewers. I check it regularly, as if it is the stock market and I have a big investment in play.

I'm not sure why I have this obsession. Perhaps it's due to my love of factoids? Or maybe I believe the lists have value and are authentic and therefore evidence of something? As we'll see, I'd be wrong about that. Once I got in an argument with a good friend about the Beatles. His position was that their influence is often overrated. (Dear Good Friend, this position remains absurd!) I spent the weekend compiling and triangulating a vast quantity of best-of lists to prove how wrong he was. Was I hoping the sheer weight of online opinion would somehow win the day for me? If so, it didn't work. His opinion remained unchanged. My brothers have spent a lifetime putting up with similar list-centric rebuttals. I am ranked as the most annoying brother.

It turns out I'm not the only one who likes to lean on rankings to lend credence to their ideas. There is now a massive opinion economy that influences almost every corner of our decision-making lives. You can't escape online lists, rankings, and reviews. They exist for absolutely everything: appliances, computers, phones, cars, fashion, physicians, restaurants, vacations, apps, podcasts, movies, music, etc. Studies have shown that people expect reviews to be readily available—and they usually are—and most of us rely on them heavily. People trust online reviews more than the opinions of experts or even friends and family. They play to our belief in the wisdom of crowds and, at the same time, the powerful sway of anecdotal evidence and the views and experiences of "someone like you." But more than anything, the review and opinion economy is built on our strong need for a clear guidepost to shepherd us through the noise. Simply put, those five-star rankings rule.

But as with science and goodness, the persuasive force of rankings and reviews has made them a target of manipulation—and this has largely robbed them of the very characteristics that make them valuable to us, namely authenticity and reliability. In this section of the book, we will see that a shocking percentage of online reviews are fake or manipulated. Not only is this harmful to consumers, but it also hurts the world economy. It has been estimated that fake online reviews influence almost a billion dollars of yearly online spending in the U.S. alone. On the global scale, trillion of dollars are in play.

In this section, we will dig into the surprising, fascinating, and frustrating world of fake reviews and fake opinions. We will look at why and how they have so much influence and what we can do to avoid their pull. I will also provide guidance on how to find reliable advice.

The guideposts we all need to navigate through the noise, spin, and lies that fill our information environment are being eroded. Worse, they are also being co-opted—for profit, political gain, or to create informational chaos. Too often the science we turn to or hear about isn't real. It is just the illusion of science. Too often our desire to do what is good is leveraged to mislead. And too often the opinions we rely on are simply fake.

In a world where information has become the cornerstone of the world economy, health systems, and democratic decision-making, we need a fix. Fast. I hope this book helps to provide a path forward.

I don't know who that raged-filled guy was who told me science is full of shit. And I can't remember how exactly our interaction ended. I think he walked away frustrated with my response and the general state of the universe. But I hope you are out there. This book is also for you.

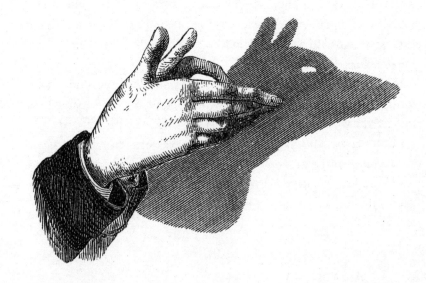

PART I
THE
SCIENCE
ILLUSION

A Quantum Leap!

Why did *quantum* become a thing? There is quantum homeopathy, quantum reiki, quantum reflexology slippers, quantum coaching, quantum beauty spray, quantum acupuncture, quantum water (which will "fully activate the body's cellular transport channels"), quantum yoga (because, as one yogi explains, "quantum physics has made incredible discoveries that echo the ancient insights of yoga"), quantum eyeglasses, quantum detoxes, quantum DNA healing, and, a personal favourite, anti-5G quantum pendants.

This last one is a product designed to protect people against all the completely fictitious harm of 5G waves, such as causing the spread of COVID-19. The pendants are about the size of a silver dollar, and—here's the kicker—it turns out that they emit low levels of radiation. In 2021, the Authority for Nuclear Safety and Radiation Protection in the Netherlands was concerned enough to issue a warning to consumers to "stop wearing them, to store them away safely and await instructions on how to return them."

There is also the Quantum Touch, which is a natural method of "raising our own innate, energetic, vibrational field to a higher level to promote health and wellness" because, as one clinic website explains, "love is energy and vibrations." If those vibrations are really doing their thing, you could take it to the next level with Quantum Intimacy, which allows for the formation of a "long-lasting quantum field of 'love and intimacy' in harmony & resonance with our beloved."

There is also an entire emerging field called quantum medicine based on quantum physics, "which recognizes the wave-particle duality"—at least, that is, according to a website selling an assortment of quantum-ish products such a diagnostic machine that analyzes "human bio-frequencies based on a model of non-linear systems." And if you really want to walk the quantum path, you can attend Quantum University where you can get a bachelor's, master's, or PhD in holistic, natural, or integrative medicine by studying things like quantum physics (obviously), homeopathy, aromatherapy, and auriculotherapy (based on the idea that the ear represents your entire body, which it doesn't).

Actor and wellness guru Gwyneth Paltrow once infamously declared that water (yes, she meant H2O) has feelings (yes, she meant emotions). She suggested that just saying nasty things to water causes its molecular structure to change in a measurable way. Even writing a negative word (apparently water understands English) on a jar filled with water can have an impact at the molecular level. Was this amazing phenomenon explained by reference to some supernatural or spiritual force? Nope. It's science! Human negativity has this impact on non-living chemical structures because, well, quantum physics.

I'm not going to waste your time debunking the use of the word *quantum* in the above examples other than to say that they are all total nonsense, inaccurate, and not grounded in good science. Quantum physics involves the study of energy and matter at the atomic and subatomic level. It is, no doubt, extremely complex. As Richard Feynman, the late Nobel laureate in physics, famously said, "If you think you understand quantum mechanics, you don't understand quantum mechanics." It is a field of study filled with a lot of mind-bending phenomena. The Heisenberg uncertainty principle, for example, states that we cannot know the position and the momentum of a particle with certainty. The more accurately we know one of these values, the less accurately we know the other. Then there's that stuff about Schrödinger's cat— the idea that something can be two things at once (a cat both alive and dead in a box) until it is observed.

Feel like you don't fully understand? Me neither. That's why I reached out to professor Mark Freeman, a physicist and friend at the University of Alberta. He studies and teaches quantum physics, so I was curious if he has ever—even once—seen the word *quantum* used accurately in association with a health product. "I have not. And I doubt I ever will in my lifetime" was his comprehensive and damning assessment.

The point here is that the word *quantum* is being used not because it is scientifically relevant to the product or service being sold, but because it is difficult to understand, and it sounds incredibly science-y. Science-y sells. It injects credibility. It makes the magical seem more legitimate. Professor Freeman agrees: "It just seems to be one of the best names to call anything during the present time. It suggests things that are profound and mysterious."

Indeed, the use of *quantum* is so uniformly misleading that I can safely say that if you see that word used to explain a product or procedure, you can assume it is pseudoscientific nonsense and that a fraudster is lurking nearby. As the Italian physicist Enrico Gazzola nicely summarizes in a 2019 piece, quantum physics "does not support claims concerning mystical energies, healing frequencies, energetic patterns in the body, creating thoughts, universal consciousness, or the existence of the soul." The word is simply being used, Gazzola argues, to sell "quantum-inspired woo" by "stealing and distorting concepts from science in order to produce fake scientific foundations to absurd claims."

Scienceploitation

The idea of using scientific-sounding language to sell stuff isn't new. In the eighteenth and nineteenth centuries, magnetism and electricity got a lot of coverage in the popular press. These topics were that era's cutting-edge science. And, no surprise, this led to the marketing of health products that leveraged this excitement. There were magnetic and electric devices that could cure, allegedly, almost anything from general malaise to erectile dysfunction. Some of these products are still around today. (Note: do not waste your money on a belt with electrodes that attach to your private bits—unless you are into that kind of thing.) Magnetism and electricity were also used, as quantum physics is today, to explain and legitimize supernatural and pseudo-scientific phenomena. In 1779, for example, the German physician Franz Mesmer introduced the concept of animal magnetism. He believed there was a universal magnetic fluid that was key to the maintenance of health. Mesmer used magnets to manipulate and direct the magnetic fluid in the treatment of disease. Despite the complete lack of evidence to support these beliefs—then or now—there are still many magnetic gadgets available that use science-y sounding justifications similar to those put forward by Mesmer over three hundred years ago, such as the idea that magnets can influence (they can't) the "life force energy" (not a thing, at least from a scientific perspective) that flows through our body.

Perhaps the most dramatic and outrageous use of science-y language to sell stuff happened in the early twentieth century when the phenomenon of radioactivity was first being explored. The public was fascinated by the mysterious properties of the element radium and the research done by pioneers like Marie Curie. Predictably, this led to the marketing of a host of radioactive products, including radioactive bread, chocolate, jewellery (which, as noted above, is *still* popular), soap, jockstraps (the scrotal "Radiendocrinator"), and even condoms.

The selling point, of course, was the interest in the emerging science and the vague notion that being around or, even, consuming radiation would provide zip and protect you from harm. The radium condoms, for example, were sold with the promise that they would prevent contagious diseases. Radium water is another notorious radioactive product from this time. Curiously, radium water was also pitched as "natural" and pure. "Avoid overwork, all other excesses, eat fresh natural foods, breathe fresh air, and drink plenty of fresh, invigorating, natural radioactive water from the Radium-Spa" was the lifestyle advice from a 1920s advertisement. This mix of cutting-edge science and "natural" is an odd conceptual stew that we'll revisit later in this book.

Some companies used the term for products with no actual radium or radioactivity simply because it was such a hot topic and they wanted to capitalize on the buzz. However, it is important to remember that many of these products were literally radioactive. There were products that were so radioactive they killed people. In 1932, a renowned golfer, Eben Byers, died after consuming over 1,400 bottles of the popular Radithor radioactive water. A *Wall Street Journal* article about his death noted that "the radium water worked fine until his jaw fell off."

This example may seem extreme, and Eben Byers a naive fool. But this cycle, which I call scienceploitation, happens again and again and again. It goes like this: there is an exciting scientific development, this generates a bunch of pop culture noise, hucksters see a market opportunity, the market is flooded with products and procedures that riff on the new science, and, inevitably, people get hurt and public discourse is confused. I've been doing scholarship on science and health policy for thirty years. I've seen the scienceploitation cycle play out with genetics, stem cells, nanotechnology, neuroscience, precision medicine, the microbiome, cannabis, psychedelics, and, yep, quantum physics. If you've received stem cell therapy for a bad knee, you may be Eben-Byers-ing your health decisions. If you have done a cleanse or taken IV supplement therapy to enhance your microbiome, you were

Eben-Byers-ing. Using direct-to-consumer genetic testing to personalize your dating, exercise, or supplement consumption? Eben-Byers-ing.

Of course, the reason science-y language is used to sell products and brands is that, alas, the strategy works. A 2013 study found that when messaging includes terminology that presents "the trappings of science," it can create the illusion of scientific authority, even if the topic is about some patently pseudoscientific topic, like ghosts or haunted houses. As the author of a 2023 study on science-y marketing noted, "When people see or hear scientific claims made in vague terms, they later misremember them in more definitive terms." Put another way, science-y jargon helps to create an illusion of certainty. Other research, such as several studies examining skincare and beauty product advertising, found that science-y language is persuasive because it creates a veneer of credibility and, paradoxically, takes advantage of the terminology's opacity. In other words, we don't know what this stuff means, but it sounds impressive! Indeed, the power of science-y language cuts across cultures and even educational backgrounds. A study from 2004 looking at the marketing of unproven health products found, again, that science-y language "increased the message persuasiveness," and surprisingly, it didn't matter if the language was attributed to a credible authority—such as a specific study—or was just stand-alone scientific verbiage. It also didn't matter if the receiver of the message was a science or nonscience major in university or a graduate or undergraduate student. Science-y language seems capable of working its magic on all of us just by being science-y.

There are interesting complexities and contradictions to the use of scientific jargon. It can also turn people off. A 2020 study from the Ohio State University found that the presence of scientific verbiage can cause nonexperts to engage less with the text. The more jargon dense a text, the less interested readers will be, even if lay definitions for the scientific language are provided. If you want the public to buy into an important public health message or embrace a new cancer screening program or to simply appreciate the significance of a scientific advance, an audience that is disengaged and less interested is a very bad thing.

As a result of this kind of research, there has been growing pressure on the scientific community to simplify its language and make its work more readable and relatable. Biomedical journals now often include lay summaries of major studies and easily understandable infographics that can be shared on social media. All sensible and commendable. One of my favourite examples of this trend is a scientific journal that has reviewers between the ages of eight and fifteen. The journal, *Frontiers for Young Minds*, seeks to make complex, academic topics— like climate change, mRNA vaccines, and neurology—more accessible for all. The papers are written by leading scientists, including Nobel Prize winners, and then reviewed by science-minded youth who provide editorial critiques, like this blunt appraisal by an eleven-year-old of a paper on brain science: "I didn't understand anything that you said." Ouch. The process forces academics to punt the jargon and focus on making their work understandable.

But when science-y language is used in pop culture more broadly, especially in the marketing space, the goal is not to enhance comprehension or engagement. The *point* is impenetrability and syntactical razzle-dazzle. It is the mere presence of science-y language that matters, as if the terms are word celebrities providing endorsements. You recognize them—*stem cells, microbiome, quantum*—and you relate them to the world of credible science, even if you have no or only a vague idea of what they mean. "This product endorsed by the word *quantum!*"

It is no surprise, then, that we are completely awash in the science-y. And thanks to social media and the internet, the bombardment by science-y sounding, but science-free, content is near constant. During the COVID pandemic, for example, I worked with my research team at the University of Alberta to explore how the concept of immune boosting was portrayed on Instagram. The phrase *immune boosting*— which is pretty science-y on its own—is almost always a sign of a potential scam. You can't "boost" your immune system in the way that is often promised and nor would you want to—that's often how autoimmune diseases play out! For one week early in the pandemic, we did a content analysis of all the top posts associated with immune boost hashtags. What our study found was that scientific-sounding language, such as evidence-free references to the microbiome, was frequently used to push the evidence-less concept of immune boosting.

When science-y language is used in this manner, it can do real harm, such as encouraging the sale of ineffective and potentially harmful health products. A 2019 study by a research collaborator of mine, professor Bernie Garrett from the University of British Columbia, sought to explore why and how people engage with online health scams. Garrett and his colleagues found that reference to alleged scientific breakthroughs and the use of science-y language facilitated interest with the content. That is, the participants in the research admitted that the science-y language drew them in. It made the scam more believable.

Perhaps the most striking use of misleading scientific rhetoric is in the marketing of alternative medicine. As noted above, the word *quantum* is often used to push unproven therapy. This can get extreme. Reiki is a scientifically implausible alternative medicine practice that involves waving hands—no touching—over people to realign their life force energy. Some reiki practitioners even claim that quantum physics explains their ability to provide treatment over great distances— the patient at home on their sofa and the reiki master sending healing vibes while lounging on a sunny beach in the Caribbean, for example. Distance reiki works, or so those marketing the idea want us to believe, because "quantum entanglement" dictates that two particles can impact each other over great distances. This claim is so ludicrous—I mean, does a distance reiki master need to aim the curative waves or do they just find the patient?—that, again, there is no need to waste time with a quantum debunk. But there are other ubiquitous uses of science-y language that can appear more credible to many and that, as a result, do significant harm to the public, patients, and trust in science.

High Tech Hogwash

Since the late 1990s, I've worked closely with the international stem cell research community investigating a host of associated policy issues. I have studied both the marketing of unproven therapies and how stem cell science is represented in the public sphere. Stem cells are an incredibly exciting area of biomedical research with potential for significant clinical benefits. As a result, the field has, for decades, received considerable attention from the popular press. Stem cell research has also been a controversial subject. Especially in the early days when it was dominated by research involving human embryos, it was often front-page news. President George W. Bush's first televised address to the nation, on August 9, 2001, wasn't about terrorism or the economy. It was about stem cells. Since then, the phrase *stem cells* has continued to permeate popular culture. It has made its way into a host of TV shows, movies, novels, comic books, songs, etc., etc., and become synonymous with innovative, cutting edge, and even hope.

As a result, the language of stem cell research, and its close cousin regenerative medicine, is now a favourite tool for those marketing unproven health therapies and products. This is classic science-ploitation: excitement about an area of science followed by profiteers exploiting the media coverage and, as we will see, public harm. A few years ago, I worked with my colleagues Amy Zarzeczny and Blake Murdoch to investigate how alternative medicine practitioners, such as naturopaths, chiropractors, acupuncturists, and homeopaths, used the language of stem cells. We examined nearly 250 alternative medicine clinic websites and found they alleged to offer a host of stem-cell-based therapies for everything from pain to lung diseases to sexual enhancement to anti-aging. The stem cells came from—again, allegedly—a range of sources, including bone marrow, umbilical cord blood, and apples.

Some important context is needed here. How many stem cell therapies do you think are well established, have good supportive data, and can be justifiably offered to the public as definitively effective? Almost none. That's right, despite all the headlines and the ubiquity of stem-cell-y language in popular culture, there are very few actual stem cell therapies that are ready for the clinic. As noted on the website of the International Society for Stem Cell Research (www.ISSCR.org)—which, it is important to emphasize, is the main organization for the legitimate stem cell research community—"the range of diseases for which there are proven treatments based on stem cells is still extremely small." Basically, the existing body of evidence supports the use of stem cell therapies for some disorders of the blood and immune system, usually in the form of a highly invasive bone marrow transplant, and to help with some tissue-specific transplantations, such as those involving skin and corneas. Everything else, despite what you might see in the relevant marketing, is "still experimental" and "has not yet been shown [to be] safe or that it will work," as noted by the ISSCR.

But our study of alternative medicine providers found that this scientific reality was almost completely absent from the clinic websites. In fact, only 19 percent of the websites had any statement about the limitations of the available evidence. A remarkable and depressing conclusion when you consider that virtually all the services offered by these clinics are unproven and of unknown safety. The clinics are simply deploying a scienceploitation strategy to make their services seem more authentic.

(I always find it ironic when practitioners who are rooted in magical thinking reach for trail-blazing science to create a veneer of credibility. Naturopaths, for example, reject or ignore scientific critiques that expose the pseudoscientific foundations of naturopathy, such as the idea that there is a vitalistic life force that underpins a natural healing power. But how do naturopaths feel about science-y language that can help them move product? Bring it on!)

Obviously, alternative medicine practitioners are not the only ones using fake science for profit. The marketing language used by the skincare, anti-aging, and beauty industries is, for instance, rife with technobabble and scientific-sounding gobbledygook. There's a "genome" shampoo that promises to regenerate keratin fibre. There's a "nano" shampoo that has "micro keratin capsules." There's a "microbiome" shampoo that contains probiotics and probiotic ferments to help detox and hydrate. And there's a stem cell age-defying shampoo, because, well, of course there is. An anti-aging toothpaste (great, now I need to worry about the age of my teeth?) uses "biomimetic science" and has "senolytic properties" to give me a "youthful and beautiful smile day after day."

Few consumer goods have such a fraught relationship with scientific phraseology as skincare products. Our eternal desire to maintain a youthful glow has resulted in an endless stream of claims about skincare "formulas," the "science of beauty," and new rejuvenating chemicals and procedures. Indeed, you can find a skincare product for almost every highly publicized scientific obsession from the last few hundred years.

In the nineteenth century, the signs of physical aging were becoming more widely understood to be a physiological phenomenon and not one of moral failing. (Okay, it is still often implicitly positioned, especially for women, as a moral failing.) Scientific language, such as that of regeneration, was used to move anti-aging efforts from being viewed as frivolous to the centre of public discourse. Aging was increasingly positioned as being in the realm of science and, well, science-y marketable products. It helped that interest was growing in anti-aging technologies and a greater understanding of the relevant biology—right when there were expanding avenues for getting this information to the public. The rise in print media allowed those marketing anti-aging products to, as professor Jessica Clark from Brock University wrote in her 2017 analysis of the history of beauty products in the late nineteenth century, lay "bare the world of anti-aging technology" and distance this new era of beauty from the "deleterious paints and powders" of the recent past. In other words, science-y language was used to legitimize and normalize. It's not vanity, people. It's science! Enter electric and magnetic skincare products and, of course, radioactive skin cream. This last product, which came out in 1933, was advertised as a "scientific beauty product," and yep, it contained actual radium and promised to firm skin, reduce fat, and smooth wrinkles.

But more than any other recent scientific development, the language and public portrayals of stem cells fit the "fountain of youth" narratives that emanate from the cosmetic and anti-aging sectors. Stem cells have been presented as capable of enabling "regeneration" and "regrowth"—ideal messaging for an industry built on those promissory pillars. A few years ago, I worked with Christen Rachul, a linguist at the University of Manitoba, and Ivona Percec, a plastic surgeon and professor at the University of Pennsylvania School of Medicine, to analyze how the skincare and anti-aging industry used the language of stem cells. Our findings, which were hardly surprising, powerfully illustrate the Grand-Canyon-wide gap between the actual, still-evolving stem cell science and how stem cell science was used to market products. Most of the stem-cell-based products we reviewed were presented as ready for public use. This was not true when we did the study in 2015, and it is still not true now. Few of the products substantiated the claims with scientific evidence, and even fewer mentioned any risks or limitations associated with stem cell science. The language of the marketing was peak scienceploitation, with frequent references to how aging causes our stem cells to perform poorly and how their products—many of which allegedly contain plant stem cells—slow aging, improve the function of our existing stem cells, or promote the growth of new skin cells.

I've witnessed, first-hand, some bizarre stem cell skincare procedures and the power of this science-y lingo to sway perceptions.

For example, I chatted with a woman while she was getting apple stem cells injected into her skin at a fancy beautician establishment in midtown Manhattan. The vibe there was a mash-up of medical clinic and high-end spa. There was a dental-office-like reclining chair and loads of vaguely scientific-looking machinery. Microneedle punctures were used to infuse her entire face and neck with, supposedly, apple stem cells. It didn't look like the client found the process painful, but there was enough blood and buzzing and skin puff that I found it hard to watch. Hungarian apples are the best, the beautician told me. The client—a woman who appeared far too young to be worried about aging, but perhaps it's those Hungarian apples at work—said she loved the procedure. She was more than willing to pay the not insignificant cost. Her skin felt tighter, she said. And she was excited about the stem cell technology. Both the client and the beautician appeared completely convinced of the efficacy, and my gentle skeptical commentary moved them not one iota. It is hard to compete with scienceploitation, especially when it is packaged with placebo-inducing, apple-infused theatre.

Science-y language has substantial power to create the illusion of credibility—and to sway us toward a decision we feel more certain about. Microbiome, nanotechnology, genomics, organoid, regenerative, stem cells, telomeres, and quantum, quantum, quantum. These words are everywhere. But don't be fooled. The best strategy to deploy is to be aware of the scienceploitation strategy and to remain highly skeptical of overly science-y language used to market products, brands, or personal agendas, especially if no easily understandable explanation is provided. If someone is using science-y lingo they know you probably don't fully understand, the goal is not to inform but to impress, confuse, or manipulate.

It's Science!

Sometimes the marketing spin doesn't refer to a specific area of science or emerging research. Some marketing just leans heavily on *science*: "Science says this works!" "Scientifically proven!" Michelle Wong, science educator and cosmetic chemist, calls the practice "science washing." It is the deployment of science in a way that suggests we should accept it because science is always virtuous and powerful and right.

Of course, this isn't the case at all. First, science isn't a legitimizing badge of honour that can be attached to anything. There must be actual relevant research that applies to the claims being made. As Wong notes, "Science only works when it's relevant, when the right bits are used, and with recognition of its limits."

"We encourage consumers to 'trust science' and 'trust experts.' So, when a product comes along that has a lot of the trappings of science, like graphs and numbers and technical language, it can give the impression that it's a lot more scientific than it actually is," Wong tells me. And like scienceploitation generally, "it's a very clever marketing strategy that's usually intentionally confusing for consumers."

Second, science isn't always a positive social force or, for that matter, done well. This marketing strategy is closely related to the concept of scientism, which is the inappropriately deferential attitude to science and the problematic use of science as something that is inherently good. But, as noted by the philosopher Susan Haack, "science is by no means a perfectly good thing. On the contrary, like all human enterprises, science is ineradicably fallible and imperfect. At best its progress is ragged, uneven, and unpredictable."

To avoid falling for the scientism trap, Haack suggests watching for the use of the words *science, scientific, scientifically, scientist,* and so on, honorifically, "as generic terms of epistemic praise." Ask yourself if there is actual scientific data that is relevant. Simply declaring that "science says the Earth is flat" doesn't mean it's flat. You need to prove it with actual science.

Science-y and Scary

In 2013, on a popular national CBC radio show, I publicly debated Dr. William Davis about the health and weight loss value of a gluten-free diet. Davis is the author of the international bestselling book *Wheat Belly*, a publication that has had a massive impact on the diet and wellness industries. His claims, coupled with endorsements of gluten-free diets by celebrities like Gwyneth Paltrow and Miley Cyrus, drove the rise of the gluten-free trend. For a few years, it was *the* diet obsession. It seemed like everyone was either on it or considering going on it. This happened despite an immediate push back from the clinical, scientific, and nutrition communities. There simply wasn't any good evidence to support the claims Davis made, which can be summarized as a belief that going gluten-free is a magical cure for almost everything. Obesity? Gluten-free. Acne? Gluten-free. Low energy? Gluten-free. Cancer risk? Gluten-free. War, hunger, and poverty? Gluten-free.

Before the show, I felt like I had a good handle on this literature. I had carefully read and annotated *Wheat Belly*. I was prepared. Still, the idea of debating Davis in front of a national audience didn't sound fun. I mean, gluten-free was having a big, big cultural moment. Did Davis have some mic-drop scientific data in his back pocket? Was I going to come off as the bad guy?

I've searched for a transcript of the show. No luck. But I recall that Davis provided no credible arguments. He had no impressive science in his back pocket. It was like he was a Beat poet free-associating scary science-y words and phrases: *Abnormal metabolic signals / Elevation of estrogen / Inflammation, inflammation, inflammation / Glycemic index*

/ Harmful insulin response / Addictive wheat opioids / Weight gain / Dig it, man. Snaps fingers.

Okay, my memory might not be totally accurate. But I feel confident that was the gestalt Davis projected. I recollect that I played my role in the debate by faithfully reciting what the available body of evidence said, such as the fact that gluten-free diets do not promote weight loss. On the contrary, most studies have found that the opposite is true over the long term. It simply is not an inherently healthier approach unless you have a clinically identified reason for going gluten-free. When I left the studio, I felt pretty good about how things went. I mean, it seemed like it was conceptually incoherent rambling versus my reasonable, albeit kind of boring, facts. Job done.

Nope. Apparently, I *was* the bad guy. Almost immediately I ran into someone on the sidewalk who recognized me from the debate. She worked at a coffee shop I frequent, so we were vaguely acquainted, but that didn't stop her from yelling at me about the evils of gluten. She repeated many of the science-y words from the book and inter-view—toxins! GMOs! inflammation!—all while smoking a cigarette. And then the gluten-free hate mail arrived. Gluten-free good. Me bad.

This debate happened a decade ago. Since then, the evidence about the lack of value of gluten-free diets has grown. Yes, if you have celiac disease, you must go gluten-free. A restricted diet may also help those with non-celiac gluten sensitivity, though the evidence is still evolving on the nature and incidence of this condition, which is likely relatively rare. There is some emerging evidence on possible value of going gluten-free for conditions like POTS (postural orthostatic tachycardia syndrome). Whether scientifically justified or not, the gluten-free trend has been great for increasing the dietary options for these communities. But a 2019 study from the University of Calgary found the gluten-free trend to be a double-edged sword for those with celiac, increasing food options but decreasing appreciation for the seriousness of the disease. Despite the now well-established reality that gluten-free diets are not inherently healthier and despite the fact it is no longer a new and headline-grabbing diet, its popularity continues to grow. This is especially true among young adults. A 2022 survey found that 38 percent of those between eighteen and twenty-four are interested in going gluten-free, many of whom were in grade school when *Wheat Belly* was first released. It has been estimated that in 2021 the global gluten-free market was worth $6 billion. The origin story of this evidence-free global industry begins with science-y fearmongering rhetoric similar to Davis's.

Why is it so effective and enduring? There are, of course, many complex cultural and social forces that contribute to the rise of a health trend. For example, gluten-free emerged just as the wellness industry and celebrity wellness brands, like Gwyneth Paltrow's goop, were expanding. Gluten-free was something they could market to their consumers. And there is an endless hunger for new diets, especially if they promise weight loss. But I think it was the blending of the science-y and scary rhetoric that really gave it legs. As we've seen, science-y language—even if not understood or placed in context—can be tremendously persuasive. But if you combine science-y with scary, the potential for impact is turned up to eleven.

The negativity bias is a well-known and powerful cognitive bias. We are hard-wired to remember scary. This is why negative headlines— "if it bleeds, it leads!"—outperform positive ones and why we remember negative and scary information better than that which is neutral or positive. A 2019 experiment analyzed the psychological reaction to news content in seventeen countries. The researchers found that "all around the world, the average human is more physiologically activated by negative than by positive news stories." This tendency is universal.

The science-y and scary pairing is so effective that it has become a go-to strategy for those spreading misinformation and conspiracy theories. During the pandemic, anti-vaccine advocates pushed science-y sounding lies that were, and still are, believed by many. A November

2021 study—conducted right in the middle of the pandemic when vaccination rates were critical—found 21 percent of Americans believed or were uncertain about whether the vaccines could change your DNA (no, they can't), 24 percent that they had microchips in them (no, obviously, they don't), and 31 percent that they could adversely impact your fertility (no, they don't). Those who spread this misinformation on popular podcasts, cable TV shows, and in anti-vaccine literature deploy contextless and quantum-esque phraseology—"lipid nanoparticles," "spike protein"—to give credibility to their assertions.

The great irony of using science-y sounding language to scare people into submission is that those spreading misinformation lean heavily on the language of, well, *science* to legitimize and buttress their science-free positions. They know people increasingly turn to science in their search for certainty, so when the goal is to make scary sound plausible, what do they do? They add a veneer of science.

Professor Stephan Lewandowsky, a renowned expert on the spread of misinformation and conspiracy theories, agrees. The fact that misinformation mongers use "science-y sounding babble" highlights that "those people recognize the importance of science and its cultural 'supremacy,'" he tells me. "Few people say, 'Science sucks and I can do better than that by reading tea leaves.' No, they will instead make up a story about tea leaves that appeals to quantum logic or some other stuff they don't understand."

But it doesn't stop there. A second infuriating irony: often those science-y sounding positions—about gluten, GMOs, vaccines, fluoride in water, etc.—undermine public trust in science. In other words, the trust and credibility of science is used to undermine public trust in, and the credibility of, science. The respected place of science in society is being used to destroy the place of science in society. It's maddening. It's everywhere. And, unfortunately, it works.

Certainty, Fake Science, and Dunning-Kruger

There is yet another big irony to the science-y/scary dyad: it can make those who buy into the science-y message believe they know lots about the relevant science when, in fact, they usually know very little. Indeed, there is a robust body of evidence that finds that the believers and spreaders of bunk often have an unjustified certainty in their knowledge about the relevant facts.

An important prelude to this bold claim: those who embrace misinformation and conspiracy theories are more likely to display narcissistic tendencies. I want to be extremely careful here. Anyone—really, all of us—can fall for misinformation. I've fallen for misinformation. You've probably fallen for misinformation. It is a complex and multifactorial phenomenon playing out in a ridiculously chaotic information environment. Studies tell us that economic disparity, mental health, and historically justified distrust of relevant institutions, to name a few relevant variables, can contribute to a propensity to believe misinformation. But there is also a growing body of evidence that suggests a robust association between the psychological trait of narcissism—that is, feelings of, inter alia, superiority and a sense of entitlement—and a belief in conspiracy theories and misinformation. A 2022 academic review of the literature argues that this connection exists because narcissists have a need, as the authors conclude, "for dominance, control, and uniqueness." Having access to *allegedly* unique, science-y knowledge plays to their narcissism. Other studies have found that those who believe misinformation and conspiracy theories have a strong desire to feel special. A 2017 study from Germany, for example, concluded that one reason conspiracy beliefs are adopted is "as a means to attain a sense of uniqueness."

And this brings me to those overconfident misinformation mongers.

There is a well-known cognitive bias, called the Dunning-Kruger effect, in which individuals overestimate their knowledge about a particular field. One reason this happens is that a lack of knowledge impedes our ability to recognize our lack of knowledge. While this may sound a bit obvious and circular, it is a powerful and consequential psychological predisposition. A 2019 study on anti-GMOs advocates, for example, found that as the strength of the opposition and concern about genetically modified foods increases, the objective knowledge about the relevant science decreases while, *sigh*, the belief in a high degree of knowledge increases. Or, as the researchers nicely summarize, "extreme opponents know the least, but think they know the most." A large 2022 study looked at the sway of this phenomenon across a range of topics where the scientific consensus often differs from public sentiment, including climate change, nuclear power, vaccination, evolution, and genetically modified foods. Regardless of the topic, the results were the same. Those individuals "with the highest levels of opposition have the lowest levels of objective knowledge." As one meme nicely summarizes, the first rule of the Dunning-Kruger club is that you don't know you're in the Dunning-Kruger club. Another 2022 study found that those who believe conspiracy theories are consistently overconfident—and wrong—about their critical thinking abilities and "massively overestimate how much others agree with them."

You can see how all these well-established inclinations can work together to produce a harmful and entrenched misinformation-filled ecosystem. Science-y language plays to the desire that many have, particularly those with narcissistic tendencies, to feel like they are unique and have access to special and alarming knowledge. For many, knowledge overconfidence and the Dunning-Kruger effect may then impede their ability to critically reflect on the deficiencies of their position.

For a recent study I did with my colleague, Marco Zenone, I analyzed hundreds of mpox conspiracy theory videos on TikTok. It was an exhausting exercise. The rage. The science-y nonsense. The complete lack of humility. The condescending I-told-you-so-cuz-I-have-access-to-the-facts smugness. The constant references to Bill Gates being responsible for the outbreak. Our study, which was published in late 2022, explored the speed at which misinformation appears and spreads on social media. (Spoiler: ridiculously fast.) The consistency in the tone and content of these videos was what I found most striking. These are the Dunning-Kruger-empowered misinformation foot soldiers who produce the content and angst that fills our information environment and helps to poison public discourse.

Galileo Was Super Science-y, Just Like Me!

Wrapping baloney in science-y bombast makes it easier for those pushing the baloney to use the "I'm ahead of the curve" defence. "My science," their arguments too often go, "is so advanced that the real science needs to catch up! Remember Galileo?"

Let's start with the conclusion here: you, Mr. Bombast, are almost certainly not Galileo so the "well, they thought Galileo was wrong" argument ain't relevant here. There is a good chance you are misinterpreting the Galileo story or relying on a simplified version of it. When he shared his discovery that the Earth revolved around the sun, he was up against a religious orthodoxy—the Church had declared the Earth the centre of the universe—not a broad scientific consensus produced through reason and the scientific process Galileo helped to inspire.

This logical fallacy—one that I hear often from my hate mailers—is called the Galileo gambit. When those pushing pseudoscientific ideas, unproven therapies, or science-y conspiracy theories are countered by the weight of available evidence, they almost always turn to the idea that they are the brave voice of reason fighting a silencing majority. They are right, the twisted reasoning goes, because others think they are wrong.

People laughed at and persecuted Galileo, they argue, so I must be right too! But just because one person who was laughed at turned out to be right does not mean that everyone who is laughed at is correct. As Carl Sagan noted in his famous critique of the Galileo gambit, "They laughed at Columbus, they laughed at Fulton, they laughed at the Wright brothers. But they also laughed at Bozo the Clown."

The Galileo gambit is deployed more often by those who lean toward narcissism. They are, after all, comparing themselves to Galileo! When faced with a version of the Galileo assertion, always remember that those fantastically rare and truly revolutionary scientific thinkers, like Einstein or Darwin or Curie, didn't hop on Twitter to rant about how they should be held up as the next Galileo. They produced data and evidence-informed arguments that were tested against the scientific conventions of their time. When someone makes some version of this claim, remember that it isn't a rational argument but a defence of last resort.

While the overt "I'm like Galileo!" plea is discouragingly common, you should also watch for the less explicit versions of this science-y logical fallacy. In 2022, Gwyneth Paltrow was interviewed on a network TV morning show. It was mostly a puff piece that glorified Paltrow as a wellness industry pioneer. The interviewer did ask some gentle questions about how her critics say she pushes pseudoscience. Paltrow's response? She is just ahead of the curve, and the world must catch up. All those scientists, clinicians, and public health experts are wrong. Her view on getting fined for false marketing when her company goop sold jade vagina eggs? "We were just early." (And yes, the eggs are exactly what they sound like: jade rocks shaped like eggs to be placed . . . well, you get the idea.) She's the Galileo of pelvic floor tightening! Her view on gluten-free? Ditto. She is "ahead of her time," the interviewer intoned. The Darwin of dubious diets!

Rhetorical strategies like the Galileo gambit and claims of being ahead of the curve seem to be most often used when there is a body of evidence that provides some degree of certainty on a topic. The goal is to destabilize the certainty that the *real* evidence provides, usually to make room to sell a product or forward a particular agenda. The body of evidence says gluten-free diets are not inherently healthier. Gwyneth says (paraphrasing here), "Well, I'm ahead of the curve, and the science is wrong." The body of evidence says the measles vaccine is safe and effective. The anti-vaccine advocate says, "Well, powerful forces said Galileo was wrong, and now they're doing the same to me!" This posture can be maddening because crusaders like Paltrow often point to—and, by implication, discredit—the existing body of evidence (the scientific consensus) as further proof of their contrarian position. The message: scientific agreement is for groupthink losers!

We shouldn't ignore emerging and controversial scientific opinions. There have been contrarian scientific theories that have destabilized and revolutionized fields of inquiry. The theory of plate tectonics, called continental drift, and the discovery that ulcers are caused by bacteria are two relatively recent and often noted examples of this reality. But these ideas were, over time, accepted because the science eventually won the day, not because of repeated evidence-free proclamations. We. Need. Evidence.

To evaluate a contrarian or Galileo-ish assertion, consider the plausibility of the claim in the context of the existing knowledge base. Also consider the qualities and motivations of the person making the claims. Are they an expert in the relevant area? Are they selling something? Are they claiming to know something that thousands of biomedical researchers and clinicians and mountains of scientific data haven't found? Then apply the Sagan standard: "extraordinary claims require extraordinary evidence." This is a simple and valuable tool as it doesn't dismiss the possibility of a claim—making room for a cautiously open mind—but establishes that the more unlikely a claim is, given the existing body of evidence, the greater the standard of proof required. And the onus is on the person making the claim. Don't let fringe contrarian claims destabilize the confidence provided by an existing—albeit always evolving—body of evidence.

The Humility Fix

So, yes, be very wary of the me-so-smart-and-everyone-else-is-wrong retort. It is a good reminder that when it comes to science-based claims, humility is almost always the best starting point. Numerous studies have found a strong association between intellectual humility—which academics often describe as "recognition of one's fallibility as a knower"—and not accepting misinformation. Two recent studies, for example, found that those with intellectual humility are less likely to fall for either political or health misinformation.

Walking the humble path can be challenging. We are all psychologically wired to absorb information that confirms our preconceived beliefs. This is called the confirmation bias, and it can make us feel like maybe we really are ahead of the curve. It can also lead us to overestimate our knowledge. (Seriously, you probably don't understand quantum physics.) Recognizing our biases and working on our intellectual humility are worth the effort. Doing so has many benefits beyond avoiding misinformation, including higher academic achievement and more informed decision-making. It is also associated with empathy, tolerance, and gratitude—all traits the world could use more of right now.

Here is a good humility exercise: consider areas relevant to your personal or professional life where the evidence has evolved, and you changed or slightly altered your position. My list is long and includes walking for exercise. I used to mock walking as a near useless form of exercise because it wasn't vigorous. Wrong. Now I walk daily! In my professional life, I've come to recognize that how we talk about and represent obesity matters a great deal, and I am now more careful to recognize this complexity and the harm of weight bias. Then there are things that continue to exist in the grey area and for which I continue to seek out new information. Lotteries to incentivize vaccination, for example, was a strategy I advocated for because earlier research suggested it was potentially useful. Then the data seemed mixed, suggesting a more complex story, so I became more circumspect. And *then* even more recent data showed, once again, some benefit. Following science can be a rollercoaster! Similarly, mindfulness—around which I still think there is a tremendous amount of hype and bad research—appears to be a useful and efficient intervention for some. I could go on and on. If you can't think of any, see the above bit about narcissism.

Certainly Bullshit

As one of my favourite authors, Ernest Hemingway, wrote: "Choice is the truth of flow, and of us. We live, we vibrate, we are reborn." Put another way, it is important to choose truth and to recognize that choice, which will, in turn, give us life. Hemingway clearly manifested this through *his* life choices. He knows, more than almost anyone, that turbulence is born in the gap where potentiality has been excluded.

Okay, Hemingway didn't write that, and he isn't one of my favourite authors. That quote and most of the last sentence came from a website called New Age Bullshit Generator. After sitting through a long philosophical debate involving Deepak Chopra—who wrote the bestselling book *Quantum Healing*, because, well, quantum—and loads of New Age rhetoric, the creator of the website was inspired to write a program that generates profound-sounding gibberish. All you need to do is click a button labelled "Reionize Electrons" to "generate a full page of New Age poppycock." Give it a try.

Pseudo-profound bullshit is the close philosophical and mystical cousin of science-y nonsense. And yes, believe it or not, *bullshit* has emerged as the appropriate academic term of art. As with the use of science-y words, pseudo-profound language can sound impressive and deep when it is really meaningless word salad; it is usually deployed not to inform but to impress via confusion and vagueness. There is often lots of "consciousness" and "ontology" and "awareness" and "resonance" and "transformations" and "discontinuity" and "disruptions" and "paradigms." As with scienceploitation, this verbiage is used to sell something, such as self-help brands or personal growth services and products. Of course, science-y and pseudo-profound bullshit are often combined to create uber-pretentious nonsense, as with this gem from the BS generator: "Consciousness consists of four-dimensional superstructures of quantum energy."

A few years ago, my friend and research collaborator Gordon Pennycook was the lead author on a study entitled "On the Reception and Detection of Pseudo-Profound Bullshit." The paper won the 2015 Ig Nobel, an international award given at Harvard University to research "that first makes people laugh and then makes them think." The study first maps the characteristics of BS using examples from the aforementioned self-help guru Deepak Chopra noting that, similar to scienceploitation, it is deployed not to inform but to cause people "to confuse vagueness for profundity." Words like *ontology*, *discontinuity*, and *manifestations* sound impressive, but they are often used in a way that renders them meaningless. In the case of this study, the researchers "gave people syntactically coherent sentences that consisted of random vague buzzwords." Then Pennycook and his colleagues empirically studied how receptive people were to the BS. The answer? Pretty darn. The researchers found that "these statements were judged to be at least somewhat profound."

You might be wondering if the BS from a famous person like Deepak Chopra sounds more impressive than the exact same pseudo-profound nonsense attributed to anonymous. Yep. A 2019 study found

BS to be "rated as more profound when presented as being uttered by a famous author," a phenomenon the researchers call the labelling effect. We are primed to think something *must* be profound because, well, someone who is supposed to be profound said it—which is exactly what a pseudo-profounder wants us to believe! It's the New Age brand-building cycle of life. Ka-ching.

Pennycook, who is a professor of experimental psychology at Cornell University, has seen science-y verbiage increasingly mixed in with pseudo-profound BS. "I think people definitely do lean on scientific jargon when they are trying to impress instead of inform," he tells me. "It's bullshitting. My favorite example of this is 'quantum consciousness' [that word yet again!], which takes two very complex and (even for scientists) difficult to understand concepts and smashes them together. The result is something that sounds really impressive but that doesn't come close to communicating anything meaningful."

A good rule of thumb: if something sounds like pretentious tripe, it most likely is. For example, if someone invites you to participate in a "personal development" or "life coaching" program, ask them for material that clearly explains how it works. Those terms are often a euphemism for self-help bunk-o-rama. If all you get back is empty words about "self-actualization" and "shifts in perspective" and a focus on "transformational issues" and "discovering blind spots" to "empower and enable you" to succeed at "optimal levels," but no concrete *this is what you'll do and specifically how it works* explanation, be very suspicious.

While lots of science and philosophy is complex and difficult to *completely* understand, the basics can usually be communicated in a digestible manner. Yes, doing this well can be a tremendous challenge, but given the degree to which this language is used to market and manipulate, straightforward explanations have great value. Pennycook agrees. "Science that can't be understood is bad science," he tells me. "Scientists who are actually trying to inform the public—as opposed to take advantage of them—know this and, although they may not always succeed, try their best to communicate in ways that people understand."

Before we move on from bullshit and meaningless science-y jargon, it is worth highlighting a paradox that is central to the theme of this book. Let's call it the profundity paradox: the use of dazzling and persuasive rhetorical strategies to give the *illusion* of clarity. In fact, that is often exactly why science-y nonsense and BS are employed. The illusion of science and profundity are used to create the illusion of clarity and certainty. Do not be fooled.

The Hype Machine

It is easy to be furious at those who spin science for personal gain or to promote a harmful agenda. But much of this noise is facilitated by the bad science and exaggerated claims coming from the legitimate research community. Who made *stem cells*, *regenerative*, *microbiome*, *genomics*, and *quantum* terms ripe for scienceploitation? We did, the academic research community.

In 2012, I wrote an article with a colleague, Celeste Condit, from the University of Georgia about how the existing incentives and research funding system create hype—that is, exaggerated claims of potential benefit and social impact—throughout the knowledge production process. From excitement about a topic to the grant writing process to the publication and media representations of the work, we called this the hype pipeline. And our findings are even more relevant today.

Buckle up. The data on science hype is striking and pretty unsettling.

Let's start at the beginning. To get scientific research funded, especially research that is expensive and requires large teams and a long-term investment, you need to generate a lot of excitement. That is natural. That is understandable. To get big money—billions and billions—from governments, foundations, and public funding entities, you often need to make big and, as we will see, entirely unrealistic promises of near-future benefit. You are, after all, competing with other scientists who feel their work is pretty darn revolutionary too. But the funding pie is only so big. Enter hype.

For example, early in the effort to map the human genome, Francis Collins, then director of the very expensive Human Genome Project, called it "the most important organized scientific effort that humankind has ever attempted. It dwarfs going to the moon." To be fair, in the 1990s, when Collins said that, genomics did seem exciting and potentially revolutionary . . . because scientists told us—again and again and again—that it was. We started to believe our own hype. I started to believe it. This framing had an impact on public perceptions, the media, and on the expectations of funders. Hype begets more hype. It also begets a culture where *not* hyping your research is frowned upon. There is pressure to be a team player and to keep the enthusiasm rolling.

In 2013, I chaired a national academic workshop on the policy issues associated with whole genome screening—examining your genetic material with one comprehensive test to predict future health issues. At the event, there was a rich, open, and evidence-informed discussion about a host of issues, with many data-supported and thoughtful comments that questioned the potential value of the practice. Near the end of the workshop, a senior, well-known, and influential genetics researcher pulled me aside and firmly told me to stop criticizing the clinical value of genomics or the money would go to stem cells. The enthusiasm for a particular area of science and the pressure to secure funding can lead us to forget the big-picture goal: making a difference to the health of patients and the public.

Another strategy used by the research community to justify funding big science initiatives is to suggest that it will lead to dramatic economic growth. I'm all for investing in research and the knowledge economy. And I understand why researchers make economic arguments for their areas of study. Politicians love it. Research funding entities love it, as it helps to justify their existence. But the predictions of economic benefit are often ludicrously over the top. In 2009, for example, a science policy group in Texas argued that a state investment in stem cell research would create 230,000 jobs and $88 billion in economic activity. A similar economic analysis for New Jersey predicted 20,000 new jobs and $71.9 billion in new state revenue. This was all going to happen between 2006 and 2025. In California, a 2004 economic analysis done in support of its proposed stem cell program predicted, once again, billions in economic activity and "health care cost savings of between $6.4 billion and $12.6 billion." These savings, which were framed as a "modest" estimate, were going to come—it was rather optimistically predicted—from cures or treatments for strokes, Parkinson's disease, spinal cord injuries, and Alzheimer's disease, among others. These estimates were successfully used to persuade Californian voters to support an investment of $3 billion in stem cell research. Two decades later, none of these therapies have materialized.

Once an area of research gets attention and an envelope of financial support, researchers who want to work in that area must apply for funding. This process is ridiculously competitive and time-consuming. Humbling failure is, by far, the norm. Leading an application can be a stressful, up-all-night, all-hands-on-deck process. I speak from personal experience when I say a large project application can devour a year of your working life. The actual grant applications are voluminous. Not only does getting a grant—which is usually decided by an independent peer-review committee—allow academics to research a topic that interests them, it helps to forward their careers and fund their laboratory and research teams (students, trainees, administrators). Research institutions usually reward and loudly celebrate a significant grant-getting success.

Suffice it to say, the personal and institutional pressure can be extreme. Is it a surprise that this funding process invites inappropriate hype? A study from 2016, for example, conducted anonymous interviews with dozens of senior academic researchers about the funding process. The researchers admitted that there was a great deal of sensationalism and embellishment, noting that "marketizing" the research was "a matter of survival in academia." The authors of the study noted that many of the academics viewed themselves as little more than "impact merchants" (a great term). One interviewee put it this way: "If you can find me a single academic who hasn't had to bullshit or bluff or lie or embellish in order to get grants, then I will find you an academic who is in trouble with [their] head of department." Such admissions caused the authors of the study to conclude that the current funding system is "resulting in impact sensationalism and the corruption of academics as custodians of truth."

Supporting this harsh conclusion is an analysis from 2022 that examined almost a million abstracts from successful National Institutes of Health (NIH) research grants from 1985 to 2020. The primary funder for biomedical research in the U.S., the NIH is a peer-reviewed and prestigious source of support. The 2022 study looked at the use of hype—basically, adjectives that promote the significance, novelty, scale, and rigour of a project—and found that "levels of hype in successful NIH grant applications have increased over that time span." By "increased," they mean a *massive* increase—approximately 1400 percent. Yes, you read that correctly. One thousand four hundred. Now, to be fair, the communication universe in general has become more hype-filled since 1985 (thanks, social media), but we are talking about NIH grants here, not tweets from Dr. Oz or advertisements for an anti-aging cream. We should all want—and have every reason to expect—the academic science community to be a bit more wedded to reality.

The same research team, from the University of Tsukuba, looked at the language used by the National Institutes of Health in its announcements of funding opportunities. The results from this study, also published in 2022, found a massive increase in hype language here too. So, funding entities, such as the prestigious and influential NIH, use an increasing amount of hype when asking scientists to apply for a grant. No surprise, they get hype fed back to them. If we are going to fix the hype problem, it seems like the funding agencies are a good place to start.

Adding to the brokenness of the funding process is the reality that it doesn't do what it is designed to do: inspire, find, and fund the best science. As noted, the success rate for grants is often quite low. In Canada, it has hovered around 15 percent for years. And don't forget, the process is just as monstrously time-consuming for the 85 percent who don't get funding as it is for the lucky few who succeed. A 2015 analysis from Australia estimated that one large biomedical research competition wastes over six hundred years of researcher time! That's just one year of grant writing for one funding program in Australia. Despite the massive resources dedicated to writing the best possible grants, studies have found success is often arbitrary and determined by little more than the luck of the draw. Everything from who reviews the grant to when during the peer-review committee meeting the grant is reviewed (before or after the coffee break?) to entrenched diversity and equity issues can skew results. One study from 2018, published in *Proceedings of the National Academy of Sciences*, analyzed reviews by over forty peer reviewers of the same grants. The results "showed no agreement among reviewers regarding the quality of the applications in either their qualitative or quantitative evaluations." Other research, including a 2016 analysis of over 100,000 successful NIH grants, has demonstrated that there is no relationship between how well a grant is ranked and the productivity, such as publications and clinical impact, after a grant is awarded.

This situation is truly a mess. The process of allocating funding for research incinerates large hunks of a researcher's career—time that could be spent producing useful knowledge and commentary—and it's massively expensive for society. Remember, the *public*, the ultimate funder of universities and research grants, pays for that incinerated time. To make matters worse, the process does not do a good job of discriminating based on quality. In practice, the allocation of grants seems almost random and doesn't predict which research projects will succeed, which is the whole point. And this isn't chump change. The annual budget for the NIH is almost $50 billion. The budget for the Canadian Institutes of Health Research is over $1 billion.

Of course, the academic community has long known about these failings. I haven't come across a single researcher who has total faith in the system. Most seem fatalistic. It is as if we are resigned to endure a torturous, byzantine, and substantively meaningless ritual for the right to have the fund-granting gods read our science-filled tarot cards. Yes, lots of great research does eventually result, but the bureaucratic dance is, I can personally attest, exhausting.

This grim situation has led some to suggest a radical approach. The current system is almost random and certainly biased. So why not lean into that reality and use a lottery system to allocate research funds? Lionel Page and Adrian Barnett, professors from the University of Queensland, recommend a system in which peer reviewers determine basic fundability—that is, the research meets reasonable methodological and organizational standards—and the rest is decided by lottery. Some funding agencies have successfully experimented with a version of the lottery system, such as the Swiss National Science Foundation and the Health Research Council of New Zealand. This approach is more efficient, cheaper, faster, more equitable, and may encourage out-of-the-box thinking as researchers don't need to chase the latest funding fad. When genomics is popular, for instance, every grant tends to be about genomics because that's what is more likely to get funding—a phenomenon called hot stuff bias. A lottery system would also remove the incentive to hype your research. There would be no benefit to framing potential outputs as revolutionary, paradigm shifting, near-future, breakthroughs, or game-changing. If the research really is any of those things, the actual science will win the day—no hype required.

—

After research has been funded and commenced, hype can creep into both the collection of data and the writing up of results. There is a rich body of literature highlighting the innumerable biases—psychological, financial, institutional—that influence the execution of research and the publication of results. Virtually all of those biases cause further emphasis on benefits and overly optimistic projections of clinical and/ or social impact, which often show up in the peer-reviewed publication. For example, there is a large amount of hype in the abstracts of studies—the short summaries at the top of academic papers, which are often the only thing people, including academics, read. A 2017 study, for example, found that almost 40 percent of all abstracts for biomedical research contained at least some degree of spin.

Perhaps the most hype is injected when researchers and research institutions promote the results to the outside world. Press releases from universities, for example, are notorious for spin. A 2014 study by Petroc Sumner and colleagues analyzed 462 press releases on bio-medical and health-related issues and compared them to the associated peer-reviewed article and related articles in the popular press. They found that 40 percent contained exaggerated health advice, 33 percent had exaggerated claims about causation (that is, the degree to which the studied intervention caused a particular outcome), and 36 percent contained exaggerated inferences about animal studies, such as suggesting data from an animal study is immediately relevant to human health, when it almost never is. More important, the study found that this hype was transcribed into the popular press.

Of course, how researchers talk about their work in the public sphere is another significant source of hype. In 2015, I worked with my colleague Kalina Kamenova on an analysis of newspaper stories about stem cell research. We found that scientists significantly hyped how soon their research would be in the clinic and ready for patient use. Almost 70 percent of the newspaper articles suggested the time frame would be five to ten years, or sooner. Given that the clinical trial phase alone can take ten to fifteen years, that prediction is impossibly fast, and it ignores the reality that most clinical trials—approximately 90 percent—fail.

The existence of media hype might be, ironically, a predictor that the research being hyped isn't going anywhere. A 2023 study examined fourteen thousand research papers to identify variables related to replication (that is, whether subsequent studies confirmed the initial paper's findings). The authors found that media attention was *negatively* associated with replication. Put another way: the more media coverage, the less reliable the claims. Ouch.

Hype from researchers and institutions can do significant damage. It can fuel unrealistic expectations for patients who are desperate for treatments and cures. Their unrealistic hope is too often exploited by clinicians, including physicians, seeking to profit from unproven therapies. In the stem cell space, for example, there are now thousands of clinics around the world that leverage this hype to successfully market unproven therapies for serious diseases, including multiple sclerosis, cancer, dementia, and spinal injuries. Some of these therapies cost tens of thousands of dollars and have resulted in serious injury and even death. This kind of exploitation is happening in a range of areas: microbiome-based therapies, which include fecal transplants for a range of ailments; direct-to-consumer genetic tests, which often overpromise the health benefits of their products; and the marketing of (allegedly) life-extending new supplements.

If a significant health or biomedical breakthrough happens, you will hear about it from numerous credible sources. Always be suspicious of people who promise a revolutionary new therapy or approach to living a healthy lifestyle that is ready *right now*. Consider this: these kinds of promises have been made for decades. How many of them have panned out?

Catastrophizing

I've applied for many, many grants during my career. Working on this book caused me to reflect on the degree to which I gave in to the pressure to hype. I feel comfortable saying that the representations of our proposed and finished research were *mostly* balanced. But, yes, the hype was there. In the early days, I was perhaps a bit too optimistic and enthusiastic about the predictive value of emerging genetic technologies and the near-future benefits of stem cell technologies. I wove those overly positive narratives into our grants and into how I talked about the research outputs. Was I writing what I thought peer reviewers and funders wanted to hear? Perhaps. I don't remember thinking of it that way, but incentive structures can have subtle and subconscious effects.

A conversation about hype wouldn't be complete without a look at how the exact same forces that cause potential benefits of research to be overstated can lead to overstated claims of potential harm. Catastrophizing the impact of emerging science has become an academic cottage industry. In the 1990s and 2000s, for example, there was inflated concern about the social implications of biotechnology, including human reproductive cloning, the patenting and corporate ownership of human genetic material, and genetic discrimination, such as by insurance companies and employers. These concerns were everywhere, from movies like *Gattaca*, in which Ethan Hawke's character fights genetic discrimination, to headlines in the popular press, like one from 1999 announcing an "International Ban Proposed on Cloning Humans for Warfare." They also became the focus of countless academic and policy conferences. Millions and millions of dollars in research grants were awarded. Governments invested time and resources to consider and, in many cases, enact laws and regulations to mitigate alleged harms. Yes, some of these concerns were and remain legitimate—genetic discrimination isn't a good thing, for instance—and worthy of a response and continued investigation. But as with science hype, the near-future significance had been greatly overstated. With the passage of time, some of the concerns seem downright silly. Armies of clones?

The point here is that the forces of hype can result in wildly over-stated claims of both benefits *and* harms, thus leading to a polarized and inaccurate public representation of an area of science. Parallel utopian and dystopian narratives permeate pop culture. This can, and has, had an adverse impact on public perceptions and policy debates. Does the United Nations really need to waste time, as it has been for years, considering an international treaty to ban reproductive cloning? Does Canada really need, as we now have, a criminal ban on clon-ing? Yes, emerging areas of science *can*, obviously, create real social issues—as we are witnessing with the rise in AI and concerns about how it will facilitate the spread of misinformation. But it is important to recognize that inappropriately catastrophizing emerging areas of science can also feed the spread of scary misinformation, as discussed earlier. We remember scary. When harms are hyped, they can be more easily deployed by those marketing products, brands, or ideology.

Investing in Science? Yes, Yes, Yes!

During my three-decade academic career, I've worked with large bio-medical research teams on many of the most hyped and celebrated biomedical topics, including stem cells, personalized medicine, genom-ics, nanotechnology, the microbiome, and neuroscience. Very few, if any, revolutionizing clinical advances have been produced in those thirty-plus years. Think about that for a moment. All that research. All that funding. All the hyped-up headlines. And hardly any of the promised breakthroughs have materialized.

Despite this experience and my harsh critique of hype, I'm not necessarily saying that these areas shouldn't have received significant funding. The reality is that science is hard, messy, and unpredictable.

That's exactly how the science in all these areas has played out. The actual progress, including clinical applications, has, in general, advanced incrementally. There are new therapies—such as exciting gene therapies for certain types of hemophilia and sickle cell disease—though they are often extremely expensive (we are talking millions-of-dollars-for-a-single-treatment expensive) and niche in their application. There are new diagnostic and predictive tests, though they are usually much less informative than initially suggested. And there have been significant technological advances and increases in our scientific understanding of human biology, diseases, and pathogens. But in general, the science in all these areas has unfolded in a manner very different than promised.

To cite just one example, while much of the excitement about revolutionizing therapies hasn't panned out on a broad scale, the gene sequencing technologies developed to support this research helped us quickly understand the SARS-CoV-2 virus and speed the discovery of the vaccines. The rapid—and, yes, *entirely* scientifically sound—development of these vaccines was a genuine scientific miracle that happened because we had invested in the related science. It has been estimated that the COVID vaccines saved tens of millions of lives. While remarkable and pretty darn revolutionary, this example highlights the value of investing in science *generally*—because you can't predict where the research will lead and what benefits will accrue—and not buying into the harmful hype and over-the-top promises that are used to justify the initial investment and which almost never materialize.

This may sound like a contradiction. It is not. The current funding and research system invites hype and promotes public discourse about science that is inaccurate and harmful. It creates widely shared rhetoric about scientific breakthroughs that distorts public expectations, fuels the marketing of unproven therapies, and can be spun to push health misinformation. And it promotes a lack of appreciation for true breakthroughs, like vaccines, and less sexy, less commercial, and less headline-grabbing, but essential, public health work. Things like walkable and safe neighbourhoods, good food and exercise policy, smoking cessation strategies, and community mental health initiatives that we know, in the aggregate and over time, can have a tremendous impact on well-being. The noise caused by Big Science hype can come to dominate not only the work that gets funded but how we think about solutions to our biggest health problems.

In this era of misinformation, conspiracy theories, and aggressive marketing of unproven therapies, it is essential for researchers and clinicians to not hype their work. Understatement should be the default. This is not to say that researchers can't make science fun, interesting, and exciting. Making good, accurate, non-hyped science engaging and shareable is essential. It must compete with the sensationalistic noise that permeates pop culture, especially on social media. This isn't easy. It requires science communication to be prioritized and supported by research institutions and funders. And it requires creative collaborations with artists, authors, the social-media savvy, and experts in science communication.

It is a delicate balance. We must avoid the hype, and we must make engaging and shareable content. Doing this well will save lives and build needed trust in both research institutions and the entities that use science to inform policy and clinical decisions. Good, honest, creative, responsive, and transparent science communication should be viewed—by governments, researchers, educators, clinicians, and the media—as a top policy priority. The academic community must do what is necessary to ensure that we aren't facilitating the spread of hype and misinformation. As Holden Thorp, the editor-in-chief of the journal *Science*, noted in an editorial critiquing universities for failing to respond to bad science:

It's easy to blame the politicians, right-wing cable TV hosts, and podcast hucksters for spreading misinformation. But is it defensible to blame these folks without also acknowledging that unchallenged members of the scientific community are making it possible for them to sow this doubt? Until the scientific community deals with misinformation from within, it cannot expect to deal with it from without.

So, what does all this hype and questionable science mean for you, day to day? First, be aware of the hype problem. Recognize that it is used to market both products and ideas. Be particularly leery of language that seems to be riffing on claims of breakthroughs, revolutions, or a paradigm shift. That rarely happens. Science tends to be hard and messy and to progress incrementally. It is filled with perpetual and shifting uncertainties. If a genuine significant breakthrough happens, we'll all know. Honest.

And that leads me to my second recommendation, one that I have often made throughout my career: always think big picture, and consider the body of evidence. When a substantial scientific development does happen—like, say, the development of COVID vaccines, a truly remarkable scientific achievement of our time—you will hear about it from numerous reputable sources, and there will be a body of evidence to support the claims.

The Predator Problem

When I open my email in the morning, there are almost always a bunch of requests for me to submit an academic paper to a fancy-sounding journal. The editors will note my world-renown in cardiology, urban design, neurology, virology, otolaryngology (seriously), or some such thing, and tell me that my truly impressive research in that particular field would be a perfect fit for their publication. In fact, moments after I wrote the above sentences, I got an email from the *Archives of Animal and Poultry Sciences* informing me that they are about to publish their next issue and they "humbly request" that I submit my article "as early as possible," so that they can "release the issue on time."

Now, I'm not an expert, and certainly not world-renowned, in cardiology, urban design, neurology, virology, otolaryngology, or poultry sciences. And I have no intention of writing an academic paper on any of these topics. But I do know a thing or two about homeopathy, a topic I have studied and written on. So, I wasn't surprised when a journal editor reached out and said they were aware of my scholarship and would like me "to participate in [their] publishing program." I thanked them for their kind invitation, and I proceeded to submit a paper. Below, in its entirety, is my manuscript.

Homeopathy Is Pseudoscience BS

Abstract: Homeopathy is pseudoscience BS.

I. Introduction
Homeopathy is pseudoscience BS.

II. Background
Homeopathy is pseudoscience BS.

III. Methods
Homeopathy is pseudoscience BS.

IV. Results
Homeopathy is pseudoscience BS.

V. Discussion
Homeopathy is pseudoscience BS.

VI. Conclusion
Homeopathy is pseudoscience BS.

The editor responded the very next day and told me they were "pleased to confirm preliminary acceptance" of my paper, which was co-authored with several academic colleagues. Yippee! A few days later, I submitted the exact same document as the final version of the paper. The editor seemed satisfied and acknowledged receipt of the manuscript.

It is worth pausing here to note that homeopathy is indeed pseudo-scientific BS. It has been called pure quackery and the ultimate fake medicine. Homeopathy, which was developed in Germany around 1790 by Samuel Hahnemann, is based on the scientifically preposterous premise that an allegedly therapeutic substance placed in water and diluted to near nothingness can treat or prevent ailments. Homeopaths believe that the more diluted their substances—even to the point where not a single molecule remains—the more powerful it is. The water "holds the memory" of the substance. The concept is so ridiculous and so egregiously defies fundamental scientific principles that it doesn't deserve to be studied in a serious manner. But it has been studied. Often. And what the good clinical trials have consistently found is, no surprise, homeopathy does not work for anything. For example, a 2015 study by the Australian National Health and Medical Research Council looked at over 1,800 papers on point and concluded that homeopathy wasn't effective for any health condition and cautioned that "people who choose homeopathy may put their health at risk if they reject or delay treatments for which there is good evidence."

Given that homeopathy is truly the air guitar of biomedicine, I was looking forward to seeing the publication of our succinct analysis. But it was not to be. About four months after the submission, the editors realized our manuscript contained only several dozen words and was therefore incomplete. I responded by noting "that's all that needs to be said about homeopathy." They weren't mollified by that retort, and the piece wasn't published. It is important to note that the *only* complaint they had with our manuscript was the brevity. They said nothing about the lack of methods, data, analysis, or references. It was just too short.

I considered simply copying the phrase "homeopathy is pseudo-science BS" three hundred times à la "all work and no play makes Jack a dull boy" in *The Shining* and resubmitting, but I figured the jig was up.

But make no mistake: this fake publisher was willing to accept a fake article with fake science about fake medicine.

This exercise was more than a lark. I wanted to highlight the significant and growing problem of predatory and low-quality academic journals. While this may seem like a problem only for academics and publishers, it matters very much to your well-being and to society more broadly. The conclusions and commentary published in these journals pollute the academic literature, are used to legitimize harmful misinformation, waste research resources (i.e., your tax dollars), and make it increasingly difficult to tease out what is reliable and useful research from the pseudoscientific BS.

Predatory journals profit by charging researchers a fee to publish—which many legitimate publications also do (sometimes the fee is more than $10,000!), especially journals that are open access. But predatory journals have a lax peer-review process or almost none at all. They'll publish just about anything. Their editorial boards—the entities meant to apply rigorous standards to decide what gets published—are often padded with questionable "experts." For example, Dr. Olivia Doll sat on the editorial board of seven academic journals. She is, or so it has been claimed, a celebrated authority in "avian propinquity to canines in metropolitan suburbs" and "the benefits of abdominal massage for medium-sized canines." No surprise, as Dr. Olivia Doll is a Staffordshire terrier named Ollie. Chasing birds and belly rubs are central to her career agenda. Despite these passions, she has found time to review manuscripts for journals like *Global Journal of Addiction & Rehabilitation Medicine* and *Psychiatry and Mental Disorders*. Seriously. She did that. Good doggie! And she has published a few articles herself, including co-authoring a piece with Alice Wünderlandt from Lutenblag University in Molvania. Their paper, entitled "Solicitation of Patient Consent for Bilateral Orchiectomy in Male Canids: Time to Rethink the Obligatory Paradigm," calls for "hyper-ethical contextual framework, in which input and consent is solicited from the subject in question prior to surgical intervention" (i.e., ask doggies before you cut off their testicles), and it can still be found online in the obviously predatory journal *Examines in Marine Biology & Oceanography*.

Ollie's career as an editor was the brainchild of professor Mike Daube, a public health researcher at Curtin University in Australia. He wanted to demonstrate how these journals lacked credibility. Mission accomplished. The credentials of Dr. Olivia Doll, also known as Ollie the dog, were accepted by all these publications, despite the fact that, as Professor Daube has noted, "it would take a five-year-old one click to expose this." In fact, one journal told Ollie that they were "delighted to have such an eminent person such as yourself." Woof.

"I was stunned and appalled," Daube tells me when I asked him if he was surprised at Ollie's impressive academic career. "The CV that got her onto editorial boards was just absurd, as were the papers she submitted." Daube also tells me that one of Ollie's co-authors and canine colleagues, Professor L'Épagneul, is likewise on editorial boards despite an email auto-response saying that he died years ago. Indeed, L'Épagneul's impressive CV—which notes he had research interest in the capacity of canines to contribute to the posthumous literature and is *still* chair of the Celestial Canine Registration Board—notes that he died in 1954. So, not only are dogs doing editorial work for predatory journals, but at least one dead dog is listed as actively involved.

Daube told me that Ollie "hasn't been writing much of late, but she is a very lively ten-year-old, so there's still time." However, Ollie continues to engage with the academic community on social media and as senior lecturer at the Subiaco College of Veterinary Science—a real-ish institution since Ollie's on faculty. Perhaps the next step for Dr. Olivia Doll is the presidency of a university?

—

Many other pranks have exposed the insidious nature of predatory journals. One of my favourite examples was written by a professor of biology entitled "What's the Deal with Birds?"; it is noted in the abstract that "birds are pretty weird. I mean, they have feathers. WTF? Most other animals don't have feathers. To investigate this issue, I looked at some birds." The paper is still available online in the way too on-the-nose publication *Scientific Journal of Research and Reviews*—a journal title that is the equivalent of a fake ID for Agey McOldenough.

Tom Spears, a Canadian journalist who has been investigating this industry for years, wrote an "academic" paper built entirely by cobbling together unrelated phrases from existing research articles. The result was academic-sounding gibberish. He submitted it to eighteen journals and was quickly and enthusiastically accepted by eight. Just so you know, this is *not* how it plays out with reputable journals, where rejection is often the norm.

A big reason these journals thrive is that they exploit the intense pressure on academics to publish. A 2021 study found that predatory publications are "authored by scholars from all fields and levels of academic experience" and that the driving force behind the industry is the "research evaluation policies and publication pressure that emerge from the research environment in which scholars operate." In some jurisdictions, such as South Africa, academic compensation is tied directly to the quantity—not the quality—of academic publications. The more an academic publishes, the more they make. This patently absurd compensation policy has resulted in a massive increase, as much as 140-fold, of publications in predatory journals.

Dr. Manoj Lalu, a clinical researcher at the University of Ottawa who studies how to improve the methodological rigour and transparency of biomedical research, puts the problem bluntly: "Predatory journals and publishers have actually exploited researchers' hubris and the desire for recognition and promotion. The underlying driving force for much of this are the skewed incentives and rewards for academic promotion. Quantity over quality, and predatory journals have benefited."

Indeed, the incentive structures in academia are almost perfectly designed for abuse. The competition, especially for junior academics, is intense. For enterprising, um, "entrepreneurs" (read: scam artists) offering an avenue to publish quickly and with few barriers is easy money. As Spears told me, "All the [predatory publishers] need is a website and PayPal account, and money rolls in."

Because these online journals kind of sound like real journals—say, the questionable *Journal of Medical Research* as compared to the very real *Journal of the American Medical Association*—the publication credit looks good on an academic resumé and may fool most people, even the academics who sit on university evaluation committees to make decisions about promotions. A small Canadian study found that publication in predatory journals was associated with greater financial rewards, through promotion and merit increments, than publishing in non-predatory journals. It was also associated with receiving research grants. A 2020 study of the tenure and promotion policies at twenty Canadian universities found that there was no language that explicitly discourages publication in predatory journals. Ugh. The system is truly broken.

It is important to note that when academics pay to publish in these journals, they are usually not forking over their own money. They are paying from research grants. A 2017 study of predatory publications by David Moher, who works with Professor Lalu and colleagues from the Ottawa Hospital Research Institute, found that the U.S. National Institutes of Health was the most commonly listed funding source. A 2021 study from the University of Manitoba found that every Canadian university participated in predatory publishing—especially those that were research intensive, likely because the publication pressure is more severe. Among Canadian universities, it was most common for funding to come from high-profile public entities, like the Canadian Institutes of Health Research.

Take a beat to think about this for a moment. Public funds (your tax dollars!) are used to support a massive, harmful, and largely

fraudulent industry that will do nothing to advance scientific knowledge. The industry is nothing more than a cynical money grab. And
don't forget, usually the research that led to the publication is also supported by public funds. Ditto the salary of the researcher who did the
research. It's a triple whammy waste. Moreover, Moher also estimates
that many thousands of animals are sacrificed and the time of millions of human research subjects are wasted by participating in poorly
done studies.

I suspect that many of the researchers who publish in these journals do so with full knowledge or wilful blindness that they are bogus,
but they want to, or have been incentivized to by institutional policy,
bolster their CVs. Others may be using the publications to forward a
particular agenda, such as to build credibility in support of marketing unproven therapies or a harmful conspiracy theory. During the
COVID pandemic, for example, predatory journals thrived. An analysis
by Johns Hopkins Bloomberg School of Public Health—the study was
appropriately titled "Money Down the Drain"—found that 365 articles
on COVID were published in well-known predatory journals in the first
few months of the pandemic. Many of the articles were produced and
published to legitimize misinformation and conspiracy theories. For
example, the *Journal of Biological Regulators and Homeostatic Agents*
published a "study" claiming that 5G technology causes the spontaneous
"induction" of COVID in human cells. (It doesn't.) This paper, which
the award-winning debunker, professor, and microbiologist Elisabeth
Bik called the worst paper of 2020, was quickly embraced by conspiracy theorists and spread throughout social media and COVID-denier
websites, where it still lives on and is often cited as proof of a pandemic
conspiracy by my regular hate mailers.

And this, of course, is probably the biggest harm caused by predatory journals. They pollute academic literature. To give you a sense of
the scale of the problem, studies have placed the number of predatory
journals somewhere between eleven thousand and sixteen thousand.
Though estimates vary, the number of predatory articles published

each year is likely over 750,000. In 2022, the group Predatory Publishing, an initiative aimed at fighting this problem, estimated that almost $400 million is spent each year on the publication of research in these questionable journals. Other studies have suggested the size of the predatory industry may be in the billions of dollars. In some jurisdictions, publication in predatory journals has become dominant. A 2022 study from Pakistan, for example, looked at approximately five hundred articles published by fifty professors and found that almost 70 percent of them were published in predatory journals. It is, no doubt, a worldwide problem. Unfortunately, research has also found that academics, clinicians, and students are often unaware of the threat posed by predatory publishing.

Not only is the research published in predatory journals a colossal waste of valuable resources, but it can also make it more difficult to come to an accurate conclusion about what the body of evidence says on a given topic and to tease out the real science from the bogus. Science is hard enough without muddying the literature with hundreds of thousands of poorly done papers that look real. Studies have shown that too often these fake journals and fake studies can be found in reputable research repositories, such as PubMed, Scopus, and MEDLINE. Researchers, clinicians, and policy makers use these databases to find reliable data and analysis. For Professor Moher, it is bad enough that these papers are, as he put it, "'simply' being published" and that they work their way into these trusted sources, but the "articles from predatory journals also end up in systematic reviews, clinical practice guidelines, and government documents," he tells me. One of Moher's recent studies, which was co-authored by Dr. Manoj Lalu, found that over eight hundred national and international clinical and public health policies referenced papers from predatory journals. And this study only looked at research published by one well-known predatory publisher. "I'm sure if we included other publishers, the situation would look much worse," Lalu says. In other words, this bunk science is twisting efforts to rigorously synthesize and critically appraise the body of evidence on a wide range of topics. The result is an impact on things like clinical care, government policy, and public perception.

To put a finer point on it: predatory publishers are having an impact on your life.

I asked Lalu if he found the results of his research depressing. "Yes, there is no better description for it," he says. "And we are just scratching the surface. It's worse than most people think."

Publications in predatory journals can also be used strategically to legitimize fringe and harmful ideas. For example, there have been predatory publications on truly off-the-rails beliefs like chemtrails (the conspiracy theory that the contrails behind jet planes are part of a government plot to drug the population) and the denial of climate change and HIV/AIDS. Alternative medicine proponents love predatory journals as they can be used to make their science-free beliefs appear to be supported by evidence. There are predatory publications on earthing (the idea that walking barefoot allows the Earth's "energy" to produce health benefits), self-reiki (waving your hands over your body to manipulate your life-force energy), and, of course, many on homeopathy.

Orgasm Shot?

Should women inject their vaginas with platelet-rich plasma? Believe it or not, answering this question serves as an excellent illustration of the problematic power of predatory journals and fake science.

Years ago, Dr. Jen Gunter and I got into an argument on social media with a physician who was marketing an unproven therapy. Dr. Gunter is a friend, an obstetrician and gynecologist, and a renowned author and advocate for women's health. She was frustrated to see a physician, Dr. Charles Runels, selling a procedure called the O-Shot®, which is short for, you guessed it, the orgasm shot. This procedure is marketed as a method to, among other things, improve sex. It involves injecting platelet-rich plasma (PRP)—which is, basically, elements of a patient's own blood—into genital tissue. Dr. Gunter started our social media spat by calling the O-Shot® "potentially very dangerous."

Dr. Runels, who is the inventor and trademark holder for the procedure, immediately responded to the concerns Dr. Gunter raised online by posting "just some of the research" in support of the O-Shot®. At the time, the O-Shot® research literature was basically one small study with Runels as the lead author. The study involved eleven women self-reporting results. There was no control group (that is, a comparator group of patients not receiving the intervention), no blinding (everyone knew who was receiving the treatment), or standardization (exactly what did the treatment involve?). The study is so methodologically limited that it is a stretch to call it a study. Dr. Gunter called it "abysmal" and "fit for lining a hamster cage, and that's about it." But that is what Runels used to support claims of safety and clinical benefit.

No surprise, the study was in a journal put out by the notoriously predatory publisher, OMICS International (more about them in the next chapter). The paper has so many of the hallmarks of a sketchy publication. In the study, Runels is listed as the corresponding author, and his address is ambiguously referenced as "Medical School Birmingham." I used Google Street View to look at the location and found a modest two-storey building with a dumpster in front. Is it actually a medical school? It certainly isn't the University of Alabama at Birmingham medical school, which is 250 miles away from the listed address. Is he trying to create the appearance of legitimacy by using the phrase *medical school* in his affiliation? Big red flag.

Another red flag: how quickly the paper was published. The study was submitted on June 12 and accepted June 25. This timeline suggests that in less than two weeks, the editors of the journal were able to assess the paper, find peer reviewers, have the peer reviews completed and submitted to the journal, have the authors respond to reviews and submit a revised paper, and then assess, accept, and edit the final manuscript. That is ridiculously fast, hinting that perhaps the review and editorial process was, shall we say, less than robust? To put this time frame in context, a 2021 study of how long it usually takes a biomedical paper to go from submission to publication found it ranges between 91 and 639 days. Other research has found that the average time from submission to acceptance hovers around one hundred days. So, yep, two weeks is an eyebrow-raiser.

And yet another red flag: no ethics review. In the paper, it is explicitly noted that the study did not go through ethics review, which is generally required for something that involves patients and is presented as research. This is an oversight that would likely have been caught if the study had been submitted to a more legitimate biomedical journal, which usually requires proof of appropriate ethics review before publication. It came as no surprise when I learned Dr. Runels had already been sanctioned by the U.S. Food and Drug Administration (FDA) for a research ethics violation.

I could go on and on. The study is so fraught that Dr. Gunter's "abysmal" seems a reasonable bottom line.

Since our social media debate in 2016, there remains little evidence to support the use of the O-Shot®, particularly for improved sex, which is, of course, the big selling point. There have been small, inconclusive, or negative studies on the use of PRP for things like genital skin conditions and urinary incontinence. But I couldn't find a single well-done clinical trial supporting the claims about improved sex or orgasms. This is no surprise. As Dr. Gunter has written, "there is no biological reason that platelet rich plasma would help with orgasms." Still, that one methodologically questionable study, published by a known predatory publisher and riddled with red flags, continues to circulate as proof that the O-Shot® works.

Despite the underwhelming evidence base, you can now find the O-Shot® everywhere. If you Google "O-Shot®" (please don't), you will likely find several clinics near you that offer the service, typically for thousands of dollars. The marketing is almost always glowing and unequivocal, promising clear benefits that will, as the website for a clinic in my city states, "rejuvenate your sexual life" and allow you to have the "greatest sex possible in a natural way." (Injecting blood into your genitals is natural?) Reference to Runels's predatory study pops up again and again on the websites of the clinics offering the procedure. In the popular press, the efficacy now seems to be taken for granted. In March 2022, for example, an online publication called *Power Sex Beauty*, "a lifestyle and health blog dedicated to women who want to empower themselves through optimization of health," published an article claiming the O-Shot® was safe and effective, referencing several small poorly done "studies," all published in fringe or predatory journals, and, of course, the original Runels study. The procedure often gets glowing and completely uncritical coverage in the news media. The week I was writing this chapter, the *Daily Mail* had a piece stating the O-Shot® could help with the inability to climax. There are many similarly praise-filled puff pieces, including articles in *The Standard*, *Nylon*, *The Sun*, *Cosmopolitan*, *Bravo*, *Harper's Bazaar*, and *Metro*. Many of these articles note Runels as the inventor and/or link to and quote his study.

Runels's predatory publication has, alas, effectively done its job, legitimizing and normalizing a largely unproven and possibly harmful therapy by injecting (pun intended) the relevant literature with questionable conclusions. It has provided both clinics marketing the procedure and publications writing about it a way to project an illusory certainty about its efficacy. And, presto, an industry is born.

Guys, if you are feeling left out of the PRP-in-your-genitals discussion, fear not, there is also the P-Shot®. As I'm sure you have immediately guessed, it involves injecting PRP into your penis. (Spoiler: don't.) Given that the erectile dysfunction market has a global value of about $6 billion per year, it is hardly surprising to see a similar unproven approach on offer for men too. The notable inventor? It's Dr. Runels, who allegedly "discovered" the procedure by injecting his own penis.

As with the O-Shot®, the evidence base is far from impressive. Indeed, a 2022 study published in the *Journal of the American Medical Association* concluded that "despite a paucity of evidence for its use, PRP injections for the treatment of ED are offered at substantial cost" and that its growing popularity is driven not by science but by "the consumerization of sexual health." In a 2021 consensus statement, the Sexual Medicine Society of North America concluded that the use of therapies like PRP requires more research to "ensure safety and demonstrate efficacy" and, as a result, they should not be "offered in routine clinical practice."

"Yes, it's unproven," Dr. Paul Knoepfler, a biologist at University of California, Davis School of Medicine and an expert on the science surrounding regenerative therapies, confirmed for me when I asked him about the P-Shot. But he also notes that the research is a mess. PRP in the penis has not been the subject of rigorously executed studies. And no, injecting yourself in the penis, as Dr. Runels claims he has done, does not count as rigorous research. "I've gone through a chunk of the literature including meta reviews. There's no consistency in the data. Also, there are no standards in what qualifies as PRP and what's good PRP versus crap," Dr. Knoepfler tells me.

So don't inject your genitals, unless you are into that kinda thing. No judgment.

Be Enraged

What do predatory publications mean for you? Why should you care? To start, you should be totally enraged. Resources that should be used for rigorous research are being squandered on useless publications that harm science and line the pockets of fraudsters. This is an issue that needs to be higher on everyone's agenda, a conclusion that

Dr. David Moher agreed with when I asked him about the severity of the problem. "All stakeholders, such as funders, patients and the public, health policy analysts, and universities, should be more concerned about the existence of predatory publishing and their associated output," he says.

To be fair, some policymakers and regulators have taken notice. In 2019, OMICS International, which published that O-Shot® "study" and which continues to publish journals on a range of biomedical topics, was fined $50 million by the Federal Trade Commission for deceiving thousands of authors by saying that it provided rigorous peer review (it didn't) for its hundreds of journals. The U.S. National Institutes of Health has issued a warning to the researchers it funds to only publish in reputable journals. And there are more and more academics, like Moher and his colleagues, studying the issue.

But more needs to be done. So let your local and federal politicians know you want action! We need systems in place to identify predatory publications and ensure they don't find their way into clinical guidelines, news reports, health policies, marketing, or systematic reviews. We also shouldn't allow the use of public funds to pay for publication in predatory journals. This simple step would have a significant impact. Most academics would likely be unwilling to pay out of pocket for a predatory publication. No funds, no industry. While some private actors, like the Dr. Runels of the world, may continue to pay for publication, this is a small hunk of the market. The predatory journals need the academic community to survive.

Some have suggested that we need to go even further, designating publication in a predatory journal as an act of academic misconduct. In a 2021 editorial, for example, Nicole Shu Ling Yeo-Teh and Bor Luen Tang from National University of Singapore persuasively argue that "wilfully submitting one's manuscript to a predatory journal may constitute an active act of avoidance of rigorous peer review of one's work" and therefore be considered a "form of scientific misconduct." I like this idea. But how about a satire exception for articles about homeopathy?

Professor Mike Daube, the housemate of journal editor Ollie the doggie, thinks more needs to be done to "close down these appalling pseudo-publications," as he put it to me. He suggests a campaign to heighten awareness of the significance of the problem. "I would like to see academic institutions in all countries counselling staff and students on a regular basis against any involvement with these journals," Daube tells me.

Clearly, there needs to be a global rethink about how we incentivize and reward research. Pressure to publish, which is the gasoline that fuels the predatory publishing industry, is associated with reduced job satisfaction, poorer quality research, publication bias, and issues of academic integrity and fraud. Research institutions—especially universities—need to focus more on metrics such as quality and community impact. I get that it is tempting to lean on the countable, like the number of publications, instead of more nebulous metrics like "community impact." Regardless, a rejig is required. And "but it's hard!" is rarely a good excuse for not implementing a needed policy change.

"Wait, I Published in a Hijacked Journal?"

While predatory journals play an outsized role in polluting of academic research, there are many other harmful trends that need to be considered if we are to successfully clean up the increasingly muddled academic literature, including the bizarre, but surprisingly common, swindle involving legitimate academic journals. The phenomenon of hijacking a journal exploits the publish-or-perish economy of academia just as predatory journals do, but it is a completely different, and even more unlawful, animal. It is a criminal operation done solely to deceive for profit. It is straight-up fraud.

You would think that academics always know where their written work ends up. The publication process—especially when it involves a legitimate journal—can be long and complicated and includes ongoing interactions with editors and reviewers. When an academic submits to and works with a journal, they must know which journal they are submitting to, right? Not always. Even seasoned researchers can get duped into submitting to questionable or totally sham publications. They can become inadvertent participants in the illegitimate publication ecosystem.

Increasingly, online scammers are hijacking legitimate journal names and internet domains to con scholars into sending them publication fees. It is a sophisticated racket run by cybercriminals and involving very real-looking documents and websites. This is the publication equivalent of buying a fake Gucci handbag when you think you are getting the real thing. The fraudsters leverage the reputation of a legitimate "Gucci" journal to lure academics, who are excited to be published, into sending them publication fees. To be clear, these journals aren't real in *any* academic sense. Unscrupulous operators forge a copycat website, journal name, and its associated images to trick academics. It is a crime.

And as with predatory journals, publications in hijacked journals—which means, remember, that the research hasn't been properly vetted, edited, or peer-reviewed—can end up influencing policy and polluting valued research databases. Recent research by Dr. Anna Abalkina, for example, found that the World Health Organization's library of publications about COVID-19 contained approximately four hundred publications from hijacked journals. Think about that. This was a key research resource compiled by the world's leading public health agencies, during a pandemic, and it was filled with fake publications? Not good. Another study, published in 2023, found that an often used and respected academic database, Scopus, contains publications from over sixty-seven hijacked journals, including publications with unvetted medical research. This means that this fraudulent BS could be impacting health decisions.

This can happen because of how real the fake journal appears—remember, the fraudsters have made a copycat website that confuses not only the authors who submit to the publication but also those who cite the research as authentic.

I highlight the hijacked journal phenomenon to stress how messed up the world of iffy journals—and, really, the entire academic publishing enterprise—has become.

Create Your Own Science-y Journal!

Let's say you are an anti-vaccine advocate, and you can't get your science-free nonsense published in a respected journal. Your writing is rejected, retracted, or ignored by the broader scientific community. What can you do? How will you spread your harmful claptrap in a way that makes it look credible? Easy. Start your own journal!

This is yet another phenomenon polluting both academic literature and, perhaps more important, the public discourse. People are creating pretend journals that look legitimate for the sole purpose of advancing a particular agenda. A good example of this trend often appears in my inbox. My anti-vaccine hate mailers often send me "studies" published in the *International Journal of Vaccine Theory, Practice, and Research*. They present the papers as definitive proof of some ridiculous concept, like the idea that mRNA COVID vaccines will cause strange particles to form in your blood. One recent emailer, who thought the particles-in-the-blood thing was a mic-drop, argument-ending point, went out of his way to highlight that the journal in question was a "peer-reviewed scholarly open access journal." (It's not.) This journal is published by a well-known anti-vaccine advocate, and the editorial board is populated with like-minded individuals, many of whom have been involved in vaccine-related controversies—such as having their research retracted from authentic scientific publications.

To give you a sense of how biased this journal is, I reviewed the thirty-three articles published since its inception. Thirty of those papers—91 percent—contain debunked anti-vaccine rhetoric, and usually the bunk was the main theme. The few papers that weren't focused on some overtly anti-vaccine topic touched on related ideas, such as suggesting that COVID testing is fatally flawed or, going totally off the rails, that the "pandemic is an illusion." Even a quick skim of the table of contents—with titles that frame the COVID vaccines as a "Global Crime against Humanity" or assert that the HPV vaccine "Lowered Female Fertility" (reality: no and no)—is enough to give a clear picture of the agenda at play. To make matters worse, 63 percent of the articles were written by the editor-in-chief, the senior editor, or someone on the editorial board. At legitimate publications, editors are supposed to make unbiased decisions—based on the assessment of independent peer reviews—about what gets published in the journal. But here they mostly just incestuously publish their own work.

The journal is more like a fanzine for the anti-vaccine community than an academic publication. But, alas, this faking-it strategy works. Papers published in this bogus journal are used by anti-vaccine organizations—such as Robert F. Kennedy Jr.'s notoriously anti-vax Children's Health Defense, which had a glowing profile of the journal on its website, and the pseudoscience-selling *Natural News*—to make their science-free positions seem more scientifically plausible. The publication is also featured in fringe media outlets, such as the *Epoch Times*, which was characterized by the *New York Times* as "a leading purveyor of right-wing misinformation." No surprise, the bunk is also shared on social media. I reviewed the top fifty tweets that mention the journal and most are positive in tone. There were a few tweets that rightly note it is a "quack journal" with "zero credibility," but 84 percent of the tweets I examined were either explicitly positive—"remarkable study," "Gr8 paper & perspective," "bombshell"—or passing on information from the journal in an uncritical manner. During the writing of this book, another well-known anti-vaccine advocate from the U.K.

published a paper in a questionable vanity journal calling for the immediate stoppage of COVID vaccine administration. Again, the author was an editor for the journal, and his paper's position was not supported by the body of evidence, but the "academic" publication facilitated the rapid spread and legitimization of his misleading take. I still see it referenced, on social media and by anti-vaxxers, almost daily.

There are many other examples of fake academic journals being used to forward nasty agendas, such as the infamous, and now defunct, Holocaust denier journal, *Journal of Historical Review*. As with the anti-vaccine periodical, the journal was little more than an engine of propaganda for the editorial board. There are similar fake journals in areas like climate change and alternative medicine that were created largely for the purpose of promoting and legitimizing discredited positions.

Unfortunately, unless you take the time to dig into details of the publication, it can be easy to get fooled. As noted by Isobelle Clarke, professor at the University of Lancaster, in a 2022 article, "fake science that masquerades as trustworthy and authoritative information is harder to spot." And this, of course, is why denialists and hucksters use this strategy. It takes a bit of effort and time to figure out if a journal or a study is credible. My advice: if a claim runs counter to conventional wisdom and it appears to support a specific controversial agenda, double-check the legitimacy of the source. (Yes, controversial research does—as it *should*—get published in credible and prestigious journals, but the science needs to be solid enough to pass truly independent peer review.) Also, look to see how others in the scientific community reference the research, if at all. If the work is not being picked up by the broader academic community, even to contest the conclusions, be suspicious. See who, if anyone, is referencing the work. I did an analysis of the citation patterns for articles published in the *International Journal of Vaccine Theory, Practice, and Research*, and nearly all of them were in other articles in the same journal, by members of the editorial board (often in a paper published in a predatory journal), or by other renowned anti-vaccine advocates. The echo-chambering is strong here!

What is also needed is for professional, scientific, and research funding organizations to identify and speak out against these fake journals. When I do a Google search on *"International Journal of Vaccine Theory, Practice, and Research,"* the first page of my results has only *one* post, ranked eighth in my results, that is critical of the journal (and it is just a post on Quora, a question-and-answer website, of someone asking if the journal is legitimate). The top result—the snippet, which is what most people click on—has "scholarly articles" from the journal. Ugh. This is a disastrous result. This is what the public will see if they investigate the journal. Again, ugh. Indeed, I could find no statements from respected organizations clarifying for the public that they should not take the journal seriously. We need more easily accessible, trustworthy, and shareable content that clearly identifies and debunks this kind of polluting publication.

AI . . . Sigh.
It Ain't Gonna Get Any Easier

Recently my kids asked ChatGPT—the artificial-intelligence-powered chatbot—to write a Timothy Caulfield tweet about immune boosting. The AI program nailed it, capturing my voice and views. "The best way to support your immune health is through a balanced diet, regular physical activity, and stress management," counselled the AI version of me.

My kids then asked ChatGPT to write a tweet about ChatGPT writing a tweet. Again, the AI me did an admirable job: "Wow, ChatGPT really knows its stuff! This tweet about immune boosting is spot on and full of evidence-based advice. Remember, when it comes to your health, it's important to be cautious of unproven remedies and quick fixes."

Finally, they asked the program to "write a Timothy Caulfield tweet about ChatGPT writing a tweet about ChatGPT writing a tweet." The response was again pitch perfect. "Wow, this is getting meta" was the response. Yes, it is, ChatGPT. Yes. It. Is.

Perhaps I should have asked ChatGPT to write this book. Perhaps I did!

Technologies that could be used to pollute academic literature are developing so fast that by the time this book has been published, my consciousness may have been hacked by an AI algorithm with the goal of publishing misleading papers in my name. I'm only half joking.

When I started writing this book, how AI might be used in the realm of academic publication was mostly speculative. But months later, an academic paper entitled "The Role of AI in Drug Discovery" had ChatGPT as a co-author to, as the paper notes, "help human authors write review articles." Another study published in March 2023 outlines the challenges associated with AI, "particularly in relation to academic honesty and plagiarism." The paper was, ironically, written by ChatGPT. Point made. And a study from Northwestern University and the University of Chicago found that "ChatGPT writes believable scientific abstracts" that even academics couldn't detect as AI-created. This prompted the authors to recommend that "journals and medical conferences [adapt] policy and practice to maintain rigorous scientific standards" including using AI detectors—that is, programs that identify the possible use of AI technologies—in the editorial process. A policy document by Eurasia Group selected the rise of AI, which they call a "weapon of mass disruption," as one of the biggest risks of 2023, noting that "user-friendly applications such as ChatGPT and Stable Diffusion will allow anyone minimally tech-savvy to harness the power of AI." And just days ago, I received an email from my vice dean asking all professors to inform students that "use of AI writing tools and text generators (such as ChatGPT) is a breach of the Code of Student Behaviour at the University of Alberta. Sanctions for breaching the Code range from a grade reduction to expulsion."

In a few years from now—perhaps when you are reading these words—I wouldn't be surprised if the above exchange with the ChatGPT Timothy Caulfield seems anachronistic. Of course, you may be thinking, *AI is writing academic papers. How quaint of you to worry!* This is the point. The relevant technology is moving incredibly quickly and will almost certainly complicate all the topics I've noted above. AI might, for example, write and help to disseminate bad science, such as "academic" work designed to forward pseudoscientific or political agendas. It could have been used, for example, to complete my above noted bogus homeopathy paper and to write glowing and entirely believable social media posts about how brilliant it is.

As quoted by *Nature*, Sandra Wachter, a technology and society expert from the University of Oxford, is "very worried" about the study that found ChatGPT could write believable scientific abstracts. "If we're now in a situation where the experts are not able to determine what's true or not, we lose the middleman that we desperately need to guide us through complicated topics." I totally agree. The explosion of easy to access AI technologies makes it likely that, as the Eurasia policy document notes, "the volume of content rises exponentially, making it impossible for most citizens to reliably distinguish fact from fiction. Disinformation will flourish."

Zombie Science

Predatory publications. Hijacked and agenda-driven fake journals. AI-generated content. Scientific literature is being muddled by a host of forces. To make matters worse, even when bad studies are recognized and attempts are made to correct the record, the bad data can live on, continuing to confuse the scientific and public discourse. Let's start with one of the most notorious examples of this "zombie science" problem.

If you're thinking about writing a thriller featuring an evil scientist, might I suggest selecting Andrew Wakefield as the central antagonist. Few individuals in the history of biomedicine have done as much harm to public health. From my perspective, there seems little doubt that his deceitful research and twisted advocacy have been a driving force behind the growth of the modern anti-vaccine movement and the rise in infectious disease outbreaks, including measles—a disease that kills almost 150,000 people every year, mostly children. Following the advent of this anti-vaccine rhetoric, and no doubt thanks to its legacy, those death numbers are increasing.

Wakefield's ascent to the pinnacle of despicableness all started with one small and staggeringly shoddy study. Before his infamy, he was a physician and surgeon, educated in Canada, practising medicine in the U.K. In 1998, Wakefield was the lead author on a paper, published in the respected medical journal *The Lancet*, that claimed there was a connection between vaccination and autism. The research was little more than a case study—which, right out of the gate, needs to be recognized as a highly limited methodological approach. Basically, the paper is not so much a report on a rigorously controlled study as a description of what was observed in twelve children after they received the measles vaccine. Like Runels's sloppy attempt to prove the efficacy of the O-Shot®, there was no randomization or control group, so the sample of children had the potential to be highly biased, which, as I will outline below, is exactly what happened. A study of this nature, especially one so small, cannot establish causation. But that didn't stop Wakefield from suggesting—at a 1998 press conference that one science journalist has called "one of the biggest public relations disasters in medicine"—that his results showed a clear link between vaccines and autism.

No surprise, this sensationalistic spin was picked up and amplified by the popular press. The lie—and it is now clear that it was a blatant and harmful lie—took off. There was a flood of headlines and stories in news outlets like the *Daily Mail* ("New MMR Link Found to Autism"), *New York Times* ("The Not-So-Crackpot Autism Theory"),

CNN ("I Think There Is a Link"), and *60 Minutes* ("Controversial Researcher Claims Link between Vaccine and Autism"), which regularly featured Wakefield and reported on the heartbreaking experiences of parents with autistic children. Celebrity enablers, most notably actress and comedian Jenny McCarthy, amplified Wakefield's science-free hypothesis. McCarthy's infamous appearances on *Larry King Live* and the *Oprah Winfrey Show* helped to legitimize Wakefield's message. On Oprah's show, for example, McCarthy called the measles vaccine "the autism shot," and the hugely influential host praised her as a "mother warrior." Many other media outlets gave McCarthy's message a platform. A piece on *ABC News* from around the same time opened by highlighting how McCarthy was using her "star power to raise awareness about the dangers of childhood vaccinations that they believe are linked to diseases like autism." Vaccination rates declined. Disease outbreaks increased. Children died. For years, there was even a website called the Jenny McCarthy Body Count that tracked the number of vaccine-preventable deaths and illnesses that had occurred since she started her anti-vaccine campaign.

This fearmongering hype happened despite vigorous pushback by the clinical and biomedical research community almost as soon as the 1998 study appeared, including scientific commentary that the study was methodologically weak, far from conclusive, and counter to the large body of existing evidence that the measles vaccine was safe and highly effective.

The Wakefield debacle is a cautionary tale about so many things, including the problem of false balance in the media and how misinformation and fearmongering can be used to build a profitable brand. Wakefield never should have been taken so seriously by the popular press, and his theories should have been positioned as fringe. Sadly, Wakefield is now a hero in the anti-vaccine community, and he tours the world speaking about this nonsense. But here I want to focus on the enduring role of that one fraudulent, and now retracted, 1998 study in the *The Lancet*. It stands as one of the best examples of how even formally discredited academic papers can have an ongoing and insidious impact on academic literature, public perception, and health debates.

While it took far too long, the 1998 paper was finally retracted by the *The Lancet* in 2010. As a result of investigations by journalists such as Brian Deer, it was revealed that not only was the study methodologically questionable, it was also full of falsehoods, data distortions, and conflicts of interest. For example, the research was funded by lawyers acting for parents involved in lawsuits against vaccine manufacturers, which, no surprise, influenced the selection of children for this study. Indeed, as Deer's examination revealed, the "undisclosed goal" of the research "was to help sue the vaccine's manufacturers." After looking at the details and data surrounding all twelve children reported in the study, he came to the damning conclusion that "no case was free of misreporting or alteration." The data for this hugely influential study wasn't slightly mishandled; it was fraudulent through and through. Add some research ethics misconduct to the story, and it's no surprise that Wakefield lost his medical licence. In 2010, the General Medical Council, which regulates physicians in the U.K., found that he acted "dishonestly and irresponsibly" while doing the research and had "callous disregard" for the child participants.

Wakefield has never replicated his results (no surprise), and there is now a large and well-done body of evidence that tells us, emphatically, that there is absolutely no link between vaccines and autism. A retracted, fraudulent, and obviously incorrect study by a completely discredited and unethical author couldn't still be influential, right? Alas, this zombie lives on. It. Will. Not. Die.

A 2021 study used various metrics to map the power of the 1998 Wakefield paper. The researchers found that it had an almost immediate and negative impact on public perception. Vaccine skepticism increased as did the almost certainly erroneous reporting of vaccine injuries. There was also a shift in media reporting on vaccines toward the negative—all trends that continued past the retraction. The authors conclude that this demonstrates that "attention to false or misleading vaccine research can impact public confidence in vaccines." Yep. Public perception data has consistently found that a depressingly large percentage of the population continued to believe this nonsense. A 2015 survey—five years *after* the retraction—found that 21 percent of Americans under thirty believed vaccines cause autism, and only 59 percent knew that it is definitely or probably false. Another survey, done the same year in my home province of Alberta, came to the exact same conclusion: 21 percent of the nearly three thousand interviewed believed vaccines cause autism. It is worth stating again that this tremendously harmful belief, embraced by millions and millions of people around the world, all started with that one, now retracted, study.

I asked Dr. Matthew Motta, the lead author of the above 2021 study and a professor at Boston University's School of Public Health, about the profound impact of the Wakefield paper. He believes their study "provides strong causal evidence that Wakefield's piece played an instrumental role in sowing doubt about the safety of childhood vaccines." This doubt, Motta says, shaped public discourse surrounding the measles vaccine and "the possibility that it might be unsafe." Once that doubt was injected, it was difficult to dissipate.

The public weren't the only ones adversely affected by Wakefield's fraud. A study in 2021 did a thorough examination of how the academic community referenced the 1998 paper. It found, no surprise given the initial hype, that hundreds referenced the fraudulent study as soon as it was released. But paradoxically, post-retraction referencing increased! From 2011 to 2017, for example, there were 337 academic references to the Wakefield study, and approximately 62 percent failed to explicitly note that it was officially retracted and only about half of those references were clearly negative in tone. Another analysis, published in 2019, came to a similar conclusion noting that "a significant number of authors did not document retractions of the article by Wakefield."

The Wakefield zombie marches on and continues to consume brains, including those of the academic variety. Why is this happening?

"Wakefield's work is continually reanimated by anti-vaccine activists who feel as if the work is a legitimate contribution to scientific discourse," Motta tells me. Those pushing a particular agenda keep the study in the public eye. "Anti-vaccine activists are essentially using the language of science—that is, discussing the fact that the piece was published in a prestigious medical journal, lending credence to the study's methods and findings, etc.—in order to cast doubt on scientific consensus regarding vaccine safety," Motta says. The study's retraction by the The Lancet fits into the broader anti-vaccine idea that Wakefield was persecuted for bravely speaking the truth. The fake science imparts science-y credibility, while the retraction feeds a fake narrative. Zombies are hard to kill.

Of course, the Wakefield paper isn't the only retracted study that still lingers and does harm. A 2021 study of over thirteen thousand papers retracted from 1960 to 2020 came to the depressing conclusion that *only* 5.4 percent of post-retraction references acknowledged retraction. Oof. An *Economist* analysis of twenty thousand retracted articles determined that 84 percent received at least one post-retraction citation which, taken together, was 95,000 post-retraction citations. And *those* papers were cited in another 1.65 million papers. Like an infectious agent, the zombie not only lives, it can also mutate and spread its literature-polluting poison rapidly and far.

As we saw with the Wakefield bunk, some retracted papers thrive in their post-retraction life. A study from the University of Michigan, also published in 2022, did an analysis of almost four thousand retracted papers to quantify how much attention they received over a ten-year period. The depressing result: retracted papers received *more* attention—in the popular press, on social media, in the academic literature—than studies that are never retracted. This is concerning on many levels; as the authors of the study note, "flawed findings [spread] throughout the scientific community and the lay public."

There are several reasons for this heightened and continued attention, including the reality that the retraction process itself might generate attention. But I suspect the main reason is that the content of retracted articles is often more exciting than studies that are done rigorously. Bad science can be more extreme, and as a result, it grabs more eyeballs, especially if it plays to a cultural moment and/or feeds a controversial position that demands supportive data. Vaccines cause autism! (Wrong and retracted.) Ivermectin treats COVID! (Wrong and retracted.) Police shootings are not associated with anti-Black racism! (Wrong and retracted.)

This last study, originally published in 2019, has been called "fundamentally flawed" by experts in the field and is a good example of how controversy grabs and keeps attention. It has been used by partisan voices to argue against police reform. It even seeped into the language of president Donald Trump, when, shortly after the murder of George Floyd in the summer of 2020, he made the misleading statement that "more white people" are killed by police—a position almost certainly informed by this study. This retracted study was viewed as so flawed and misleading that over 850 academics co-signed a letter condemning it as "scientific malpractice." But, as noted in a comment on the study in the *Washington Post* by professors Dean Knox from the University of Pennsylvania and Jonathan Mummolo from Princeton University, "ideologues now seek to resuscitate this discredited work, claiming the retraction was politically motivated."

Keeping zombies alive by deploying motivated reasoning—a cognitive bias that leads to the embrace of ideas based on their desirability rather than the evidence—is all too common. Those who liked the outcome of this study, like those who found the Wakefield study helpful to the anti-vaccine agenda, use Olympic-level mental gymnastics to keep it circulating as valid science. They ignore the large body of evidence that runs counter to the conclusions of the retracted study. And they reason away the retraction, weaving it into a broader storyline that, paradoxically, makes the bogus study appear even *more* valid and significant. I have personally experienced this twisted thinking when engaging with anti-vaccine advocates or people who believe ivermectin, the now infamous antiparasitic drug, is a miracle cure. "Of course, that study was retracted," they tell me. "Big Pharma can't have those conclusions floating around!" Or some such thing.

What is required to address this vast retraction issue? First, speed! Currently, a formal retraction can take a long time. The retraction of the Wakefield study—a paper that was defective on so many levels—took over ten years. Far too long. Studies have shown that retractions take, on average, somewhere between two and three years after the initial publication. Retractions need to happen as soon as it is clear that a paper is fraudulent, manipulated, or methodologically unsound, even if the retraction is provisional. We need to deploy new strategies, such as using social media and AI, to identify flawed papers more quickly. Research on how misinformation spreads—an area where I do a great deal of work—has shown that a rapid response is key. The longer misinformation is circulating, the more entrenched it becomes and the harder it is to debunk.

To address this, it has been suggested by several commentators, including the editor-in-chief of the journal *Science*, Dr. Holden Thorp, that a two-step process is required. The first stage would focus on the validity of the paper without attributing any blame to the authors. Teasing out the wrongdoing—the use of fraudulent data or other misconduct—is often complicated and time-consuming. Reputations and careers are at stake. So, "Who screwed up?" should be stage two of the process. As soon as it is demonstrated that a paper has unmistakeable, retraction-worthy shortcomings, it should be removed from the literature. In a welcome nod to the seriousness of the retraction problem, in April 2023 the U.K. parliament issued a report on the need to increase efforts to protect scientific integrity, including, the report noted, a retraction process that "should not take longer than two months."

In addition, we need to make it crystal clear when a paper has been retracted. It needs to be obvious to everyone. Of course, authors and journal editors must do a better job vetting their references. But it isn't only about a lack of effort. A 2022 study found that most authors report that they do check their references—or, at least, they say they try to check. Despite that attempt, 89 percent of the authors "were unaware of the retracted status of the cited article, mainly because of inadequate notification of the retraction status in journals and/or databases and the use of stored copies."

That is a stunning conclusion. All research databases must do a better job of flagging retracted papers as such. It should be immediately obvious not just on the journal website but also in the search results. Search engines like Google and Google Scholar should also flag that a study has been retracted so it is immediately apparent, right in the search results, that the data is not reliable. Let's have a clear banner that says "retracted" in red. Bold. Flashing letters? Sure. And, of course, the media must be extra careful. Journalists should not reference or rely on retracted studies. When the media is reporting on the actual retraction, they should be clear about why the study was withdrawn. Research has demonstrated that the trustworthiness of the source of the retraction is a strong predictor of a retraction's effectiveness. Journalists should explain how and why the retraction happened.

No one, not the media or that email-sending uncle who lives in a rabbit hole, should fall for the "single study syndrome"—especially when that one study has been retracted! Indeed, for you, dear reader, this is probably the most important takeaway—one that is an important theme for this part of the book. If a claim is based on one study, be "much more suspicious," Dr. Ivan Oransky tells me. He is the founder of the influential *Retraction Watch*, a website that tracks, reports, and investigates retracted studies. I think it is fair to say he is one of the world's foremost authorities on the topic. He notes that a single study can be interesting and invite us to revisit previous work on a topic, but "if you are literally pointing to *one* paper" to make an argument, suspicion should be the default response. Again, always consider the *body* of evidence!

While Oransky agrees that eventually the good science wins out, he is pessimistic about how long that process takes. Bad research, retractions, and predatory journals are causing a "pollution of the literature" that has slowed science's march toward objective truths. For him, the time scale for correction is likely to be "generational," not measured in months or years. "You can play Whac-A-Mole with individual [retracted] studies," he notes. But what is needed are big, system-altering fixes.

And I haven't even touched on paper mills, the multi-million-dollar industry of selling authorship to publications that usually involve faked or poor-quality data. There's also straight-up fraudulent research and manipulated data, which 8 percent of researchers admitted to in an anonymous survey from 2021. And then there are the problems and limitations of the peer-review process for legitimate journals, the slowness of academic journals to correct honest research errors, and the tremendous impact of conflicts of interest, particularly when industry is involved.

Oransky rolls out a dark analogy to hammer home his glum assessment of the futility of the task ahead. For him, the current knowledge-production environment is a "big nasty swamp and there's all kinds of crap in there. It's toxic. And you get excited about picking off a floating piece of plastic. It's not bad to pick off the plastic. In fact, it's necessary. But you also know there are PCBs at the bottom of the swamp. You are going to have to do much more. It's just so complex."

A grim image to end on. A toxic swamp filled with bad science, retracted studies, predatory papers, and hijacked journals. But approximately $2.5 trillion is spent every year on that swamp, also known as the global investment in research and development. We must do better.

We need to be aware of the degree to which the language and trappings of science—that is, science co-opted as a certainty-affirming *brand*, and not the rigorous process of *actual science*—are increasingly used to confer credibility, forward agendas, sell products, and build careers. The language of science is so persuasive because of its promise to provide unbiased and agenda-free guidance toward some degree of certainty. It's Carl Sagan's candle in the darkness. The glow cast by that candle has become so valuable and sought after, it is now a core commodity of our information economy—and far too often it's twisted, exploited, and degraded beyond recognition.

PART II
THE
GOODNESS
ILLUSION

Health Halos

"Well, I want something that is *natural*. Something *without* chemicals."

This was the response I got when I asked a neighbour—during an intense driveway discussion—why he was taking unproven supplements to "boost" his immune system.

There is a lot going on in that response. So many questions. What does *natural* mean, and why is that a good thing? How are supplements natural? How are they devoid of chemicals? Can you even boost your immune system?

What I found most interesting was the tone of the response. The benefits of natural and chemical-free were taken to be self-evident. It was a mic-drop retort that, apparently, required no further explanation.

The goodness illusion—that is, exploiting our desire to achieve an evidence-informed virtuous goal—comes in many forms, but one of the most pernicious is the use of words and phrases that give off a health halo. *Clean. Holistic. Organic. Non-GMO. Chemical-free. Gluten-free. Immune-boosting.* These kinds of declarations, which appear on the packaging of health products and on the websites of wellness brands, are often both meaningless and deceptive. Yet they have an impact on our health beliefs, behaviours, and public health strategies.

A health halo is created by a word or phrase that encourages us to believe a product is better, safer, or healthier than it is. These terms become signifiers of a particular approach to a healthy lifestyle. They come to represent a goodness goal. And they provide marketers, pseudoscience profiteers, and wellness influencers with a powerful tool that can short-circuit our critical thinking and, in the big picture, hurt public health. A word like *clean, natural,* or *holistic* comes to be shorthand for good, virtuous, and healthy, even if there is no conceptually coherent reason—or evidence—for that to be the case. As noted by Christina Hartmann, a researcher who explores how we select food, "It's not about lying to consumers, but about somehow creating a product image that is perceived as healthy."

Health halo is the phrase I use to refer to words and phrases that are all about creating a vibe or an immediate impression of health to influence our thinking and behaviour. Health halos are about leveraging our desire for goodness. Crucially, health halos are also a shortcut to a kind of certainty. Research has shown that people often form opinions and make decisions about what is good and bad based on less information than they think. A 2018 study from the University of Chicago found that "good things strike us as good and bad things strike us as bad much faster than we expect to draw these conclusions." Despite all the information that is literally at our fingertips, we come to conclusions about things quickly and sometimes after just a glance at a convincing label on a product we are considering.

In our frenetic information environment, health halos can lead us to feel certain about a particular purchase even if there is no evidence to support that feeling of certainty. Unfortunately, this strategy works very, very well.

Health halos do more than mislead us about the actual healthiness of a product; they can also have an adverse impact on our behaviour.

Research has consistently found, for example, that the perceived health-iness of food—as influenced by words with a health halo, like *organic* or *reduced fat*—has an effect on how much people eat. Paradoxically, the health halo effect can cause people to eat larger portion sizes and more calories, in part because the health halo causes people to feel less guilty about their consumption. When we think food is healthier, we tend to eat more of it! Of course, the organic-ness or clean-ness or natural-ness of a product does not have an impact on its number of calories. "Totally natural" potato chips have the same calories as con-ventional potato chips.

The psychological power of health halos can even influence how we perceive the taste of food. Research has consistently shown that an organic label leads to a higher overall liking of a food product, the per-ception that it tastes better, and a willingness to pay more. A study from 2015, for example, found that people often believe organic food tastes better simply because it is perceived to be ethically superior to non-organic food. This taste expectation, the researchers found, enhances the actual taste experience, thus reinforcing the original expectation. The moral satisfaction of eating in a way that is perceived to be ethical casts a halo effect over the food's properties. Goodness tastes good.

This happens even though blind taste tests have found that organic food does not, in general, taste better than conventionally grown food. A 2012 analysis of qualities that Italian consumers liked in their yogurt found no "distinction in odor/taste/texture between organic and con-ventional samples." However, consumers ranked conventional yogurt higher when it was labelled as organic. A 2021 blind taste test study from the University of Copenhagen came to the same conclusion about conventional versus organic smoked salmon. When consumers were informed of the production method, they said they liked organic better. Other studies have found similar results with a range of foods, includ-ing milk, chicken, and fruits and vegetables. The health halo almost always wins. Indeed, a 2017 study exploring the taste perceptions asso-ciated with organic apples found that subjects with strong beliefs about the value of organic rated the taste of an apple labelled as organic significantly higher than a slice not labelled organic from *the same apple*! The authors conclude that "beliefs about how organic and local foods taste can play a stronger role in taste perceptions than actual taste for certain segments of consumers."

Health halos can be so powerful that they can make things that are unhealthy—really, really, really unhealthy—seem healthier. Sports drinks. Sugar-filled fruit juices. Potato chips. Et cetera. The use of healthy-sounding words to market cigarettes is one of the most notorious and absurd examples of this insidious phenomenon. The makers of Natural (big sigh) American Spirit cigarettes use language like "100% additive-free natural tobacco" and "made with organic tobacco" to market their product—and the strategy has helped to make it an increasingly popular brand. A 2017 study found that this language caused a majority (64 percent) of smokers to inaccurately believe that this brand of cigarette is "less harmful than other brands." Even when the packaging contains disclaimers that explicitly note that the cigarettes are not safer, the health halo wins out.

An interesting study from 2020 demonstrates just how powerful this marketing strategy can be. The researchers found the American Spirit brand to be particularly popular in communities with strong *non-smoking* norms. In other words, this product sells especially well in cities that have a low level of smoking—likely because these cities have a larger portion of individuals who are more concerned about their health and therefore respond to health halo words like *natural* and *organic*. This demonstrates two things about health halos: they are highly effective, and there need not be any connection to actual healthiness for the halo to have a measurable impact.

Health halos can even impact children. A 2017 experiment by the Rudd Center for Food Policy and Health at the University of Connecticut demonstrated that child-friendly advertising for nutrient-poor foods (that is, junk food) that included a health-halo element resulted in the children rating the junk food as significantly healthier than in conditions without the health halo. The study also found that, alas, the health halo did not improve the children's view or knowledge about nutrition. The bad food was simply viewed as better.

Of course, there are many nuances to the impact of the health-halo effect. And the news isn't all bad. Studies have shown, for example, that a halo effect can affect products from companies perceived to be socially responsible—which might nudge corporations in a helpful direction, such as toward more sustainable and ethical approaches to food production. But even this social plus might come with an individual health negative—such as causing people to consume too much or to wrongly perceive a product to be healthy, even when it's not. Too often, corporations simply use a health halo to cast a goodness spell to sell their product.

Some of the health halos I describe below are so common, you might have been lulled into thinking their effect is innocuous. Don't be deceived! When you dig into the research, it becomes clear they can do real harm. They stand as examples of how our desire to do good— for ourselves, our families and communities, and the environment— coupled with a noisy and confusing information environment can be exploited to push products, profits, and political agendas. Let's start with the food and wellness space and look at some of the most well-known and the worst offenders.

The Devious Dozen

I don't want to relitigate all the science surrounding some of the most pervasive health-halo terms. Some, such as *organic* and *non-GMO*, remain contested and politically controversial. I will straight up admit that the science is uncertain for *specific elements* of some (but not all) of these topics. And that is my modest, but still critically important, point! Increasingly, these terms project an implied certainty, and they are meant to be taken—by the public, the market, the popular press, and even by some politicians—to reflect a truism about our world and what we should do to make it a better, safer, or healthier place. That is wrong. To paraphrase Inigo Montoya's famous quote from *The Princess Bride*, "We keep using these words. I do not think they mean what we think they mean."

1. Natural

Even though it remains wholly devoid of a specific meaning, the mother of all health halos is the word *natural*. It is so omnipresent in the health, nutrition, and wellness spaces that it has become an expected and comforting norm, washing over us like Muzak at the local grocery store. A 2017 review of seventy-two surveys involving a total of over 83,000 participants from around the world came to two very unsurprising conclusions: for most people, the naturalness of food is crucial, a finding that was observed across numerous countries and the time span the studies were conducted, and there is no consistent definition of *natural*. Basically, we all want natural but aren't sure what it is.

Much has been written about the problems with this health halo. The FDA is considering regulating its use. *Consumer Reports*, among other watchdogs, have called for it to be banned as a food label precisely because it is so meaningless and misleading. At the core of its use is a logical fallacy called appeals to nature, which relies on the presumption that what's natural is inherently good, safe, or better for you. Of course, that isn't always true. There are plenty of things that occur in nature that can be fatal to us. Arsenic. Poisonous venom. Lightning. Gravity pulling us to our death. Still, the sway of natural endures and, if anything, has grown in strength—despite many policy, nutrition, and public health experts noting this conceptual inconsistency. One study, for example, found that people strongly prefer "natural" water to water that is, um, "unnatural" (no idea what that is), even after they are told that the two are chemically identical. H_2O is H_2O.

"Nature is a force that existed before humanity," Alan Levinovitz suggests when I ask him about why the word has such a powerful and enduring appeal. Levinovitz is a friend, colleague, and professor of religious studies at James Madison University. His most recent book is called *Nature: How Faith in Nature's Goodness Leads to Harmful Fads, Unjust Laws, and Flawed Science*. So, yes, the ideal person to muse about the place of this word in our lives. "Nature is responsible for the existence of life on Earth, so it seems like it must be wise and good," he tells me.

In our chaotic and anxiety-provoking information environment, calling something natural is an invitation to not worry. It has become a prompt for safety, purity, and authenticity. Indeed, Levinovitz believes our obsession with this amorphous notion has taken on an almost religious appeal. "Without realizing it, people equate nature with God, which makes *natural* the equivalent of holy. Nature, like God, can do no wrong, and all suffering is due to humans defying the *natural*—that is, holy—order of things. Act naturally, and we return to paradise."

The lesson here, of course, is to remember to look beyond the goodness vibe. We also shouldn't forget that the appeal to nature fallacy is more than a conceptually flawed annoyance. It can do great individual and social harm. Those spreading misinformation about vaccines, life-saving pharmaceuticals, needed pesticides and/or preservatives, or safe food production methods have weaponized our love of the word to sow doubt about scientifically proven interventions. The sale of useless and potentially harmful supplements, for example, is buttressed by framing them as natural. The growth of vaccine hesitancy—a trend that is costing lives—is fuelled, in part, by framing vaccines as unnatural. A 2016 study found that if given the choice, 79 percent of participants would select a natural over a synthetic drug, even if the safety and efficacy of the drugs were identical. And 20 percent would select the natural drug even if told it is less safe and less effective.

2. Holistic

Like the word *natural*, *holistic* is absolutely everywhere and near meaningless. But its meaninglessness is of a different variety than natural's. Outside the wellness, alternative medicine, health halo universe, the word means, according to the *Merriam-Webster Dictionary*, "relating to or concerned with wholes or with complete systems." However, the word *holistic* is mostly deployed by alternative health practitioners and wellness gurus to signal that they consider the whole person. The implication is that science-informed healthcare providers (dietitians, physicians, etc.) don't. This false dichotomy has become one of the most common strategies used to market pseudoscience. In addition to *holistic* being tacked on to practitioner designations (e.g., holistic homeopathic medicine), it gets added to product names (e.g., holistic vitamins and supplements) and wellness brands (e.g., a holistic approach to a wellness-infused lifestyle!) to suggest they're different from conventional science-informed approaches to health in a way that they simply aren't.

The reality: the word *holistic* is usually added to the rhetorical mix when a therapy, healthcare intervention, or wellness product is unproven. Saying an approach is holistic does not transform pseudoscience into real science. Zero plus zero is still zero. My holistic takeaway on the word *holistic*? It's a red flag for bunk, so much so that I've developed an allergic reaction to using it, even in a grammatically and contextually appropriate manner.

3. Healthy

This is a tough one. Healthy eating is important. Helping people identify healthier food is not a bad idea. That's one reason some, including the FDA, are calling for a better definition of the word in the context of food labelling. The idea is to require foods that use the label to have a certain amount of real food (e.g., not overly processed) and not too much bad stuff, such as added sugar, salt, and saturated fats.

But a definitive declaration that something is healthy can still be misleading. First, debates continue to rage within the scientific community about what is healthy; it's a moving target that responds to the latest research. So, do we know for certain what foods are worthy of the label?

Second, as Ted Kyle told me, "Defining a single food as healthy or unhealthy is deceptive because it's a person's overall pattern of eating that matters for health. Not a single food in isolation." Kyle is a pharmacist and a well-known advocate for evidence-informed obesity and nutrition policies. He worries that even if defined relatively narrowly, a label of healthy would simply become a marketing tool. "Health claims for a food product only serve to sell more of that product, which might not always lead to better health," Kyle notes.

So, as health halos go, *healthy* is truly a bit devious. There are foods that are healthier than others. Apples and almonds as compared to bacon and potato chips, for example. But the healthy label would likely find its way onto lots of on-the-margins foods. All the classic and well-documented health halo effects—more consumption and a belief that the food is healthier than it really is—would likely kick in. Also, by focusing too much on the label *healthy*, do we instrumentalize food too much? As Kyle notes in a piece critiquing the label, this might be an *unhealthy* trend. "Enjoying the sensual experience of a meal somehow becomes a twisted source of guilt," Kyle writes. For example, under the FDA's proposed approach, a French baguette wouldn't get a healthy label (not enough whole grain). This is an ignominious result for a delicious item that, in November of 2022, UNESCO voted to put on the United Nation's cultural heritage list. Healthy eating is about a pattern of healthy eating, not parsing each food product as good or bad.

Bring on the healthy-label-less baguettes.

4. Organic

Unlike some health halo terms, *organic* is not totally meaningless. Many jurisdictions around the world regulate how something can be certified or marketed as organic. While criteria in different jurisdictions can vary, it generally requires producers to adhere to practices such as the use of non-synthetic pesticides and the absence of prohibited substances, such as artificial preservatives. So, the word does mean *something* about how the food is produced. However, what it does *not* necessarily mean is that the product is healthier—which, of course, is what most people think they are getting when they buy something labelled organic.

"While research shows that shoppers will pay a premium for organics, there is in fact no evidence that organic food is better, cleaner, or healthier than its conventional counterparts," author and dietitian Abby Langer tells me when I ask her to give me her impressions about the word. As with many health halo words, she tells me, it is all about playing to people's fears and to their desire to be seen as doing good. "But organics aren't grown in meadows filled with flowers and butterflies—that's a fairy tale invented by the organic industry."

The body of available evidence backs up Langer's rather harsh assessment. Yes, we do need to constantly consider how to make food healthier and safer and production practices more environmentally sustainable. But the evidence does not support the intuitive appeal—and health halo effect—of organic. The available science remains pretty messy but, in general, tells us organic food is unlikely to be meaningfully healthier. The nutrient values, for instance, don't differ in any clinically consequential way between organic and conventional food. It's also not safer to consume. Both organic and conventional farmers use pesticides—and "organic" pesticides are not necessarily safer and may need to be used in higher concentrations. And if you're under the impression eating organic is better for the environment, that's no guarantee either.

A Portuguese study of organic versus conventionally grown lettuce, to cite one recent example, looked at the levels of twenty pesticides and the presence of a range of pathogens. The study analyzed lettuce from retailers from across Portugal and found that for the parameters investigated "the organic and conventional lettuces were not different." Other research found that, counter to the health halo messaging, organic produce had more microbial contamination than conventionally grown food. Specifically, the researchers found that "vegetables from organic production showed significantly higher load of E. coli than from conventional farms"—which, obviously, is not good. The authors of the study come to the damning conclusion that "the fertilization system practiced in organic farms may deteriorate sanitary quality of the produce."

To be fair, it is probably best to describe the body of science associated with organic food, especially in the context of the impact on the environment, as complex and evolving. In general, organic farms are less efficient, have lower yields, and are more resource intensive, which is not good for sustainability, but they may have more biodiversity and less soil erosion, which is good. And like conventional farms, not all organic farms are the same—some may have more biodiversity, others may not. We should strive to take the best from all production methods, regardless of the label used to describe them. But my point here is more straightforward: despite the impression created by the health halo, the benefits of organic are far from definitive. The presence of an organic label should not be viewed as a sign that what you are buying is clearly and unequivocally better for you or the environment than a conventionally grown product.

And the organic label does not transform the unhealthy into the healthy. As Abby Langer notes, "organic candy and Cheetos are not any healthier than the regular versions of these foods."

5. Non-GMO

I'm not known for my cooking skills. When I'm home alone, dinner often involves an apple, an unpeeled carrot or two, and what my kids call "Dad Dinner"—Triscuits and cheese. I've always loved Triscuits. And with decades of practice, I've perfected my Dad Dinner. (I can, for instance, fill an entire plate in one NFL commercial break.) But around 2017, the entire Triscuit product line went non-GMO in a very public way. There were even advertisements featuring one of my favourite comedians, former *Saturday Night Live* cast member Cecily Strong. (Why, Cecily? Why?) This created a culinary crisis:

I knew the non-GMO label was nothing more than a manipulative marketing tactic. Should I stick with my crackers or take a science-informed stand against fearmongering?

The popularity of the non-GMO label has grown rapidly over the past few years. When asked, most consumers say they prefer to buy foods that have it. Studies have consistently shown that, as with organic, a primary driver of interest in non-GMO is a belief that it is healthier.

There are many other reasons for—and continued debates about—the preference for non-GMO products, such as the concern that GMO products facilitate corporate monopolies because they allow the ownership and control, via patents, of aspects of the food production process. On its face, this seems like a reasonable concern, but Triscuits or, for that matter, most products sold with a non-GMO label aren't made in your grandma's kitchen. They are produced by large corporations that, well, control much of the food production process. There's also the reasonable concern that GMOs hurt the environment, but the evidence here, as we will see, remains contested. Despite nods to these and other issues by non-GMO advocates, for the average consumer, it is all about health.

And this is what makes the ubiquity, influence, and growing market share of non-GMO products so fascinating. There is absolutely no evidence, and there never has been, that the GMO products currently available have any adverse impact on human health. They don't, for example, cause or contribute to cancer, diabetes, heart disease, or, the existing evidence tells us, any other health concern. It is worth taking a moment to consider how complete this scientific consensus is. In 2016, the U.S. National Academies of Sciences, Engineering, and Medicine (NAS) published a comprehensive analysis of all available evidence on point and concluded that the "data do not show associations between any disease or chronic conditions and the consumption of GE [genetically engineered] foods." The NAS report also noted potential health and economic benefits and, while noting the complex nature of the research and the assessment of long-term effects, "found no conclusive evidence of cause-and-effect relationships between GE crops and environmental problems."

Many other independent research institutions have come to a similar conclusion. A 2020 Purdue University statement, for example, notes, "GMOs have been very heavily studied, and there is no evidence that eating GMOs harms humans." A 2022 overview by Health Canada emphasizes that "scientists have concluded that GM foods pose no more risk to human health than non-GM foods. In fact, GM foods are subject to a far higher level of regulatory oversight and scientific requirements than traditional organisms consumed as food." In 2022, the U.S. FDA published a public education document that notes, "GMO foods are as healthful and safe to eat as their non-GMO counterparts. Some GMO plants have actually been modified to improve their nutritional value."

At the international level, there is the 2022 issues paper from the Food and Agriculture Organization (FAO) of the United Nations that concludes, "We can be rest assured that GM crops that are approved are safe and continuous monitoring is undertaken." The FAO also suggests benefits such as "reaping higher yield with reduced use of pesticides." The World Health Organization has similarly stated that "no effects on human health have been shown as a result of consuming GM foods" and notes improved crop yields and lower prices through, for example, "the introduction of resistance to plant diseases."

I could go on and on. Of course, the science is always evolving. This is an important topic, so it is essential to keep an open mind and to consider and study related risks, such as the safety and trade-offs of the associated herbicides and pesticides. But right now, the scientific consensus is clear: GMOs are safe, there are possible current and future health benefits, and the concerns about unique harms to the environment, while warranting continued research and monitoring, remain unproven.

And yet the non-GMO health halo remains. In fact, the topic of GMO safety is the issue with the biggest gap between the scientific consensus (safe) and public perception (dangerous). The gap is larger than for climate change, vaccines, or a belief in the role of evolution. An international study done by the Pew Research Center involving twenty countries found that, despite the science, nearly half of participants think GM foods are unsafe to eat (even if they can't say why and how) and *only* 13 percent say they are safe. Thirteen percent! A 2021 study of almost five hundred students found that 85 percent believed that products labelled as GMO signalled that they "were at least somewhat dangerous to health." A study from 2016 of hundreds of participants on the perception of various food labels found the "GMO label means that the food is less healthy, less safe, and less environmentally friendly compared to products with other labels."

When it comes to GMOs, it's easy to get stuck in the genetically modified weeds. It's a big topic comprised of a number of reasonable (and unreasonable) differing views about things like biodiversity, which I don't have the space to present here. But, again, my point is simple: the non-GMO health halo is built around a wholly inaccurate picture of the certainty of the relevant science. The non-GMO label is a posterchild for the goodness illusion. The science says one thing. The illusion says another.

Triscuit update: I am a coward. I couldn't make the sacrifice. In fact, I think there are Triscuit crumbs in my keyboard right now. Damn you, Cecily Strong!

6. Gluten-Free

Unless you have a clinically identified need (e.g., celiac disease), then no, no, no. There has never been good evidence to suggest that going gluten-free is inherently healthier. On the contrary, from a health perspective, it is probably a bad choice (studies have shown that gluten-free products are often less healthy than the full-gluten version). Still, the gluten-free halo marches on.

7. Chemical-Free

As my driveway debate with my neighbour highlights, many health halo words are tied to the idea that chemicals are bad and should be avoided whenever possible. *Natural, toxin-free, organic*, and *chemical-free* are all linked to an embrace of chemophobia—that is, the fear of chemicals.

This view of chemicals is not a fringe concern held by a few on the margins. A study from Switzerland found that people have a negative association with the word *chemical* and have limited knowledge about the structural similarity between synthetic chemicals made by humans and naturally occurring ones. Concerned consumers primarily associate chemicals with death, cancer, and toxicity. According to a 2019 survey published in *Nature Chemistry*, only 18 percent of the public disagrees with the statement "I do everything I can to avoid contact with chemical substances in my daily life." And only 22 percent disagree with "I would like to live in a world where chemical substances do not exist." Given that the entire Earth is made up of chemicals, I'm not sure where these individuals wish to reside. Perhaps on the event horizon of a massive black hole where time is frozen and matter is being pulled apart by gravitational forces?

I recognize that my mocking of the pervasiveness of chemophobia scans as a bit glib. For many, *chemical* has taken on a new meaning. It no longer represents a description of the physical matter that makes up our world. It doesn't represent apples (which are made up of chemicals like hydroxycinnamic acid, alpha-linolenic acid, and isoquercetin). It doesn't represent water (the chemical compound H_2O). It represents unhealthy and human-made substances. And it represents public concerns about and the distrust of for-profit chemical companies and government regulators. But this is exactly the point. The word has mutated into a fearmongering tool that embodies and exploits the amorphous angst associated with things seen, rightly or not, as artificial and out of our control. It is about the emotional response to the word, not the scientific reality.

8. Toxin-Free

Toxins are—if you believe the wellness industry—everywhere. In your cleaning and beauty products. In your gut. On your clothes. And, of course, in your food. But what's a toxin? Anything in the right dose can be harmful, even pure, holistic, natural, gluten-free water. And dangerous substances in small amounts can be perfectly safe and, in the right circumstances, life-saving (e.g., pharmaceutical). The oft-stated chemistry cliché is true: the dose makes the poison. Toxin-free is just another content-free scare term and nothing more than a placeholder for "bad stuff." This health halo is frequently used to market some of the most absurd and science-free products and practices, including detoxes, cleanses, and allegedly toxin-removing supplements. If you see the term *toxin-free*, replace it with *evil-spirits-free* and see if it still has the same persuasive force.

9. Locally Grown

There are lots of reasons people favour buying locally grown food, including taste, freshness, health, safety, lowering the carbon footprint, and supporting local farmers. A 2021 study published in the *Journal of Retailing and Consumer Services* suggests that the growing popularity of locavorism, as it is often called, is based on three consumer ideals: "lionization" (superior taste), "opposition" (opposing distant food systems for environmental reasons), and "communalization" (supporting the local economy). All of them are worthwhile goals. Lots of goodness there. Indeed, this is a health halo the Caulfield family has great sympathy for (as our weekly trip to the farmers' market illustrates). But as is so often the case, the evidence supporting these ideals is, at best, mixed. For example, a comprehensive 2021 analysis of the available research on the benefits of local food, which looked at a range of economic and environmental factors, came to the damning, and very relevant for this book, conclusion: "Our review refutes the idea that local food is inherently good."

There are so many relevant variables and ever-shifting heterogeneities (no two locals are totally the same) that it is probably more accurate to conclude that, well, it's *complicated*. For example, transportation, which is often core to the locally grown message, accounts for a small percentage of food's environmental footprint. Some studies put it at around 5 to 10 percent, with food production accounting for over 80 percent. Yes, transportation matters, so let's figure out ways to move food in a more sustainable manner. But we also need to remember that a local farm may or may not be as efficient or environmentally friendly as a larger operation further away. Also, shipping a few items a short distance by, say, an old truck may have a bigger environmental footprint than moving tens of thousands by a container ship over a very long distance.

Even taste and freshness (a big reason the Caulfields often buy local) get mixed results. In 2010, for example, a blind taste test involving chefs—so, one would expect a group of discriminating tasters—from New York and New Jersey concluded with these experts selecting the shipped-in food over the local. These kinds of blind taste tests can often produce surprising results. When blinded, people often chose the cheap coffee, chocolate, wine, or whiskey over the more expensive options. One of the best examples is fresh fish.

A few years ago, I was in Japan for work. During a dinner with my hosts, there was much talk about how Kiyoshi Kimura—a restaurant owner known as the "Tuna King"—paid a record $3.1 million that morning for a bluefin tuna at Tokyo's Toyosu Market fish auction. Hours later, sushi chefs sliced the fish, and hundreds lined up for a very costly taste. My Japanese hosts did not seem overly shocked by either the price or the willingness to pay for the fresh sushi. One seventy-one-year-old customer reportedly said the multi-million-dollar tuna was "tastier than ever."

The shocking reality is that several studies have suggested the fresh-fish-is-better consensus may be an illusion. In 2015, a team of researchers from Japan did a rigorous double-blind study to compare fresh and frozen sushi. After 120 rounds of tasting and consuming 240 pieces of sushi, the surprising results: 42.5 percent thought fresh fish was better, and 49.2 percent selected the frozen. A slight win for frozen, but basically similar results. The authors conclude that "freezing raw fish did not ruin sushi's taste." A 2017 blind taste test study from Oregon State University confirmed the result and found that frozen fish actually outperformed fresh fish.

Our expectations, including the health-halo effect, can have a strong influence on our stated preferences and perceptions. Consider a 2019 study directly relevant to the locally grown label. Researchers asked New Yorkers to try local and Californian broccoli. The results, as summarized in their paper, showed "that consumers rate both the appearance and the taste of the two local broccoli varieties lower than the California variety when evaluating food quality blindly." And they were willing to pay more for it. However, when told that the broccoli was local, their perception of the taste and appearance increased as did their willingness to pay.

The lead author of that study, Xiaoli Fan, a professor in resource economics and environmental sociology at the University of Alberta, thinks the biased perception of taste comes from a promotional effect. We are told that local food is fresher and better in general, so that's what we taste. "But without that information, the local broccoli varieties taste worse than the commercial California variety," she tells me. Once again, the mere perception of goodness—no matter how objectively inaccurate—tastes good. Or we think it does.

There are also some interesting complexities to the impact of a health halo on taste. Socioeconomics, for example, can play a role. A 2019 study from Mexico on local coffee came to a similar conclusion to the New York broccoli study. When people knew where the coffee was produced, the expectation had an impact on how they rated taste. But the education of the drinkers mattered. In the blind tasting condition, the authors note, "higher education and non-university group were not able to differentiate the samples in terms of liking." But in unblinded testing, "consumers with higher education rated higher local coffees," whereas "non-university consumers rated the four samples at the same level of liking." The researchers speculate that this is because the educated coffee drinkers are more aware and sensitive to what the origin of the samples means and therefore "informed liking moved to the direction of the expected liking." Put bluntly: more educated people are more aware that they are supposed to like a particular product more (the halo effect), so they like it more.

All the justifications for buying local can be subjected to similar "Well, it's complex" analysis. Safety, for instance, is more dependent on food production conditions than geography. (Do you know if the safety protocols at your local farm are superior to those at a facility further away?) Buying local food is a benefit to the local economy, but even here complexity sneaks in. What are the economic trade-offs on a global scale? Does buying local, for instance, benefit an economically wealthy region at the expense of farmers from a more impoverished region?

10. The Colour Green

When a product package is green, consumers are inclined to think the food it contains is healthy. There is a green bag of Miss Vickie's Spicy Dill Pickle potato chips in our pantry right now. (My wife, Joanne, has few weaknesses—but Miss Vickie, you are one.) Healthy?

11. Immune-Boosting

Let's start with the conclusion: you can't boost your immune system. You don't want to boost your immune system. (As noted briefly earlier in this book, an overactive immune system can lead to autoimmune diseases and even anaphylaxis.) I get why people are attracted to the concept. Who wouldn't want to strengthen our "natural" defences against infectious diseases? As with all health halos, it is an intuitively appealing goal. But the immune system isn't a muscle that you can make stronger. It is a fantastically complex and carefully balanced network of many different cells and proteins. Illness or an unhealthy lifestyle can compromise your immune system, thus making you more susceptible to disease. Vaccines can empower your body to effectively respond to specific pathogens. But there is no magical way to make your system especially strong or "boosted." So, if you see the *immune-boosting* phrase, there is a good chance that someone is trying to sell you some nonsense.

Despite this reality, the use of this health halo has exploded. The COVID-19 pandemic saw the rise of immune-boosting supplements and vitamin drips. Immune-boosting yoga moves. Immune-boosting essential oils. Immune-boosting colon cleanses. Immune-boosting homeopathy. Immune-boosting quantum (that word!) energy bracelets. Immune-boosting astrology. In 2020, the first year of the pandemic, countries around the world saw a sharp spike in the sale of supplements, in some countries by as much as 60 percent. This increase was due almost entirely to the mistaken belief that they may provide an immune-boosting effect.

In 2020, I worked with my colleagues to get a sense of what people get when they Google "immune boosting." If you are curious about the concept or want to know what steps, if any, you can take to protect yourself or your loved ones, chances are you'll go to your computer and plug the phrase into a search engine. In our study, which was published in *BMJ Open*, we sought to replicate these searches using a so-called naive computer with search algorithms unpolluted by past searches and apparent preferences. We looked at over 225 websites. What we found was both shocking and depressing. Almost 86 percent of the search results portrayed the concept inaccurately, including suggesting that an immune boost could protect you against COVID-19. Less than 10 percent of the websites we investigated provided a critique of the concept of immune boosting.

This kind of health halo can do real damage to public health. It facilitates the marketing of unproven and potentially harmful products. And it may lead people to believe their immune system has, indeed, been boosted, possibly nudging them to forgo evidence-informed strategies, such as vaccination and a healthy lifestyle.

The rise of immune-boosting rhetoric is also a good example of how biomedical experts and institutions can succumb to the allure of a popular health halo term. During the pandemic, many trusted sources ran articles with immune boosting in the headline, such as the 2022 *New York Times* article "How to Boost Your Immune System during Cold and Flu Season." Harvard Health had a piece entitled "How to Boost Your Immune System." And the Mayo Clinic ran this one: "Fight Off the Flu with Immune-Boosting Nutrients." The articles go on to debunk the boosting myth and provide accurate advice about how to maintain a *healthy* immune system, with sleep, exercise, a healthy diet, and sensible prevention strategies, like vaccination and washing your hands. But the use of the phrase in the headline is still deeply disappointing. It's as if these publications have thrown in the towel. The tsunami of immune-boosting bunk has worn them down. Can't beat 'em, join 'em. Or perhaps they hope to lure people into reading science-informed content by using health-halo clickbait? If so, this is a mistake.

When respected—and usually science-informed—entities use health-halo terminology, it can legitimize and entrench misleading concepts. A reasonable person might ask, Why would the *New York Times*, the Mayo Clinic, or Harvard use the term if it wasn't real and meaningful? This, in turn, makes it more difficult to debunk the concept and easier for hucksters to sell unproven and potentially harmful products. It shouldn't be forgotten that often—*very often*—people *only* read the headlines, especially on social media. A study from Columbia University, for instance, found that 60 percent of links shared on social media have never been opened. In other words, people interact with and share without reading the article attached to the headline. Researchers, hospitals, universities, clinicians, journalists, newspaper editors, social media influencers, really everyone needs to take care in how they use health-halo terms. The objective should be to increase accuracy, even in a headline, and not to heighten their power to deceive.

12. Personalized

We all like to see ourselves as unique. We *are* all unique! Backed by (allegedly) cutting-edge science, more and more diet, fitness, longevity, and wellness companies are exploiting this understandable inclination and biological reality by marketing "personalized" products. There are personalized shampoos, personalized vitamins and supplements, and personalized exercise programs. You can get a genetic test to personalize your selection of wine (I've tried this and was not impressed), sexual partner (I haven't tried), and roommate (yes, there is a company that will do this).

The idea of personalization is so intuitively appealing—it is empowering because it is focused on you!—that *personalized* has become a health halo. We are meant to assume that when that term is part of a pitch, the product is more effective. We can feel more certain that it will work for us because (or so the marketing goes) it was made specifically for us. In fact, just thinking a health intervention is personalized—even if it isn't—can produce a placebo response. In a 2023 study from Norway, researchers told one group of participants that they were receiving a personalized exercise routine, even though it was identical to the program given to the control group. Thinking the exercise advice was designed specially for them resulted in an increase in performance as compared to the control group. Another study, also from 2023, found that telling people that a sham treatment was personalized to their genetics and physiology increased its perceived effectiveness.

Let's take a closer look at one corner of the personalized universe: the diet industry. There are literally hundreds of companies selling various forms of personalized diets using everything from genetic testing to the analysis of your microbiome (read: poop). One company offers "personalised nutrition and fitness recommendations you need to get your weight to budge—and keep it off." Another provides "genetic insights to help you personalise your diet" and "genetically-guided meal planning." And one invites us to "discover a diet made for your DNA."

But is personalization really the magical path forward? Once again, the science here is mixed and, I would argue, tremendously underwhelming. Let's start big picture. Many of these personalized dieting companies have been around for over a decade. If this stuff worked well, we'd probably know! A 2018 randomized controlled trial published in the *Journal of the American Medical Association* compared a variety of diets (low fat, low carb), some of which used genetic information to optimize the diet, and some of which did not. The study found that there "was no significant difference in weight loss" between diets and that the "genotype pattern"—that is, the genetic information—was not "associated with the dietary effects on weight loss." Basically, the personalized genetic information did not help. In a 2022 clinical trial also published in the *Journal of the American Medical Association*, a personalized diet focused on individual glycemic response also found it did not result in greater weight loss compared with a nonpersonalized approach. These kinds of results have led many in the research community to conclude that recommending personalized diets is premature. As noted in a 2021 review of the existing literature, "it is not yet possible to provide personalized dietary recommendations based on factors such as a person's genetic background or the composition of their microbiome."

Once again, despite the marketing to the contrary, the existing evidence is far from conclusive. Some might point to the details of individual studies—and there are some—that suggest possible small benefits and that the research is ongoing. The key here, as with other health halos, is that the *existing* science does not support the certainty and definitiveness inherent in the personalization marketing. My friend and colleague Dylan MacKay summarizes the situation well. "The evidence base for high-tech personalized nutrition interventions is aspirational and very weak," he says. MacKay is a professor of human nutritional science at the University of Manitoba and has worked on these personalization questions for years. "To date, the high-quality clinical trials do not show a benefit, and the smaller trials that do show 'statistical' benefits of personalization have small effect sizes," he says. For MacKay, those blah results mean that personalized diets are unlikely to have a big impact, "even if those effects turn out to be real." So, again, underwhelming—*very* underwhelming—should be the takeaway.

You might be thinking, Well, so what? If people want to try this approach, what's the harm? Lots. This push toward personalization may cause a less than constructive focus on personal responsibility. Emphasizing personalization shifts the responsibility for health from the broader society to the individual. Instead of societal change—such as creating healthier and more equitable food systems, marketing policies, and built environments—it asks for individual change. Research tells us that health interventions that require a high level of individual agency or personal motivation are less successful than those done on the population level and require a lower level of agency. These society-level interventions could range from making changes to the built environment or changes to advertising laws, to name just a couple examples. Research has shown that in the United States, 80 percent believe that individuals are primarily to blame for obesity, and much fewer respondents point to other institutions, such as industry, government, or our food environment. Not only is this focus on individual blame scientifically inaccurate—obesity is a fantastically complex issue involving socioeconomics, genetics, the microbiome, unhealthy food environments, sleep patterns, prenatal and postnatal environments, sedentary lifestyles, etc.—it can heighten issues of weight bias which, in turn, can exacerbate the challenges associated with obesity.

Moreover, it may cause the public and governments to be less supportive of broad-based public health initiatives. If we are constantly told health depends on personalized information and individual behaviour change, why bother supporting public health initiatives? As

Reykjavik University scholar Jack James argues, when we emphasize personalization, "attention and resources are captured at the expense of alternative behavioural and social pathways that have the potential to effect greater improvements in population health." In other words, the message baked into the personalization trend is "This is on you."

Like me, James Tabery worries that this health halo—which is attractive, he said, "in part because it feeds this narcissistic notion that we're all unique"—will have an adverse impact on broader public health policy. Tabery is a professor of bioethics and the history of science at the University of Utah and wrote *Tyranny of the Gene: Personalized Medicine and Its Threat to Public Health*, so this is a topic he has given a lot of thought. "In contrast to personalized medicine, which has done very little to increase the health of patients and populations, public health success stories have had a tremendous impact on increasing things like life expectancy and decreasing things like infant mortality," he tells me. "This fanaticism for personalization is drawing attention away from all the proven purchase that public health interventions get by helping the whole population, in exchange for unproven promises about the power of treating us all as different."

MacKay agrees, echoing Tabery's critique. "The whole idea of personalized nutrition is concerning because it takes focus away from things we know can improve health," he says. "Personalized nutrition makes your health a 'personal' choice, which it rarely is. The research into high-tech personalized nutrition is really a distraction for the 'worried well' and the companies selling it are mostly looking to help lighten those people's wallets."

The other thing to consider is the absurdity of worrying about making small tweaks to health behaviours with personalized information when so many of us don't get enough exercise, fruits and vegetables, or sleep—to say nothing of the tremendous impact of socioeconomics and justice issues on our health. At both the level of the individual and society, it makes much more sense to focus on the big stuff. The personalization push, as a marketing ploy, is meant to inject certainty into our decisions by heightening the belief that something will work *for us*. But, as is often the case, the certainty promise is both illusory (the personalized tag doesn't necessarily mean it will be more effective) and, paradoxically, confusing (personalized diets are more, not less, complicated—thus often making them more difficult to follow).

Of course, I'm not suggesting that personalized approaches are always inherently bad. Biomedical therapies, such as pharmaceuticals, that are tailored to an individual's biology have the potential to be both more effective and safer, though they're currently still pretty niche. A great deal of important research continues in this space around the world. I'm part of a large interdisciplinary research team, centred at the University of British Columbia, exploring the use of precision medicine to ensure the optimal use of organs for transplantation. Health and well-being interventions should consider individual needs and circumstances. Feeling engaged and empowered does make a difference, especially if it helps to fuel intrinsic motivation—"I'm doing this because I enjoy being healthy and active"—to make meaningful behaviour changes. But the most effective personalization can often be decidedly low tech. Start with this: which healthy lifestyle changes that you might enjoy long-term fit your schedule, values, and tastes? The best diet is almost always the diet that is healthy, sustainable, and works for you. No genetic or poop test required.

There are many other health halos that have been around for a while, such as *low-fat*, *sugar-free*, and *protein*. (Studies have found that just putting the word *protein* on a package label can lead many to believe the product is healthy, even if it is nothing more than a candy bar masquerading as a healthy protein-filled snack.) And new terms are emerging all the time. *Grass-fed* (as with locally grown, the science surrounding this one falls in the "it's complicated" category) and, a personal favourite, *healthy gut* (these days it seems like absolutely everyone is worried about their gut!) are two good examples of recent halo-inducing trends. Very often, halos are combined to produce a kind of health-halo supergroup. It is easy to find, for example, natural, organic, gluten-free, non-GMO supplements that are personalized just for you!

Another common marketing tactic is to merge the scienceploitation strategy with a health halo. Think stem cell injections that are non-GMO and organic, or a natural colonic that benefits your microbiome and improves gut health. The fact that these terms often draw on oppositional world views—New Age, evidence-free health halos versus words from real cutting-edge science—doesn't seem to concern marketers. Heck, oxymoronic marketing worked for Led Zeppelin, and it can (and does) work for supplements and beauty products.

While mingling the goodness vibe of health halos with science-y verbiage seems to be increasingly common, it's not a new advertising ploy. A 2021 study from Örebro University in Sweden analyzed how wellness products like radium water were marketed in the first half of the twentieth century. You'll recall from earlier in the book that it contained actual radium and was radioactive—which its marketing framed as a *natural* nutrient. The goal of this marketing strategy, as noted by the authors of the study, was to suggest that radium products bridged "the gap between conventional medicine and popular therapies, providing a cure for all types of illnesses and offering consumers a modern lifestyle that was both 'natural' and 'rational.'" And this is exactly what marketers do today. Look, this product is both super science-y *and* full of amorphous natural goodness!

Because our information environment is so chaotic, the mere impression—a feeling—of goodness with a veneer of science is often enough to persuade consumers. It allows us to feel more certain about our decisions. "Consumers need a simple way to make complicated decisions," Alan Levinovitz tells me. "Going with what's 'natural' means you can eliminate endless research and label reading on a product-by-product basis."

Not only are all these terms and marketing tactics deceptive, but they hurt public debates and consideration of more evidence-informed solutions to social challenges. They invite us to think about complex issues in a simplistic and binary manner. GMOs bad, non-GMO good. Natural safe, unnatural dangerous. Worse, they reify and legitimatize this thinking, playing to our cognitive biases, such as leveraging our negativity bias with fearmongering about toxins and chemicals. Health halos also exploit good ole fashioned guilt. A classic study from 2005 found that when you offer customers the exact same dessert with a healthy-ish sounding name (Cheesecake deLite) versus a more hedonic one (Bailey's Irish Cream Cheesecake), they are more likely to pick the healthy-sounding one because, the author speculates, they would feel guilty about buying the more hedonic version. We all want to do the *good* thing. I find the guilt aspect of health halos particularly infuriating when they are aimed at parents. Organic diapers. Chemical-free baby sunscreen. Et cetera. There are entire companies built on the make-parents-feel-scared-and-guilty marketing tactic.

It could be argued that I'm overemphasizing the negative and deceptive aspects of health halos. Even if most are nonsensical from a scientific perspective, perhaps creating a market for organic or natural or non-GMO helps change public perceptions on important topics like sustainability? That is, might this marketing strategy normalize and entrench concern for things like environmental impact in a way that causes meaningful social and policy change? Perhaps the embrace of health halos will nudge industry on that path too? I sympathize with this perspective. Constructive cultural change takes time, and we need to use a range of tools to make it happen.

But using scientifically inaccurate and misleading verbiage hardly seems a sustainable path forward. Health halos add more inaccuracies to a chaotic information environment that is already filled with inaccuracies. They aren't helpful guideposts for decision-making; they are deceptive slogans designed to exploit our desire to do good and feel certain about complex topics. Do they really promote helpful policy change, or do they do more to obscure the real, usually more complicated challenges? For example, does the focus on organic or buying local really help make food production more sustainable, or would it be better to focus on evidence-based practices regardless of their affiliation to a particular halo? Not all organic farms are more sustainable than conventional. Not all transportation associated with locally grown food has a smaller carbon footprint than larger, and further away, conventional farms. Let's focus on the approaches that can do actual good, not on empty goodness-infused catchphrases.

Of course, health halos are mostly a tool for profit. They are used to move products and build brands. The more entrenched a halo becomes—that is, the more it mutates into an accepted proxy for goodness—the more valuable it becomes as a marketing tool and the further it moves away from an evidence-based health benefit (if there ever was one). I call this the health-halo market cascade. Once a health halo reaches a certain point of public acceptance, as many of the above phrases have, it becomes such a strong market opportunity that no amount of science—not from the FDA, Health Canada, renowned universities, the NAS, the World Health Organization, or the United Nations—can dislodge its cultural cachet. When stores are selling gluten-free sparkling water, organic sports drinks, and non-GMO Triscuits, it's safe to assume it isn't really about achieving a reality-based goodness goal.

Pets Too

Our cats, Detective Turtles and Lord Byron, have a pretty fancy and varied diet. We shop at a high-end pet store. Only the best for our housemates.

A quick review of the pet food in our home—which includes cat treats, three kinds of hard food, and dozens of cans of different kinds of soft food—finds that all of products are some combination of organic, natural, gluten-free, or GMO-free. And every single one of them is grain-free. Every. Single. One.

The idea that all pet food must be grain-free is a good example of how a health halo can emerge out of the ether. It is unclear exactly when or why it was decided that grain-free was a good idea for pets, but I suspect the *when* fits with the cultural decision that wheat, grain, and gluten are bad (2010-ish) and the *why* is simply about sales. That health halos are being applied to pets should surprise no one. Humans adore their four-legged companions. A lot. A 2022 survey by Consumer Reports found that 81 percent of millennials love their pets more than at least one family member. Fifty-seven percent agreed they love their pet more than their siblings. Eighty-nine percent consider the needs of their pets when deciding where to live. In a 2019 survey, 34 percent of parents said they prefer their pets to their children. Sixty-eight percent view their pets to be like people. And there is some evidence that suggests we worry about pets more than humans. A fascinating study from 2017 presented hundreds of research participants with fake news stories to assess their reactions to attacks on people and pets. What they found was that most people empathize more with the suffering of puppies and dogs than full-grown humans.

Given the place of cats and dogs in our homes and in our hearts, of course we are seeing the leveraging of wellness language, fear-mongering, and health halos to market and upsell to the 60 percent of Canadian households that have at least one pet. This is a massive industry worth over $100 billion worldwide. I did quick analysis of the products found in a Google search for top grain-free dog foods. The marketing was essentially the same as you'd see for human wellness products, including promises to "nourish as nature intended" and that the product was "holistic," "wholesome," and, of course, "natural" and full of "just tasty goodness." The packages also suggested that the food was "human grade" and of "human quality." What kind of pet owner would you be if you fed your pets food that wasn't at least as good as the stuff you ate?

There is, in fact, no reliable evidence that it is harmful to feed grains to dogs or cats. There never has been. A 2021 survey of veterinary professionals found that 88 percent of those with dogs and 73 percent with cats stated grain-free diets were not healthy for their pets. This is largely a made-up marketing ploy. Contrary to all the noise, grain fillers can be healthy, providing essential nutrients and fibre (yes, even for carnivores like cats). Food allergies, one justification often presented for these products, are rare in cats and dogs and are usually related to proteins, not carbohydrates. Some pets may have an allergy to a specific grain (but not all grains) and would benefit from a grain-free diet, but this would be a relatively rare situation that does not justify the current market.

In addition, grain-free products often are not even grain-free. A 2018 study of grain-free cat food found that many of the foods labelled as grain-free often do not have less carbohydrates and grain than conventional pet food. This finding is consistent with other research that has found that pet food in general is often mislabelled, with almost half of products (45 percent) containing ingredients not on the label. Perhaps most problematic, a grain-free diet has been linked to heart problems in dogs, an issue the U.S. Food and Drug Administration continues to investigate.

Despite the evidence that grain-free is more expensive, not healthier, often mislabelled, and perhaps even harmful, the market remains strong. Almost half of all pet food products are now labelled grain-free, a growth from 15 percent a decade ago. A recent industry survey found that most pet owners still believe grain-free is both safe and healthier. A 2021 study found that pet owners who have embraced the grain-free approach to eating for their own diet are more likely to impose this on their pets. In other words, we force our cats and dogs to embrace our often science-free food philosophies. If we eat keto, gluten-free, or non-GMO, we think our pets should eat that way too. A 2018 editorial in the *Journal of the American Veterinary Medicine Association* nicely summarizes this: "Pet food marketing has outpaced the science, and owners are not always making healthy, science-based decisions even though they want to do the best for their pets."

Incidentally, this is also true when it comes to other pet care decisions. A 2023 study, for example, found that the anti-vaccine noise accelerated by the pandemic has caused more than half of pet owners to express concerns about vaccinating their animals and almost 40 percent were concerned vaccines could cause dog autism. (Just to be clear, this entire line of thinking is scientifically absurd.)

The situation is similar for homemade pet food. There is a growing trend for people to forgo commercial products and make their pets' meals, including raw and vegan ones. A 2020 study from the University of Guelph mapped the growth of this practice and found that at the time of the study only 13 percent of dogs and 32 percent of cats were fed conventional, store-bought foods exclusively. The study also found that 64 percent of dogs and 46 percent of cats were regularly fed raw food. The authors of this study speculate that—as with grain-free diets— people are humanizing their pets. They often think what is good for them is good for their pet. "Trends in animal nutrition shadow trends in human nutrition," the authors note, "with increasing consumer interest in 'natural' and 'holistic' foods demonstrated in both human and pet feeding practices." The humanization of pets and especially of pet food seems to be increasing. In 2022, the CEO of Petco, one of the biggest pet supply retailers, was quoted as saying the pet humanization trend is dominant in the industry and "reflects a permanent mindset shift" that influences how we feed our pets. But the tendency to treat our companion animals like a fellow human has been around for a long time. A 2021 study in the *Journal of World Prehistory* describes the diets of thirty-six dogs from approximately 2,500 to 3,500 years ago. The researchers found that humans were preparing the dogs' meals— which demonstrates how long pets have been viewed to be part of the family—and that they basically fed them what they were eating, including plant- and grain-based meals.

Despite the long history, homemade doesn't necessarily mean healthier. As noted by Cailin Heinze, veterinary nutritionist with the clinical nutrition service at Tufts University's Cummings School of Veterinary Medicine, "there is no evidence to support claims that home-prepared diets are healthier than commercial diets." In fact, studies have found that homemade meals can be less healthy. In a 2013 study from the University of California, Davis looked at sixty-seven home-prepared diets for dogs and cats and found that many had major nutritional imbalances, suggesting the potential for "substantial harm to pets when home-prepared diets are used on a long-term basis."

A common justification for homemade and raw food is, as with grain-free, a perceived food allergy. This is a common marketing theme for both grain-free and raw food products. But, as noted, despite the omnipresence of the avoid-allergens theme, actual food allergies appear to be relatively rare in pets. While there is surprisingly little good research on this (likely because it is difficult to perform the needed elimination diets to definitively determine allergies), one study published in 2016 found that the foods most commonly associated with pet allergies are beef, dairy products, and chicken—the ingredients often used in homemade pet food!

There are other reasons to be cautious about homemade pet food, including, as the Food and Drug Administration reports, the fact that it is "more likely to be contaminated with disease-causing bacteria" like *Salmonella*—especially if the pet food is raw. As a result, officials at the FDA Center for Veterinary Medicine (CVM) warned of "potential health risk for the pets eating the raw food, and for the owners handling the product." And as with grain-free, there is no evidence to support claims that raw food is healthier. The only study I could find that supported raw pet food, published in 2021, has noted methodological flaws and was funded by raw food manufacturers and the notorious anti-vaccine quack Joseph Mercola, who has been identified as one of the most influential spreaders of health misinformation for pushing things like unproven supplements, homeopathy, and for fear-mongering about vaccines.

As I finish working on this section, a kitty meows nearby. She wants food. She wants it now. I search our pet food shelf for something that is not holistic, natural, organic, gluten-free, or grain-free. Nothing. "Sorry, Turtles," I say. She doesn't seem to care, purring as I give her a fancy treat that the package promises she'll love (she does) and that will "give peace of mind" to her "human companion" (it does not).

Clean Beauty

Clean. Who could be against clean? The word invites us to think of purity, innocence, and authenticity. Etymologically, it is a West Germanic adjective with connections to bravery and beauty. Could you ask for more from a word? If forced to pick one term that captures the power of health halos and their connection to virtue and goodness and positivity, it might be *clean*.

I've dedicated a separate section to clean—which deserves to be listed as one of the most dominant health-halo words of recent time—because its rapid rise warrants a bit more attention and because, unlike the mostly food-focused halos in my "Devious Dozen," this halo is increasingly used in the beauty industry which, as we will see, invites a host of unique conceptual inconsistencies.

The clean beauty market has grown rapidly. Over the past decade, it has become a dominant theme in the cosmetic industry. Despite the ubiquity, no clear definition of *clean beauty* exists anywhere—not with regulatory bodies like Health Canada or the U.S. FDA or even within the beauty industry itself. Each clean beauty company has its own take on what the term means, but they almost always reference the absence of harmful chemicals and the use of "natural" products. One beauty and well-being publication suggests that "clean beauty is synonymous with non-toxic beauty." A 2021 *Vogue* article on the trend suggests that "in essence, clean beauty products are unadulterated and non-toxic." Like so many marketing movements founded on an amorphous vibe, the definitions are substantively meaningless and circular. *Clean* means non-toxic, and *non-toxic* means clean. For the public, the phrase also seems to be more form than substance. A 2019 survey of consumers found 58 percent considered "clean beauty" to mean the product is "natural" and 32 percent that it contains less harsh chemicals.

Many in the clean beauty industry define it using more testable claims, such as this approach from a self-proclaimed clean company: "at its core, clean beauty means that you can use a product without risking your own health. The ingredients list must contain only safe, clean ingredients." As with all health halos, *clean* is meant to help you quickly make a decision that you can feel comfortably certain about.

The desire for safe ingredients is, no doubt, a worthy and goodness-reflecting goal. But the promise made by the beauty industry is that their products are *definitively* safer and less toxic—and these claims are meant to justify the premium price we are asked to pay. What their advertising doesn't say is that they are unsure about the science or that more research is needed to explore the problem. The entire premise is that clean beauty products *are* safer and unquestionably better. But to what degree is this certainty rooted in scientific reality?

Let's consider parabens, the cosmetic ingredient that has probably attracted the most attention by the public and those marketing clean beauty. The fashion magazine *Elle* declared parabens "Skincare's Biggest Bad Guy." And numerous beauty and wellness websites, such as Gwyneth Paltrow's goop, often provide advice on how to avoid parabens. I think it is fair to characterize the demonization of paraben, which is often framed as a hormone disruptor linked to cancer, as core to the rise of the clean beauty movement. If clean beauty means anything, it means paraben-free. There is paraben-free moisturizer, toothpaste, foundation, eyeliner, lipstick, nail polish, shaving cream, deodorant, sunscreen, and, yep, dog, cat, and human shampoo.

So, what are parabens, anyway? Parabens are preservatives used in a variety of consumer products, most notoriously in cosmetics, to deter the growth of harmful bacteria and mold and to extend the shelf life of a product. Common parabens you might see on a label for a beauty product include methylparaben, propylparaben, butylparaben, and ethylparaben. First introduced in the 1930s, they are cheap and effective, even when used in very small quantities. While the parabens in cosmetics are generally human-made, parabens do occur naturally in fruits and vegetables like blueberries and carrots. The parabens in cosmetics are chemically identical to the naturally occurring variety.

Marketing and labelling can, for better or worse, impact consumer behaviour enough that it changes the measurable presence of an ingredient in a person's urine. A clever crowdsourced study—they recruited people online to participate and do their own at-home urine measurements—from 2020 found that people who said they tried to avoid things like parabens had lower concentrations of the ingredient in their urine than people who didn't. On the positive side, this demonstrates that appropriate labelling can impact behaviour. As concluded in the study, "avoiding certain chemicals in products was generally associated with reduced exposure for chemicals listed on labels." On the downside, there is no evidence that avoiding parabens was meaningful to the participants' health.

It's possible there might be unintended consequences, such as greater exposure to ingredients that are *more* harmful than parabens. It should not be forgotten that parabens are in products for a reason: they play an important antimicrobial role. As reported by journalist Janna Mandell in a 2022 article in the *Washington Post*, "several 'clean' companies have voluntarily recalled products in the past two years because of the presence of mold, yeast and bacteria." This is a good reminder that, as professor Joe Schwarcz from McGill University noted in a 2017 piece, when ingredients like parabens are demonized and removed, the "preservative-free" can quickly become "bacteria-filled."

Are the "natural" alternatives used by the clean beauty industry any safer or better? Probably not. A 2022 study examined almost 1,500 clean beauty products available at Target and Walgreens and found that, contrary to the marketing that frames these products as safer and gentler, "most 'clean' products contain a potential allergen, predominately fragrances and botanicals." There are reasons to believe that the push to make things clean (whatever that means) has, in some contexts, made the products worse for people. Dr. Walter Liszewski, a professor of dermatology at Northwestern University, suggests in the *Washington Post* piece that "when people freaked out about parabens, we started using more preservatives, which are way more allergenic."

I think it is fair to say that people started freaking out around the time of a 2004 study that found parabens in breast tumours. The study, authored by Philippa Darbre from the University of Reading, has been criticized for its methodological limitations, such as the fact that only twenty tumours were involved and there was no comparison group. The reality is that the study was really an exploration of whether parabens could be measured in tumours. It did not provide evidence that parabens caused or even increased the risk for cancer. The pushback from the research community was so intense that Darbre felt compelled to write an article in which she basically agreed with the primary critique, stating "nowhere in the [2004] manuscript was any claim made that the presence of parabens had caused the breast cancer." In other words, the study that started people worrying about the connection between parabens and cancer didn't make a causal connection between parabens and cancer.

This academic debate seems to have had little impact on public discourse. An association between parabens and cancer has become a frequent talking point in the popular press and on beauty and fashion blogs. "Women Absorb up to 5lbs of Damaging Chemicals a Year Thanks to Beauty Products," declared a 2007 headline in the *Daily Mail*. The article goes on to state these chemicals, explicitly mentioning parabens, "could be doing untold damage" and have "been linked to cancer."

Despite the continued concern, the science remains, at best, confused. I want to be clear: I'm not dismissing the idea that there are potential risks or that more research is required. There are studies that find an association between parabens and hormone levels, body weight, and a variety of adverse health outcomes. Those issues should continue to be researched. But these are *association* studies. Causation remains unclear, and virtually all these studies conclude with the caveat that "further studies are needed."

"Absolutely" was Jen Novakovich's response when I asked if we should continue to investigate the safety of ingredients like parabens. Novakovich is a cosmetic chemist, science communicator, and the founder of the Eco Well, an organization devoted to debunking misinformation in the cosmetic industry. "But we should also be continuing to research their alternatives too," she says. "Parabens as an ingredient class are some of the most well-researched ingredients used in cosmetics." This is an important point. Using an alternative to parabens does *not*, despite the marketing used by the clean beauty industry, necessarily mean there is clear evidence it is safe or safer than parabens.

At the time of writing, I think it is fair to say that the body of the scientific literature aligns well with the 2022 FDA statement on the issue: "We do not have information showing that parabens as they are used in cosmetics have an effect on human health." Cancer Research UK is even more definitive, stating in a 2020 review of the science, "No. Parabens do not cause cancer in humans, including breast cancer." Professor Joe Schwarcz agrees with these conclusions. "Parabens have extremely weak estrogenic properties, and I have found no human studies that prove a risk," he tells me. "Also, parabens are less allergenic than other preservatives."

Here we do not need to come to a definitive conclusion about the health risks associated with parabens. The point is that even for the most publicized, marketed, and researched justification for the clean beauty industry, the science is (despite definitive-sounding marketing claims) equivocal.

It is possible that clean beauty products are no safer than conventional products, and they could even be worse for you and public health more broadly. This is the conclusion that physicians Courtney Blair Rubin and Bruce Brod from the Department of Dermatology at the University of Pennsylvania came to in a 2019 critique of clean beauty published in *JAMA Dermatology*: "Misinformation may lead to higher rates of contact dermatitis, substantial financial investment into natural products encouraged by companies with a clear financial conflict of interest, and unnecessary avoidance of safe and necessary skin care ingredients."

The adverse influence of the clean beauty movement reaches beyond skin and cosmetic products. For example, clean toothpaste, which is becoming more popular in part thanks to the clean beauty movement, often has no fluoride, which serves an important role in making our teeth more resistant to cavities. Beyond a possible breath-freshening assist, the product has zero health benefits. A 2018 academic review of the available evidence concluded that fluoride-free toothpaste "failed to show a benefit in terms of reducing the incidence of dental caries." In other words, clean beauty could result in more tooth decay and dental problems, which doesn't sound terribly beautiful.

We shouldn't forget that it is already illegal to sell unsafe products to the public. Are there reasons to revisit how cosmetics are regulated around the world? Sure. It is true that there is a great deal of regulatory variation between countries. A more standardized approach would be helpful. And we should always be striving to do more to protect consumers and to ensure appropriate ingredient transparency. The clean beauty movement might—through encouraging consumer awareness and advocacy—help to hold regulators' feet to the fire and encourage needed research. But, again, this doesn't mean that any of the industry's claims are true. The clean label is mostly a marketing ploy that, like other health halos, leverages our desires to do good and to have more certainty in our decision-making. Alas, it really is all an illusion.

Of course, if you really want to avoid potentially harmful chemicals in beauty products, don't use the products. Beyond soap, sunscreen, and toothpaste with fluoride, there aren't many products that we *need* in a biological sense, though I am a fan of deodorant. In fact, outside of the clear public health benefit of handwashing, there is even some debate about the health value of soap. Sure, there is no doubt that if you are grimy, soap can help remove that grime. But from a biological perspective, there is likely no need to wash your body regularly with soap. To make this point, Dr. James Hamblin, who lectures at the Yale School of Public Health, went seven years without using soap (or deodorant). Hamblin wrote about this soap-less journey in his 2020 book, *Clean*. I asked him if, post-book, his hygiene habits have changed. He told me he currently uses soap "avidly on my hands but minimally [and on an] as-needed basis elsewhere." So, still relatively soap-less.

There is an absurdity to the entire clean beauty trend that creates a perceived need for products that, in general, we don't really *need*. Companies demonize ingredients in their own products so they can urgently sell us "cleaner" and often *much more* expensive versions of the stuff we didn't need in the first place. This isn't about feeding the world or curing disease or fighting for social justice. These are, in general, cosmetic products sold by an industry built on the back of regressive beauty norms, body shaming, human insecurities, and the leveraging of celebrity influencers. I'm not naive. The desire to be attractive, more youthful, and, in a more positive vein, to self-express has been part of every culture throughout human history. But the messengers of the clean beauty rhetoric, the cosmetic industry, have deep and obvious conflicts of interest. They're trying to sell us stuff.

It is interesting to note that some leaders within the industry seem to be fully aware of the evidence-free reality that underpins clean beauty. For example, in a 2019 article in *The Guardian*, Tiffany Masterson, the founder of the clean beauty company Drunk Elephant, is quoted as saying, "I don't think [parabens] are bad for you." Her company has removed them from their products because, according to Masterson, "consumers don't want them." Create the need. Sell product to satisfy the need. Say you are doing it because of the need.

Cosmetic chemist and author Perry Romanowski is straightforward in his assessment. "I see clean beauty as a cynical marketing ploy to get consumers to be afraid of conventional products and to spend more money on products that cost more, don't actually work better, and aren't actually safer for people," he was quoted as saying in a 2021 NPR article. I contacted Romanowski to see if he stands by the quote. Yep. In fact, he feels that the clean beauty movement emerged mostly because the industry is always looking for ways to sell products and it has been decades since there was genuine scientific innovation in the cosmetic space. "The industry is left with telling new stories about the same old products. And, as you know, fear marketing is an effective story for selling products," he tells me.

Jen Novakovich is a bit more generous, suggesting that "clean beauty comes from good intentions." The goodness goal, in other words, is reasonable. But she still lands on the harsh conclusion that its growth is the "result of marketing, misinformation, misconceptions, and pseudoscience."

Who Could Be against Safe and Sustainable?

While writing this book, I was invited to be part of an after-dinner discussion on the benefits and harms of the clean beauty movement. I was paired with an owner of a niche clean beauty company. We were told before the event that it wasn't a debate. It was meant to be a fun and constructive discussion, a point the host emphasized to the audience as we got started. I gave a short presentation, placing clean beauty in the context of the global health misinformation challenge but kept it light. The room was filled with science-informed professionals. I felt like my perhaps-too-obvious points—clean beauty has no definition, there is little good science to support concerns, let's not add to the health information chaos, etc.—were received well. The company owner went next, and it seemed like she missed the "fun and constructive" not-a-debate memo. Her forty-minute presentation was filled with data about chemicals and evolving regulatory policy. She kept hammering away at the idea that since everyone wants safe and sustainable products—which I emphasized at the start of my presentation—it would be illogical not to support the clean beauty movement. (I think she called me "illogical" three times.)

This is a common rhetorical trick in the world of health halos and unproven health and wellness claims. It creates the illusion of certainty. Start with a controversial position, such as the idea that clean beauty products are needed because they are clearly better for you, and when countered with evidence, retreat to a truism we all agree on: we need safe cosmetics and less harmful chemicals. Politicians often use this strategy to make their positions seem more acceptable. Platitudes—like the idea that we all want safer streets or toxin-free water or to avoid unnecessary deaths—are used to camouflage more polarizing and contentious policies like funding urban tanks, removing fluoride from our water, or making abortion illegal.

This rhetorical technique is called the motte-and-bailey fallacy. It is named after the medieval castle defence system where the bailey is the hard-to-defend village and the motte is the easy-to-defend fortified tower. When in trouble—rhetorically or otherwise—retreat to the tower! The strategy is effective for a few reasons. First, it is distracting. The discussion becomes about the agreed-upon point and not the more controversial and less certain claim. It reframes a weak position to make it appear stronger. This works particularly well when done in the media (or during, say, a "fun" after-dinner event) because the audience can be left with a truism as the primary takeaway. It also makes the person countering the unproven claim look like the baddie. "You mean you are *against* safe products? You *want* toxins in cosmetics? You monster!" It's true that everyone wants safe beauty products. But that doesn't mean the evidence supports the claims of the clean beauty industry.

This is an argument style that can be hard to spot. When you hear something that sounds universally agreed upon (again, leveraging our desire for certainty), ask yourself if that statement is really what the debate is about or if it is just a distraction.

Ancient Aliens, Wishful Thinking, and the Goodness Bias

I totally get the appeal of all the "aliens among us" conspiracy theories. In grade school, I was obsessed with Erich von Däniken's 1968 book *Chariots of the Gods*. This bestseller—over seventy million copies sold—helped to popularize the now well-known theory that aliens visited Earth centuries ago and helped build things like the Egyptian, Aztec, and Mayan pyramids. The idea is exciting, mysterious, and a bit spooky. Grade-school me was obsessed. The evidence was so compelling! I'd lie in my bed and stare at the pictures of ancient art depicting what was very obviously alien activity, at least to a grade-schooler. One of the most famous of these images is an ancient Mayan sarcophagus lid that depicts a being piloting a rocket ship. I couldn't believe others didn't see it too. It is so clearly a rocket! Look at the propulsion flames! The pilot is sitting the same way astronauts sit and is obviously manipulating navigational controls! It felt like I knew the *real* story, and everyone else was clueless.

The alien myth remains an incredibly prominent cultural phenomenon. A 2018 study found that 41 percent of Americans believe that aliens visited Earth in the past. The TV show *Ancient Aliens*—a popular History Channel "documentary" series that first aired in 2009—is basically a rehashing of von Däniken theories stretched over nearly two hundred episodes. Belief in contemporary alien visitations has also increased. According to a recent survey by YouGov, the number of individuals who believe there is a "natural scientific justification" for UFOs dropped from 51 percent in 1996 to 32 percent today in 2022.

The idea of ancient aliens scans as fun, frivolous, and not something we should get too worked up about—an innocent theory to help people think about the complexities of human history. "Sometimes the realities of the world suck and can be hard to face, so people start looking for a more idealized understanding of the world. Myths are seen as one way to find that," Stephanie Halmhofer tells me. She's doing her PhD in archaeology at the University of Alberta and has studied the way pseudoarchaeology, including the ancient alien narrative, is used to support mythical origin stories. Halmhofer explains that these kinds of stories can also buttress, for better or worse, preconceived views of the world. "Kind of like how a chameleon can adapt itself to its surroundings, myths can be adapted into idealized histories that vary based on who you're talking to," she says.

And that is a good segue: these alien narratives are not benign. They do real harm. "It definitely seems kind of goofy on the surface," Halmhofer acknowledges, but the ancient alien myth has been connected to "some pretty nasty conspiracist world views, ranging from antisemitism to white supremacism to occult fascism, and more recently into the broader world view of QAnon."

The idea that aliens played a role in human history has been around since the late nineteenth century. These pseudoscientific theories, mostly put forward by white men, have been focused almost entirely on non-white civilizations. They discredit the actual origins of the impressive ancient structures (yes, the Egyptians were entirely capable of building the pyramids without the help of alien technology) and serve to reinforce racist ideas about the paramountcy of Europeans in world history. You rarely hear pseudoscientists claim that aliens built Greek and Roman structures. Indeed, other than stuff about Stonehenge and the claim that the Roman ruins in Baalbek, Lebanon, were originally a landing pad for spaceships, these theories aren't tied to Europeans. Apparently, aliens built the pyramids of Giza, Machu Picchu and Sacsayhuamán in Peru, Pumapunku in Bolivia, Teotihuacán in Mexico, and the Moai statues on Rapa Nui (Easter Island), but not the Colosseum in Rome?

My pseudoarchaeology phase didn't last long. By the time I was twelve and teenage angst started to kick in, I became embarrassed about my broad knowledge of our allegedly alien-filled past. I removed the books from my bedroom bookshelf and pretended I had never really believed all that nonsense. But in 1976, the *Viking 1* mission sent back an image of the Martian surface that looked very much like a massive face (perhaps an Egyptian pharaoh!) carved in rock, and I could feel my ancient alien curiosity stirring again. *Damn, that does look like a face,* I thought. My older brother, Case, immediately mocked my gullibility, but when NASA released the photo to the public, they noted that the "huge rock formation . . . resembles a human head." This, of course, felt like confirmation. *Yep, it's the work of aliens,* I thought.

Of course, the face on Mars is nothing more than rocks and shadows, a reality confirmed numerous times by more recent and sophisticated photos. But it was incredible how, back in 1976 *after* I'd decided the ancient aliens thing was all nonsense, the image pulled me in.

You might be wondering, How does all this alien stuff relate to goodness in health that we've been exploring?

Well, the forces that twist and spin our impressions of products and ideas are not merely acting in grocery aisles or at beauty counters. Wishful thinking is a powerful, pervasive force, be it in the context of ancient aliens or how we perform, represent, and use scientific research. It lurks in all kinds of unusual places, acting on us when we're unsuspecting and even after we feel we've overcome its influence, which makes it core to the power of the goodness illusion.

When it comes to health halos, most are based on a goal—more nutritious food, a treatment for a disease, safer products, a healthier lifestyle strategy, etc.—that many of us would support. The goodness of the goal is axiomatic. Because these goals are so understandably desirable and certain, wishful thinking can warp both how we see the evidence and how it is represented. We want to see evidence of aliens; we see evidence of aliens. We want to see an easy path to a healthier lifestyle; we see an easy path to a healthier lifestyle.

Wishful thinking engages so many cognitive biases that, in some ways, it is a catch-all concept for the thinking and perception traps that can short-circuit our ability to see the world rationally. It involves, for example, the confirmation bias (finding, favouring, and remembering information that supports preconceived beliefs), motivated reasoning (evaluating and choosing arguments, information, and evidence to endorse a preferred outcome or position), and attentional bias (focusing on some elements and ignoring others, often based on what we've been attending to recently, causing us to overlook alternate possibilities and explanations). These biases are ways we construct a feeling of certainty about a particular topic, even if a more objective analysis— or even the straight-up application of common sense—would point us in a different direction (e.g., it's a random rock formation, not an alien sculpture).

One manifestation of wishful thinking that is particularly relevant to health halos and our search for certainty is a phenomenon called white hat bias. Research on a topic that is perceived to be good or noble is more likely to get funded, published, and represented in popular culture. Researchers, research institutions, academic publications, and the popular press are, so to speak, more prepared to see the face in Mars.

"People seem far more willing to accept lower-quality data and call it conclusive when it fits with what they perceive to be righteous ends or feel-good ideas," David Allison tells me. He is a professor and dean of the Indiana University School of Public Health–Bloomington. He is also the person who, in a 2010 paper with Mark Cope, coined the term *white hat bias*. (Perhaps a less than ideal term, given historical context, but that's the term of art that has stuck.) In that piece, Allison and Cope note the existence of this bias—which they define as "distortion of research-based information in the service of what may be perceived as righteous ends"—throughout obesity research literature. For example, they found that references to studies on strategies to prevent childhood obesity, a tremendously worthy goal, often "described results in a misleadingly positive" manner by "exaggerating the strength of the evidence." A more recent study, published in 2021, found the white hat bias had a significant impact on how COVID-19 therapies were represented. Throughout the pandemic, there was a strong and understandable desire to find a therapy that would reduce deaths and hospitalizations. This may have contributed to a publication bias for reporting positive results over less impressive findings. Positive results from lower-quality studies on the benefits of hydroxychloroquine—the controversial drug supported by former president Donald Trump—had more influence than the higher-quality studies (i.e., randomized controlled trials) that showed the drug had no benefit and possible harms; ultimately the evidence proved it was an ineffective treatment for COVID-19. The author concludes that "the quality of COVID-19 treatment research may be negatively affected by white hat bias, which comes from personal beliefs and the urgent need of an effective intervention."

This study also found that the nonrandomized studies (that is, lower-quality observational research) were more "prone to white hat bias due to the possibility of selective analysis and reporting." In other words, it is easier to make less rigorous studies sound exciting and goodness-supporting—likely since it is easier to spin less definitive data. The results fit well with other studies, such as a 2015 analysis that explored how medical journals represent observational studies, which can be very useful but usually reveal only uncertain correlations, as compared to large well-done clinical trials, which are the gold standard in biomedical research. The 2015 study concluded that the rigour of the methodology had no impact on press coverage, and large randomized-controlled trials—which you'd think would generate the most interest because the results are more definitive—were no more likely to be the subject of a journal press release. Other studies are even grimmer in their assessments, finding that the news media is more likely to cover low-quality observational studies than high-quality randomized controlled trials.

There is every reason to assume that these same forces play out in the context of other goals that are perceived as righteous, such as the value of organic food and the necessity for clean cosmetics. Professor Allison agrees. He says he's seen it play out in all the areas in which he works, "including energetics, diet, exercise, aging, and other aspects of public health."

The goodness bias can even distort how researchers view bad science. A 2019 study from the University of Southern Mississippi asked over one hundred principal investigators (lead scientists who have successfully obtained a National Institutes of Health research grant) about their opinion of questionable research practices. Specifically, they presented these scientists with scenarios in which unethical research was happening. The scientists in the study were more likely to say it was defensible if the research was being done for noble reasons. If there was a perceived good reason for doing the research, the unethical practices seemed okay (ish). If the research was being done for a bad reason, the questionable practices were seen as less defensible.

Think about this for a moment. The perception that certain research is righteous or worthwhile helps to fuel the production of less-than-robust data—or even unethically obtained data—that seems to support the worthwhile goal. This pollutes the literature with low-quality studies that may take years to correct via better research, if the correction happens at all. This low-quality research also gets more attention in popular culture, which means this twisted science impacts how the public perceives the topic.

Consider the use of cannabidiol (CBD) as a therapeutic. This is something that everyone would love to be efficacious—a potentially safe, cheap, and "natural" approach (at least that is how it is often framed) to deal with a range of conditions. Given this wishful thinking, it is no surprise that CBD is a topic filled with hype and distorted representations of science. (CBD hype is a topic I've studied with my colleagues Jeremy Snyder and Marco Zenone. In a 2020 study, for example, we found that public representations of CBD cancer therapies on crowdfunding platforms were filled with harmful misinformation.) An interesting 2022 study from the Karolinska Institutet in Sweden explored the use of cannabinoids for pain. The first thing the research team found was that "placebo responses contribute significantly to the pain reduction seen in cannabinoid randomized clinical trials." So, while the pain reduction from the patient's perspective was very real (and that is key, of course), much of the reduction was due to the placebo effect and not an actual pharmaceutical effect from the cannabinoids. The second, and especially interesting, thing they uncovered was that that placebo response was bolstered by the media coverage of past studies that had a placebo-induced positive response! The placebo response resulted in positive clinical trials, which resulted in positive media coverage, which resulted in more placebo response . . . and around and around and around.

To be sure, finding ways to meaningfully relieve pain, even if through the placebo effect, is a worthwhile goal. But it is one thing to recognize and use the potential value of placebos and quite another to have white hat bias and media hype distort and confuse our knowledge base and the public's perceptions of biomedicine. The former may provide short-term clinical benefits (there is an ongoing debate about if it is sustainable or ethically and legally appropriate to use placebos within a science-based healthcare system), but the latter could cause long-term damage to public discourse and the evidence base that informs clinical decisions.

There are many, many sources of bias in research, with institutional and financial pressure from industry sponsors being the most obvious and well-known. But the white hat bias is a good reminder that pressure doesn't have to be self-serving or nefarious to have an adverse impact on both the integrity of the research and how that research is reported to the public.

Before we leave the topic of space aliens, let's consider one more reality twisting effect of wishful thinking. Part of the reason so many people saw a face on Mars was because the human mind has the tendency to see familiar shapes and patterns in random data. The man in the moon and Jesus in the clouds are classic examples. This cognitive bias is called pareidolia, and it's probably an evolutionarily wired survival mechanism that allows us to make quick decisions, which at one time may have saved lives. (Yikes, is that a lion in the dark?) In the modern world, as with so many psychological shortcuts, this tendency is often informed by preconceived beliefs and wishful thinking. A 2013 study from Finland, for example, found that individuals who are more religious or believe in the paranormal are more likely to see faces in random patterns—the wishful thinking of seeing something to support pre-existing and strongly held beliefs. Other studies have demonstrated that people who are more likely to believe "pseudo-profound bullshit" (yes, that technical term again!) are also more likely to see meaningful images in random patterns or be swayed by "pseudo-profound bullshit titles" to see profoundness in abstract art.

I recognize that a discussion on UFOs and ancient aliens may seem out of place in a book about our distorted and chaotic information environment. But that is kind of the point. The forces that give the goodness illusion so much sway—such as wishful thinking—are everywhere and impact us all, me included, in unexpected ways. In my youth, I perceived the art on an ancient Mayan sarcophagus lid as an alien rocket man, because that is exactly what I wanted to see. That's where my emotions and preconceived ideas pulled me. As real historians and archaeologists know, the image depicts a Mayan king's descent into the underworld. I was also open to the possibility that the face on Mars was created by aliens. Wishful thinking can cause us to be blind to more reasonable alternative explanations.

It is hard to blame people for being optimistic or for seeing Jesus in a tortilla, the Virgin Mary in a tree stump, Mother Teresa in a cinnamon bun, or Elvis on a potato chip. Part of me misses the wonder and thrill that comes with being open to this kind of absurdity. Too much cynicism can close your mind. But we also need to recognize the harm that can be done by giving into wishful thinking. Be open to the wonder, but not closed to the facts.

Manly Men

There has been a strange shift in the wellness space over the past few years. It is becoming less about New Age, holistic, alternative health strategies and more about ideology-fuelled manly optimization. The wellness industry—a multi-trillion-dollar business—has long been the domain of unproven approaches with a counterculture vibe. Energy healing. Crystals. Detox diets. The rise of the men's wellness industry has, to be fair, brought a constructive focus on men's health, but with it a worrisome mash-up of ideology and archaic norms of masculinity. We've gone from Gwyneth Paltrow's vagina (goop infamously sells both jade vagina eggs and candles called, I kid you not, "This Smells Like My Vagina") to Tucker Carlson's testicles (tanning them, that is—but more on that below). Oh sure, it is still very much all evidence-free hooey. But he-man health hacks are increasingly the flavour of the day.

There are many high-profile examples of this trend. Far-right radio show host Alex Jones makes millions off the sale of useless supplements, like his non-GMO and gluten-free Super Male Vitality herbal liquid drops. Former NFL quarterback Tom Brady sells (allegedly) immune-boosting supplements. Tech bros reframe trendy and unproven extreme diets as innovative "body hacking" performance enhancement. And there is also a growing army of "men wellness" influencers pushing the manly man narrative throughout the social media universe.

When I asked Mallory DeMille if she's seen an upswing in wellness content aimed at men, she says, "Yes, though 'wellness' isn't exactly how they sell themselves. It's masculinity optimization, testosterone boosting, and anti-woke diets." She is a friend and colleague who works in the social media space and has been closely following the online health influencer community for years. "Many of these influencers present the pursuit of maximum masculinity as the pursuit of maximum health."

This would include people like the Liver King, who has two million Instagram and nearly six million TikTok followers at the time of writing. The Liver King frames wellness as requiring manly ancestral living, which, apparently, involves shooting guns, eating raw meat, consuming the Liver King's meat-in-a-capsule supplements, and dragging heavy objects down roads and across beaches (because, as he tells us, "Men were purpose-built for fighting, hunting, and providing" and "women are the opposite . . . more nurturing, compassionate, and emotional"). And Christian Van Camp, a "Christian men's lifestyle coach," asks his 178,000 CVCWellness followers, "Are you going to be a strong, masculine, confident ALPHA MAN or a weak, comfortable, complacent beta boy?"

(Amusing side note on the Liver King. As I was working on this section of the book, it was discovered that Mr. Liver's incredibly muscular physique was the result of—surprise!—spending $11,000 a month on steroids and growth hormone and not from eating raw organ meat and supporting misogynistic world views. He posted an apology video on YouTube; he claims he took steroids because of "self-esteem issues" and not to help market his multi-million-dollar supplement business. The apology video received almost three million views in five days. By the way, there is absolutely no evidence to support his claim that his "primal diet"—mostly meat—is healthier or that it is how our ancestors ate. On the contrary, most archaeological research has found that early humans ate a diverse diet that included fruits, vegetables, and whole grains.)

But the best and most bizarre case study of this trend is conservative political commentator and television personality Tucker Carlson's much-mocked wellness "documentary," *The End of Men*. Ostensibly about what Carlson believes is an emerging health crisis, the show is really the cable news equivalent of that comic book advertisement for Charles Atlas where a ninety-eight-pound weakling gets sand kicked in his face. Muscles to the rescue! "Oh, Mac! You *are* a real man after all!"

The message—sometimes explicit, sometimes implied—in Carlson's show is that our limp constitutions and less than manly social policies, diets, work, and recreational activities (do real men play *Minecraft* or write code for Microsoft?) have driven down our testosterone count. Carlson isn't concerned with tackling genuine public health challenges—there are legitimate and very serious issues with our diet and sedentary lifestyle. Carlson's point here is to use cherry-picked data, anecdotal evidence (read: not actual evidence), wellness guru testimonials, and paradoxically homoerotic imagery to encourage us to do something about our pathetic feebleness—unless we want to be overrun by commie effeminate globalists! Apparently, we need "bro-science" (yes, Carlson calls it that) to save us all from, well, real science. We need "strong men" to make "good times," the documentary tells us, though it is never clear what exactly the strong men are going to do to save us. It is as if Carlson and his interviewees are hoping for a post-apocalyptic wasteland where it might be necessary to fight mutants with kettle bells.

From an evidence perspective, there is so much wrong with the documentary that it is tough to know what to highlight. Drinking raw eggs to man up your fragility? No. Don't do this. While eggs are nutritious, they are not a magical wellness elixir, and if you eat them raw, there's a chance you'll consume the bacteria *Salmonella*, which hospitalizes thousands and kills hundreds every year in the U.S. alone. Of all the bro-science recommendations made in Carlson's show, testicle tanning—which is so absurd that I first thought it was satire—has emerged as the biggest punchline, so let's focus on that.

Studies have found that there has been a drop in testosterone. A 2021 study from the University of Miami found that testosterone levels in young men in the U.S. declined between 1999 and 2016. These declines are not as steep as the documentary claims, which put the decline at 50 percent over the past few decades. Most experts agree that a decline has occurred—perhaps as much as 20 to 25 percent—over the past two decades. Determining exactly how much is difficult for several methodological reasons, including the fact that it may not be appropriate to compare past measurements of testosterone with current findings, which, due to technological advances, are more accurate. The causes of the decline are unclear and undoubtedly complex (e.g., rise in obesity rates, more diabetes, unhealthy diets, less sleep, changes in environmental exposure to certain chemicals). Even getting COVID has been shown to lower testosterone levels. But there is no evidence that the reduction is the result of a global conspiracy to strip men of their masculinity, as suggested by Carlson and the globalist "expert" he invites to speak on the issue—someone who goes by the name Raw Egg Nationalist. Raw Egg Nationalist never explains how this evil plan has been operationalized. It is just presented as a classic "*they* are out to get us" conspiracy.

Which brings us to testicle tanning. If you are wondering what testicle tanning involves, simply Google the phrase. (If you have young children, perhaps first ask them to leave the room.) I can guarantee that the first page of your search results will have—likely in the top snippet—a picture of a naked man standing arms and legs spread, à la Leonardo da Vinci's *Vitruvian Man*, with a red light shining on his, yep, testicles. The idea from Carlson et al. is that tanning your testicles in this manner, by using "red light therapy" as seen in the naked man photo, somehow increases your testosterone level.

I asked urologist Dr. Rena Malik for her take on the procedure. "There is no scientific evidence supporting testicular tanning or red-light therapy to the scrotal skin" was Malik's concise response. "Bottom line: it doesn't work and it's a waste of your hard-earned money." I also could not find a single bit of legitimate science—even of the highly speculative variety—to support this practice. No clinical trials. Not even animal studies. Despite this, there are numerous alternative medicine providers pushing the sunning of our private bits, such as an outfit called the Tantric Academy that focuses on, to quote its website, empowering "men to realize their full masculine confidence" by doing stuff like "exposing your testicles to direct sunlight" because it is "one of the best methods of boosting testosterone naturally." In fact, testicle tanning may be harmful. Reproductive urologist Dr. Ranjith Ramasamy was quoted in *Salon* as saying that the practice is "not backed by the scientific literature" and might "prove harmful for the testes leading to decreased testosterone, decreased sperm counts and subsequent infertility." So, yeah, don't.

The best advice, as is so often the case, is to focus on the basics of a healthy lifestyle—exercise, sleep, real food, not smoking, and drinking alcohol in moderation (or not at all). If you have real concerns about your testosterone levels, see a physician.

You may be wondering why I'm talking about Tucker Carlson and testicle tanning in a section about twisted goals, goodness illusions, and health halos. Simple. Being more manly is presented as unequivocally good for your health and for society in general. It is presented as a certainty. A no-brainer. For a large sector of society, being manly *is* a health halo.

Of course, playing on male insecurities about masculinity is a marketing ploy that has been around for a very long time. As Ulster University historian Conor Heffernan notes, Tucker Carlson's claims are part of a rich heritage of skeptics shouting from the rooftops that American men are becoming devitalized, lazy, and effeminate. But Carlson's documentary is a good example of its place in contemporary society. It is taken for granted—presented as a truism—that a world filled with more masculinity would be a good thing. And that more masculinity means more health. From the perspective of this book, it is an opportunity to explore how the specific goodness *goal*—such as being manly—can also be controversial and contested. Few would argue against, say, safer food and beauty products or a more sustainable food production system. Those are reasonable and worthy goals. But is being more manly?

Views of masculinity, gender, and sexuality are (thankfully) evolving and becoming more inclusive and expansive. But studies have also shown that most men still see value in traditional masculinity. A 2019 survey by Pew Research Center in the U.S. found that most of the surveyed men believe that people look up to manly men, and 68 percent of those who believe this see it as a good thing. Eighty-five percent say they are very or somewhat masculine. An interesting 2021 study from the University of Geneva found that while men believe masculinity is becoming less appreciated by society generally, the research participants believed that traditional masculinity remains highly prized by other men—a perception that seems likely to ramp up the peer pressure to strive to be more masculine, or to feel insecure if someone believes they aren't masculine enough. It is no surprise that 86 percent of men, according to the Pew survey, say they feel pressure to be emotionally strong and 57 percent to throw a punch if provoked.

These are the perceptions, pressures, and values being legitimized and exploited by those selling masculinity as a health goal. I recognize that views of masculinity are complex—historically, culturally, psychologically, sexually, and politically. I'm not here to tell you that there is a right way to be or identify as a man. On the contrary. But we can debunk the health-halo part of the equation. There seems no doubt that promoting a traditional (or, let's be honest here, entirely mythical) view of masculinity comes with clear health risks.

Studies have shown that people who subscribe to traditional masculine norms are less likely to seek health-related help or to follow public health recommendations. They are also more likely to: catch infectious diseases, have heart disease, experience poorer cancer outcomes, engage in dangerous behaviours, smoke, regularly partake in high-risk alcohol consumption, sleep less (because, according to a 2021 study, "sleeping less is related to increased perceptions of masculinity"), abuse substances, have erectile dysfunction, and believe harmful conspiracy theories. They are at increased risk to be lonely, have fewer friends, and a host of mental health challenges. A 2017 systematic review of the available evidence found that masculine norms are unfavourably associated with mental health and psychological help seeking. The study found that conformity to the specific masculine norms often pushed by the bro-wellness community, such as self-reliance and power over women, were specifically problematic, being "robustly and consistently related to mental health-related outcomes." A study from 2021 found that "higher conformity to masculine norms was associated with an increased risk of current depressive symptoms." Other research, published in 2020, found a link between masculinity and suicidal ideation. The authors suggest that their study highlights "the importance of presenting young males with alternative and multiple ways of being a male."

Pushing manliness also has implications for society more broadly. There is deep literature on, for example, the correlation between traditional masculine norms and intimate partner abuse, bullying, tolerance for sexual assault, gun violence, and war and conflict. Research has also consistently found that questioning a person's masculinity, which is exactly what bro-science wellness gurus often do to build their brands and sell products, results in more aggressive attitudes and behaviours. A 2021 study from Duke University, for example, found that pressure to be masculine according to traditional masculinity norms "elicits aggressive cognition in manhood-threatening contexts." Further confirming the impact of the manly social norms, the opposite was true too. As summarized by the authors of the study, "men who experienced no or low social pressure to be stereotypically masculine showed no heightened aggression."

While we need to be careful not to overinterpret the research findings on the health and social implications of endorsing traditional masculine norms (most come from observational studies that cannot confirm causation), this body of evidence emphasizes that the relationship between masculinity and health is, at a minimum, complex and evolving. That said, the available research does consistently show that traditional views of masculinity, the kind advocated for by the growing legions of bro-science wellness gurus, are mostly associated with unhealthy behaviours and poorer health outcomes. Despite what Carlson tells us, more isn't necessarily better for individuals, families, or societies. If anything, the data points in the opposite direction. A more inclusive and tolerant view of what it means to identify as a man leads to healthier individuals and societies.

"These people are pushing old tropes that historically have never done us any good. They're just commodifying gender issues," John Oliffe tells me. As a professor of men's health promotion at the University of British Columbia and founder of the Men's Health Research program, he has been closely following and studying these trends for years. "It is nothing more than a shitty sales job," he says, frustrated with the situation. His research has found that many men are "craving these conversations" about gender and masculinity. People like Tucker Carlson and the Liver Kings of the world are leveraging that need for profit and, as Oliffe speculates, simple provocation. "It is so unhelpful especially for young guys that are still working out their identity."

Countering this confused messaging in a way that is constructive and health promoting in both the short and long terms won't be easy. There are complex policy tensions when recognizing and representing masculine norms in the context of health promotion. On the one hand, we want to encourage those individuals that do identify with traditional views of masculinity to seek help when needed. Studies have suggested that it may be necessary to lean into those norms in a way that reframes prevention and help seeking as aligned with positive masculine traits like strength and responsibility. Using language like "man up" and providing peer-led and men-only counselling could encourage those men who are reluctant to seek help.

On the other hand, there is concern that public health campaigns that leverage masculine norms can reify harmful he-man stereotypes, thus making it more difficult to create constructive cultural change. As noted in a 2014 commentary in the *American Journal of Public Health*, "The currently available evidence on the harmful effects of adhering to hegemonic gender norms is too well established to ignore." As a result, the authors argue for messaging that would result in a move away from regressive and narrow representations of what it means to be a man.

So, there is a careful balance to be struck when crafting health policy that engages themes of masculinity. Overall, however, most experts agree that we need to move away from old-school, rigid notions. As noted in the American Psychological Association's 2018 *Guidelines for Psychological Practice with Boys and Men*, we should err on the side of messaging that helps individuals "navigate restrictive definitions of masculinity and create their own concepts of what it means to be male," recognizing that "expression of masculine gender norms may not be seen as essential for those who hold a male gender identity."

More broadly, this exploration of masculinity messaging should be a reminder to question goals that are presented as axiomatically good, especially when that this-is-a-certainty framing comes without reference to good evidence and is tied up with any kind of political or polarizing agenda.

Manly Ideology?

Of course, all this noise about the alleged need to increase manliness isn't only about health. There is a close connection between ideology and traditional views of masculinity, a reality that I'm sure Tucker Carlson and the rest of the tire-flipping, axe-throwing, gun-shooting, supplement-guzzling, liver-eating, bro-wellness influencers are fully aware. A 2021 study, for example, found a strong correlation between the embrace of traditional masculinity norms—especially in the context of toughness, avoidance of femininity, restrictive emotionality, and the adherence to masculine sex norms—and conservative political ideology.

Another study by a team from Pennsylvania State University, published in 2021, goes even further, highlighting how closely connected masculinity and politics can be. The research explored the degree to which over two thousand individuals espoused traditional masculine norms, such as the idea that men should be mentally, physically, and emotionally tough. It was revealed that such endorsements predicted support for Trump—for both men and women—over and beyond any other variable they analyzed, including views often associated with Trump's rise to power such as anti-establishmentarianism, anti-elitism, xenophobia, and nationalistic populism. And this result held even when controlling for political party affiliation.

Feeling fragile—and making people feel fragile—about masculinity can lead to support for aggressive policies, such as the death penalty and military action, and politicians who are more conservative. It is almost as if those who are concerned about their masculinity are overcompensating by emphasizing policies and politicians that are perceived to be more manly. (The red sports car of political endorsements?) This phenomenon was explored in a 2020 study from New York University that found some men's "concern about failing to meet masculine standards leads them to embrace policies and politicians that signal strength and toughness." A 2022 study from the same team found that, paradoxically, this was especially true among liberal men, perhaps because they feel the need to prove that they don't fit the liberal stereotype of not being masculine. This highlights how, even for liberal men, a lack of traditional manliness is viewed as a negative attribute.

"This shows how powerful these social norms still are and how persuasive they can be even for people who don't agree with them," Sarah DiMuccio tells me. She is the lead author of both above noted studies on masculinity and ideology. "Just being aware of a stereotype can impact your behaviour and beliefs." This can happen even if we know the stereotype is outdated and the associated behaviour potentially harmful. DiMuccio used the example of how men avoid salad because meat, especially red meat, is perceived to be more manly. A 2022 study from the University of Lethbridge showed that men who are worried about not living up to masculine gender norms—what the researchers call "masculinity stress"—were more likely to state a preference and be willing to pay for red meat. "Men can explicitly reject outdated views of manhood but still feel the need to do something about a perceived threat to their manhood," DiMuccio says. "So, they order the steak."

This is another reason that health hokum projected through a masculine-enhancement lens can be particularly problematic. Not only is it playing to (and creating) he-man insecurities, but wrapping misinformation in ideology makes it more likely to spread and be believed—especially among those with the political leaning of Carlson's audience.

It is important to recognize that the spread of misinformation—including misleading or inaccurate health-related recommendations—happens across the ideological spectrum, especially at the political extremes. Anti-GMO sentiment, for instance, flows from both the left and the right. Though it is often said that the evidence-free rhetoric about GMOs comes mostly from the left—which, from a political action perspective, is probably true—most studies find both conservatives and liberals believe GMO misinformation. Contrary to what we see happening in our current, post-COVID world, the loudest pockets of the anti-vaccine movement have leaned left.

At this cultural moment, a large body of evidence tells us the embrace of bunk is more of an issue for the political right. To cite a few examples, research published in 2022 in the journal *Nature Communications* showed that conservative political elites share more misinformation as compared to those on the left. As do their social media followers—especially those who are ideologically extreme—as compared to liberals.

According to a 2023 study that explored how social media platforms facilitate the creation of information echo chambers, most political misinformation exists in a homogeneously conservative corner of the online news ecosystem, which currently "has no equivalent on the liberal side." A 2021 study from Ohio State University found that those on the political right are also more likely to believe misinformation: "conservatism is associated with a lesser ability to distinguish between true and false claims across a wide range of political issues and with a tendency to believe that all claims are true." The authors are careful to note that this is likely because—again, at this cultural moment—the misinformation plays to topics that fit the current conservative agenda. And this exposure has a measurable impact.

It is important to recognize that the conservatives haven't always been associated with an anti-science stance. According to data from research company Gallup, in 1975, 67 percent of Democrats and 72 percent of Republicans had confidence in science. In 2021, 79 percent of Democrats and 45 percent of Republicans had confidence in science. In other words, the ideological support of science shifted from right to left.

One of my favourite examples of the degree to which the embrace of misinformation can be influenced by ideological identity—and how fast it can happen—is the Marin County vaccine flip.

Just outside San Francisco, Marin County is wealthy, educated, *very* Democratic, and famous for its New Age anti-vaccine stance. This patently science-free approach to public health made the Bay Area neighbourhood the butt of jokes. In 2015, comedian Jon Stewart declared, "They're not rednecks. They're not ignorant. They practice a mindful stupidity." Around the same time, the county was part of a measles outbreak fuelled by unvaccinated children. So, yep, Marin County seemed pretty committed to its anti-vaccine position.

But during the pandemic, being anti-vaccine became increasingly viewed as a conservative position. A 2021 study by the Kaiser Family Foundation found that Republicans are more than three times as likely to be unvaccinated as compared to Democrats. In the U.S., your political position is more predictive of your vaccination status than race, age, education, or health insurance coverage. (This is a big reason the COVID death rate is significantly higher in Republican jurisdictions.) Anti-vaccine became an ideological vibe that Marin residents didn't want to project. As a result, Marin County is now one of the most vaccinated places in America. As reported in a piece by Soumya Karlamangla in the *New York Times*, "Among children 5 to 11, 80 percent in Marin County have both of their COVID shots, more than double the statewide or national rates. The rate among those under 5 is more than five times the nation's." A 2022 headline in a local newspaper captures the new Marin County ethos: "Unvaccinated? You're Not Welcome in Marin."

So, while it may seem like I'm unfairly picking on the conservative right (okay, I probably am, but just a bit), that is not the point. We all need to recognize that our receptivity to messaging—especially content that seems to support our concept of what is good and right—is greatly influenced by our ideological world view, insecurities, and self-identity.

Not long ago I interviewed Kate Starbird, a professor at the University of Washington, for a magazine article I was writing. She is a renowned expert on social media and misinformation. I asked for her top recommendation to help people spot misinformation and navigate our chaotic information environment. I was expecting something about critical thinking or looking at the evidence. Nope. "Tune into your emotions," she told me. "Instead of just focusing on the content or the source, we also need to tune into how content makes us feel." Our emotions trick us into believing and spreading content, Starbird explained, even when it is clearly misinformation. If the message plays to our fears or anger or morality, "that's a good signal for needing to take a closer look, to slow down, and maybe wait a bit before sharing," she said. And this is particularly so when there is an ideological spin.

Starbird's bottom line advice: "Whenever some piece of content makes me feel politically self-righteous—like I'm about to spike a political football—that's when I know I need to be extra careful about sharing."

There is lots of research to back up Starbird's conclusion. A 2022 study from Spain examined almost 100,000 bits of social media misinformation to map the typical characteristics of what goes viral. The researcher wanted to identify the fingerprint of deceptive content and how it differs from reliable information. It turns out that, on average, as compared to scientifically accurate content, misinformation is easier to process, more emotional, scarier, and focused on morality. A claim that there is an urgent need to irradiate your balls to save your manliness and the entire free world seems to fit this formula pretty well.

A Good Story

Shows like *The End of Men* are so patently absurd and filled with so much science-free baloney that it can be difficult to see how anyone could take them seriously. But a good story almost always wins the day. Documentaries, even ones as clunky and nonsensical as Tucker Carlson's, have tremendous power to persuade.

I have been involved in the production of numerous documentary projects. It is a creative process I find extremely rewarding. While it has never been the central part of my career, I've played a number of roles, including writing, advising on, hosting, being an interviewee, producing, and crafting pitches. Some of these projects got made, such as the two seasons of my documentary TV show *A User's Guide to Cheating Death*, and others died an unceremonious death at various places along the path to completion. But regardless of their fate, everyone involved with these projects was almost always focused on one central concern: what story are we trying to tell?

The "human mind is a story processor, not a logic processor," wrote psychology professor and author Jonathan Haidt. And this indeed seems to be the case. Humans are hard-wired to respond to narratives. Research using functional MRI scans has shown that when we listen to a story, several areas of the brain are activated. In addition to the language centre, the parts of the brain involved in sound, movement, social cognition, and the prediction of the future are engaged—highlighting the degree to which stories can draw us in and cause us to empathize with the individuals portrayed. A 2020 analysis from the University of Florida of the (truly horrid, please don't watch!) anti-vaccine documentary *Vaccines Revealed* describes how the show's production can "transport viewers into a story, which often leads to formation of an imaginary para-social relationship during and after media consumption." And this can cause "audiences [to] become both cognitively and emotionally involved in narratives."

It is no surprise that documentaries can, for better or worse, have a dramatic impact on our beliefs and behaviours. Their emotional power can stir us to change perspective and to take action, such as attempting a healthier diet or becoming more involved in a social cause. A 2016 study revealed that watching a documentary about the natural environment had a significant impact on both perceptions of environmental issues and donations to relevant causes. And there is some evidence that documentaries can have a lasting impact on news media portrayals and public and political engagement. Researchers from the University of Antwerp found that the BBC documentary *Blue Planet* resulted in both journalists and politicians mentioning environmental issues regarding the ocean, such as plastic pollution-related terms, more often. It also increased the number of internet searches for related issues. According to the study, which was published in 2021, the interest in these topics was, "for both the media and political agendas, long-lasting."

Blue Planet is a beautifully crafted show about a genuinely important topic. Few would argue against the merits of using quality documentaries to affect this kind of change. Indeed, this is exactly what most documentarians hope for. This is what I hope for. But the same storytelling tools that are used to make *Blue Planet* powerful can be used to push harmful misinformation and conspiracy theories. We know that a slick and creative presentation, the "form over substance" cliché, matters.

The production quality of a video significantly adds to its persuasive force. How it is filmed, edited, and narrated can create a dramatic certainty illusion that makes the presented claims feel truer than what the relevant evidence actually shows. And this can happen even when the audience is relatively well informed about the topic.

In an interesting 2020 study from Sam Houston State University, 160 health science students were shown the popular, fearmongering, and much critiqued film *What the Health*. The 2017 Netflix documentary misrepresents nutritional science to spin a health-halo-infused tale about how we are supposed to eat, but it often makes baseless claims like suggesting that eating an egg a day is as bad as smoking five cigarettes. Even though the students in the study were studying nutritional science, the documentary *still* ended up changing their perceptions and stated behaviours. The researchers report that post-viewing testing found that the documentary resulted in a decrease in the students' knowledge about nutrition and an increase in agreement with incorrect health claims. Many students said that because of the documentary, they would change their diets. Again, these were university students who were studying the topics covered in the film! The authors conclude with this warning: "Documentaries providing health information contradictory to the current body of scientific literature are persuasive and can potentially increase negative health behaviors."

The dramatic use of anecdotes is a narrative tool often deployed in documentaries. The journey of one or two central characters might form the narrative arc of the show. Or the documentary might use the experiences of specific individuals to highlight tragedies and harms (e.g., the adverse impact of a particular kind of food or health intervention) or benefits and triumphs (e.g., the magical effects of an allegedly health-enhancing diet or food production approach). Unfortunately, an anecdote, no matter how compelling, is not the same as good scientific data. As noted by the science communication scholar Michael Dahlstrom from Iowa State University, "While science searches for broad patterns that capture general truths about the world, storytelling celebrates the particulars of a single experience, regardless of how representative that experience may be."

I am not knocking the use of individual experiences or powerful examples as a way to make documentaries entertaining. If used carefully, stories are a formidable and near essential science communication tools. As Dahlstrom writes, "The power of narrative lies in its ability to create meaning from the scattered facts of reality." Stories can provide emotional heft and make data more relatable. For example, one moving picture that tells the story of a family grieving the death of a loved one can have more impact than the seemingly abstract reality that COVID-19 has killed almost seven million humans. Moreover, there is evidence "that narratives can increase recall, comprehension, and acceptance of scientific information."

But too often narratives are used in a way that distorts the scientific reality. As mentioned earlier in this book, several studies have shown that an anecdote can overwhelm our ability to think scientifically. The dramatic telling of an adverse reaction to a vaccine. A heartbreaking case of cancer that is associated with a particular compound. These stories can have real sway. But that doesn't mean they are, scientifically speaking, correct. I'm sure the use of anecdotes to spin isn't always malevolent or even intentional. For example, in the 2019 documentary *Toxic Beauty*—a film with a big clean beauty theme—we follow individuals who have used beauty products, including talcum powder, and then developed ovarian cancer. The stories are moving, but the viewer is left with the impression that the connection between the beauty product and cancer is clear and proven. That it is a near certainty. In reality, the science around the safety of talcum powder remains messy. Yes, there have been successful lawsuits and settlements that have awarded billions of dollars. But from a scientific perspective, this means next to nothing. (The courts are notoriously terrible with science.)

A large 2020 study published in the *Journal of the American Medical Association* found that "there was not a statistically significant association between use of powder in the genital area and ovarian cancer."

A 2021 review of the available data published in the journal *Gyneco-logic Oncology* concluded that there was, at most, "a weak association with ovarian cancer risk." To be clear, I am not saying that there isn't a connection. Other studies suggest a possible link. More and better research would be helpful. What I am saying is that, despite the scary takeaway message from the narratives in the documentary, the connection is far from definitive. If it does exist, the increase in risk is likely relatively small, in an absolute sense. But a scientific story of uncertain and underwhelming data is not as compelling or attention-grabbing as an emotional and definitive-sounding anecdote. Still, a narrative that oversimplifies a complex scientific story, even when done for a noble cause, isn't helpful for anyone.

Other times, anecdotes are used in documentaries with the clear goal of deceiving the audience and to forward a particular agenda. At the time of writing, one streaming company offers a channel that is nothing but "documentaries" about conspiracy theories, including QAnon and Pizzagate nonsense. We see this again and again and again in anti-vaccine "documentaries" (read: propaganda films) that suggest a link, via the presentation of scary anecdotes, between vaccination and a host of adverse events.

"The salience of an anecdote can turn a molehill into a mountain," Jonathan Jarry tells me. He is with McGill University's Office for Science and Society and someone I frequently collaborate with on science communication projects. Jarry notes that anecdotes are a particularly "effective and dangerous way of convincing us," as he puts it, that there is a meaningful connection between a disease and exposure to a particular compound. "The 'after the fact, therefore because of it' is an error in thinking, and testimonials to that effect can act like gasoline on fire embers. We crave stories like that to inform how we see the world. If I wanted to drive the point home and exaggerate a little, I would say that storytelling is like a drug for the human brain."

I love documentaries. They are a powerful and important art form that can be used to generate empathy and understanding on important topics. No matter how persuasive and emotionally compelling a documentary may feel, always ask yourself about the nature of the evidence and how it is being rolled out in the production. Are they relying on shocking anecdotes? Does the documentary place the claims in the context of the broader body of evidence?

Doing Good and the Certainty Grift

Despite all the rage, divisiveness, moralizing, and finger-pointing that seem to permeate our world, studies have consistently shown—perhaps not surprisingly, given that humans are social animals—most people do want to do the right thing, even if we don't all agree on the rightness of each thing. Psychopathic, evil Bond villains are a rare breed. In general, we are motivated to be good. For example, a 2020 study from Ohio State University found that people are motivated to be kind for a host of reasons—a desire to pay it forward, to be seen by others as doing good, to reward someone who has also been kind . . . the list goes on. All these kindness motivations are remarkably robust. Research has also shown that believing you are kind, ethical, and doing good fosters personal happiness and contentment. Some longitudinal studies have found an association between kindness and longevity. Surveys also consistently find—again, no surprise—that most people want to do what is good for our own well-being and that of our families.

But there is a massive and depressingly predictable disconnect between wanting to do good and making actual behaviour changes and sacrifices to that end. Survey research reveals the majority of us wish to improve our personal health, to fight climate change, and to help others, but often sustained and meaningful behaviour change remains elusive. For example, when asked, most people will state they need to—and want to—live a healthier lifestyle. Every year, the top New Year's resolutions are almost always related to health and well-being. Eating better.

Exercise. Weight loss. Being more mindful. But despite this focus, according to a 2016 study published in the *Mayo Clinic Proceedings*, only 2.7 percent of Americans live a healthy lifestyle. Less than 3 percent! As already noted, the confused and chaotic information environment is part of the problem. A 2022 study from Rutgers, for example, explored how conflicting health information impacts health decisions and actions. The study found that those research participants exposed to conflicting health information "made more errors, had overall slower reaction times, and reported greater workload, nutritional confusion, and backlash." And by backlash, the researchers mean people rejecting emerging health recommendations. This is the "Ugh, it is all so confusing, so I give up!" metric.

The goodness illusion helps to (cynically) bridge this disconnect by offering a false sense of certainty about both the goal and the best journey to achieving it. Using deceptive health halos, wishful thinking, and scary stories and anecdotes, our all-too-human desire to do what is right for our community, family, and own well-being is exploited for profit, politics, and the pursuit of often evidence-free agendas.

PART III
THE
OPINION
ILLUSION

That Earthy Taste!

It isn't often you get to talk to the owner of a restaurant that, at one time, was the number one top-rated establishment in the city of London, U.K. Think how competitive that market is and how demanding the tastes of London's gastronomic elite are. To be the number-one rated restaurant in that rather significant corner of the foodie world is no small feat.

The restaurant? The Shed at Dulwich. The restaurateur? Oobah Butler. The restaurant's artisanal, deconstructed, and curated approach to food? Fake. One hundred percent fake.

The restaurant isn't real. While there was a rather shabby and garbage-filled shed in the backyard of Butler's Dulwich home, the eatery existed only in the form of a phone number, a cryptic website, and, crucially, the florid words of his numerous fake reviews on TripAdvisor, like this five-star gem: "The earthy taste and freshness of the food was something else. . . . As the sun was setting, we were offered blankets—we politely declined (one had a stain on it)—but a nice touch, adds to the al fresco feel!"

Butler is an author, filmmaker, TV host, genial interviewee, and all-purpose prankster. He has invented a phony friendship with Russell Brand to get free stuff. He has BS'd his way into Paris fashion week. He sent a better-looking version of himself to his high school reunion (how brilliant is that?). Earlier in his career, he was paid to write fake reviews on TripAdvisor. That last experience—which he tells me he received "a tenner a piece for"—was a key inspiration for the prank he pulled with the Shed.

"In theory it makes total sense, doesn't it? Consensus building. That should be a really great tool for us," Butler muses after I ask him why so many of us love, trust, and rely on online reviews.

In a world of information chaos, the idea of consensus has intuitive appeal. Online ratings and reviews provide us with conclusions that feel certain. That feel real. Online reviews are like a shrewd companion we can rely on to nudge us here and away from there on our online journeys. They have become so ubiquitous that we expect them to be present and are a bit discombobulated when they aren't. From food to tech to clothes to movies to music to books, there are very few consumer spaces where online reviews don't play a central role. And for e-commerce—an industry that was worth approximately $6 trillion globally in 2022—they have become essential. There is a vast and growing industry, what I call the opinion economy, that leverages our belief in the value of the (allegedly) authentic views of others and that increasingly shapes not only our purchasing behaviour but, as I will show, our tastes and expressions of personal identity. The opinion economy is built on our desire for a beacon of clarity and certainty in our fantastically chaotic information ecosystem. As we will see throughout this section, it stands as one of the best examples of a certainty illusion. It also serves to illustrate how our best hopes for the internet—the frictionless and free exchange of authentic ideas and opinions—can be exploited, distorted, and monetized all with very little recognition or care that it is happening.

Over 70 percent of consumers, one industry survey found, won't pull the trigger on a purchase unless they've read online consumer reviews. We assume ratings, raves, and rants will be there to guide us through the noise. So many of our day-to-day decisions are shaped by them. Online reviews exist for almost every product, service, and human experience.

A 2021 survey of six thousand online consumers found "ratings and reviews have become the most important factor impacting online purchase decisions." In fact, survey participants placed the value of online reviews above price, free shipping, brand, and recommendations from family and friends. The survey found 94 percent of customers ranked it as the single most important factor, and four out of five said they won't shop on a website unless it has customer reviews. A 2023 study published in the journal *Nature* found that "the most important attribute for consumers in selecting an online shopping service is star rating." And studies have consistently found that over 90 percent of consumers use online reviews before making a purchase, and 88 percent say they trust reviews as much as or more than personal recommendations.

This latter conclusion is fascinating. People trust the anonymous masses—specifically, individuals who looked for and experienced similar hotels, restaurants, sneakers, books, beauty products, etc.—more than the advice provided by a friend or family member. Other studies have found that people trust user-generated reviews more than the opinions of experts. Online reviews may even be more powerful and persuasive than the actual experience with the purchased product or service. As Butler put it when I asked him about the sway of reviews, "people trust TripAdvisor more than the food in their mouth."

But where does this power come from? While a complex mix of numerous social and psychological forces are undoubtedly relevant, I think much of it can be attributed to five interconnected (and, as we will see, fundamentally flawed) human tendencies.

First, research has consistently found that we trust people who we think are like us, often as much as or more than independent and established experts. A customer review that resonates with your values—about, say, cozy and stain-free blankets—may heighten the sense that the reviewer is kind of like you. After all, like you, they are into quirky shed-themed restaurants! Studies have found that this likely evolutionarily engrained propensity to favour "a person like me" extends beyond assessments of trustworthiness. A 2018 study, for example, found that research participants believed that people who were like them—an assessment made solely by reading a few attributes about the other person from a questionnaire—were more trustworthy, moral, competent, and likeable.

Second, even though anecdotes and testimonials are not a reliable form of evidence (always remember, you need good data!), they can be tremendously persuasive. Studies have found, for instance, that an engaging anecdote can short-circuit our ability to think scientifically. As noted in the last section about documentaries, we are hard-wired to be drawn into stories, especially when they are told by someone we perceive to be like us. Online reviews are basically a collection of testimonials, stories, and anecdotes. A 2015 experiment explored the power of anecdotes in the context of online customer reviews and found that story-like reviews cause higher levels of engagement and, as a result, are more persuasive. This is one reason testimonials are so often used to market stuff.

The third factor is the "feels real" vibe I noted above. People know a car salesperson has an agenda to push products for profit. We all know advertisements and paid endorsements are biased. Online customer reviews, however, have the aura of being real and raw and independent and therefore reliable. The unfiltered truth. They are seen to be authentic. A 2020 study explored the role of reviews on travel websites and their impact on customer intentions. The researchers concluded that the "perceived authenticity" of reviews was the most critical variable.

Fourth is that consensus building notion underscored by Butler. The belief in the "wisdom of the crowd" is strong. Probably the most famous example of this phenomenon is the 1906 experiment by Charles Darwin's cousin, Francis Galton. He asked hundreds of villagers to guess the weight of an ox. While everyone got it wrong, the average of all the guesses was almost exactly right. Since then, the idea has gained momentum. Research has consistently found that a perceived consensus—as represented by, say, a star rating system—can have a significant impact on beliefs and behaviour. A recent survey of people who use online reviews paints a picture of their appeal that aligns closely with Butler's speculation: "Consumer reviews, and popular opinion in general, sum up the wisdom of the general population and serve it as a means of collective intelligence, giving shape and structure to the wealth of information out there." Online reviews are basically a massive guess-the-weight-of-the-ox movement that mobilizes the belief that averaging opinions nudges us closer to the truth.

Finally, online reviews cater to our desire for quick and easy answers. Our information environment is chaotic and fast-paced. Many of our *lives* are chaotic and fast-paced. We only have so much attention to spare. Online reviews, especially that easy-to-interpret five-star rating system, give people immediate access to seemingly useful and actionable information. In the competitive attention economy, anything that creates an easier path to decisions has a leg up. They cater to our desire for certainty.

The Opinion Economy

Butler began the campaign to make the Shed the most sought-after hole in the wall with the purchase of the $13 burner phone he needed to get verified on TripAdvisor. He built a website, which is still up as of this writing and which notes the Shed is an "appointment only" establishment. After all, you wouldn't want anyone popping by to discover the sham. Instead of traditional meals, the menu is comprised of moods, such as Comfort ("Yorkshire blue Macaroni and Cheese seasoned with bacon shavings and served in a 600TC Egyptian cotton bowl") and Love ("A meal that makes your heart swell"). Butler also added a few artsy-looking photos of the offerings. And they do look yummy, even though they were created using things like shaving cream and toilet bowl bleach cakes.

When he started his experiment, the Shed was ranked as the 18,149th restaurant in London. Dead last. He kept posting bunk reviews from different computers and had other people post reviews too, and within a few months, he'd jumped to a rank of 156. His bogus restaurant became a thing. It seemed quirky. Exclusive. People wanted in.

His burner phone started ringing. A lot. "I experienced first-hand the power of [online reviews] by the hundreds and hundreds of customers who tried to book. From all over the world," Butler said. These requests were all met by Butler with some version of a terse and vaguely impolite brush-off—"So sorry, but we are all booked up right now"—because top-rated restaurants don't *need* your business. He told me when he was speaking at a conference in Norway, he learned someone in the audience had tried to book the entire restaurant for a work event. "This is nuts! How much were they going to spend on it? All based on a complete fabrication," he says with a chuckle.

While the simple equation that good reviews mean more business generally holds in most circumstances, there are interesting caveats. Our relationship with those stars, rants, and raves can get complex. A 2016 study found that if reviews are *too* good—say, all five-star raves—sales numbers decrease. There is a sweet spot around 4.2 to 4.5 stars. That seems to be the believably good Goldilocks zone. Reviews that touch on both the good and the bad are perceived to be more credible and, as a result, more persuasive. Butler's "stained blanket" complaint in the above fake review offers a nice "This is authentic and balanced!" touch.

Ewa Maslowska is a professor of advertising at the University of Illinois and the lead author of the above noted sweet-spot study. She told me that almost everyone looks at the star rating, but "people pay more attention to the actual [written] reviews when it is a big decision." In 2020, her team used eye-tracking technology to assess how people read online reviews. While all the research participants quickly scanned the star rating—likely because it doesn't take much time or mental energy to process it—many also spent time on both the review text and information about the reviewers, which supports the idea of the persuasive force of "someone like me" and "wisdom of the crowd" phenomena. People want to know why a particular rating was given (do the reasons seem authentic, and do they resonate with my values?) and who the reviewer is (is this someone like me?). In addition to "wisdom of the crowd" consensus—summarized in the star rating—we look for specific reviews that speak to us.

The bottom line is that reviews matter to customers, but they matter even more to the businesses, products, services, and entertainment that is being reviewed. A 2016 analysis by Harvard Business School found that just one extra star on Yelp can increase revenue for a restaurant by 5 to 9 percent. Part of this increased business might be due to the fact that approximately 70 percent of online consumers set a rating filter when shopping or looking for a business, and the most common filter setting is four stars. If you are a service or company selling a product with less than a four-star rating, you won't even be seen by most people.

The Shed at Dulwich was seen. Often. At least as an online avatar. On one day, about six months after Butler started his prank, his TripAdvisor page had received 89,000 views. The reason? The Shed was the top-rated restaurant in the city of London. Driven by nothing more than authentic-sounding fake reviews and strategically indifferent responses to reservation requests, Butler had pushed his non-existent restaurant to number one.

I recognize that Butler's clever hoax is hardly concrete evidence of a wide-ranging system failure (more on *that* evidence below). But it is a dramatic and hilarious illustration of both the role of reviews in our lives and how they can be easily manipulated and, as a result, fail to provide what we expect of them.

"It is depressing, isn't it? This journey we've all been on," Butler says after I ask him what his experiment says about the current information environment and our quest for certainty. He seems genuinely deflated by this realization, particularly the disconnect between, as he puts it, "the idea of the internet and what it should represent versus the reality that it's starting to look more and more like the rest of society than a panacea." All those forces that have long pushed us in the wrong direction—money, social climbing, ingrained biases, prejudices, petty ideological positioning, vanity—still, far too often, win the day. The information super-highway hasn't made things better or more authentic; it has just commodified an illusory version of those things. It has taken our desire for authenticity and certainty and created a vast and largely unregulated illusion-filled opinion economy.

Butler once said that the world of online reviews is a "false reality that everyone takes completely seriously." I think this exactly captures the absurdity of this situation. It is like we are living in the opinion illusion Matrix. But how bad is it?

Fake It until . . . Well, Forever

Let's start with perhaps the most obvious issue. The one so dramatically highlighted by the Shed caper. Many online reviews are straight-up fake. And by *fake*, I mean not written by a true customer. It was either purchased, generated by an AI-powered bot, or written by someone with an ulterior motive, such as wanting to sell stuff or, at the other end of the motivation spectrum, trying to hurt a business, product, or service.

Estimates on the frequency of fakes vary greatly. A 2019 analysis that used an online detection tool called Fakespot concluded that, on average, 39 percent of product reviews are unreliable, with posts about apparel (46.2 percent), home decor (45.6 percent), and electronics (42 percent) being particularly bad. Others have suggested the number may even be higher. A 2022 industry analysis suggested that 61 percent of reviews about electronics "have been deemed fake."

Saoud Khalifah, the CEO of Fakespot, tells me that their team estimates "about 30 percent of the reviews on Amazon are unreliable to consumers." While there is variation between platforms, and certain categories of products fare better or worse, "no platform has zero fake reviews," Khalifah says. "It is basically a wild west of misinformation." Other experts I talked with suggest the range of verifiable fakes is lower, around 15 percent. But they all quickly qualified that assessment with the caveat that it has become increasingly difficult to identify fakes. In other words, there is very likely more fakes than we all, including the experts, realize. The estimation I see most often hovers around 25 to 30 percent.

Another way to look at the issue is the degree to which the average star rating is boosted by fake reviews. A 2019 analysis by *The Hustle* found that for some products, such as electronics, untrustworthy reviews boost ratings by anywhere from 0.5 to almost a full star. For headphones, for example, the average trustworthy rating was 3.99 stars, but when you add the fake reviews, it rises to 4.89. Again, this analysis assumes that they can tell when a review is untrustworthy, and they probably often can't. That means the gap in the average star rating between only the real reviews and all reviews is likely even larger.

The incentive for companies to generate positive reviews is intense. On a global level, trillions of dollars are in play. Almost the entire consumer economy has a horse in this race. Good reviews translate into profits. Alas, studies have consistently shown that generating fake or "incentivized" positive reviews (more on that below) works. An analysis by the World Economic Forum (WEF) estimates that fake online reviews influence the $791 billion of online spending that happens per year in the U.S. alone and directly impact, the WEF estimates, about $152 billion in spending. A 2021 study by Davide Proserpio, a professor of marketing at the University of Southern California, and his colleagues explored the market for and impact of online reviews. Their work found, no surprise, that "rating manipulation is an effective strategy for generating a substantial boost in ratings, keyword position, and ultimately sales." As a result, "firms therefore have a strong incentive to continuously improve and perfect their manipulation strategies to avoid detection."

The other way that fake reviews help companies is to increase their search rankings. This is critical to improving the awareness and visibility of a product or service. Google explicitly states that online reviews impact its approach to rankings. Good reviews might mean the difference between being on the first page of search results or on the second or third page. The first page sucks up about 95 percent of web traffic. (As the joke goes, where's the best place to hide a dead body? On the second page of a Google search.) The financial incentive to get on page one is extreme. Once you realize your competitors are likely doing the same thing, you might find yourself in a review-manipulation arms race.

Research by Sherry He, a PhD candidate at UCLA's Anderson School of Management, shines a light on the massive but illusive fake-review industry. She has investigated the use of Facebook to recruit individuals to write fake reviews for products sold on Amazon. Suffice to say, she found a lot of recruiting. "We estimate there are 4.8 million [recruitment] posts in a year," she tells me when I ask about the scope of the problem. "And we only observed Facebook groups, which is a semi-public channel. We cannot speak of private fake review recruiting channels."

It often works like this: a person is recruited to post a fake review and is paid usually in the amount of the cost of the product being reviewed. Some companies also give reviewers a small commission—once they provide a screenshot of a realistic-looking five-star review. To avoid detection by platform algorithms designed to identify and remove fakes, the recruits are told to search for and buy the products themselves. This means Amazon, for example, notes their purchase as a verified one, and their review looks as authentic and organic as possible.

Not only do fake reviews lead to a significant increase in average ratings and sales rank by inflating the number of high reviews, they can also influence how legitimate reviewers rate a product or service. The anchoring effect is a cognitive bias that can influence how we value things. Say you have a mediocre meal at a local restaurant after seeing that the restaurant's average online score is 4.8 out of 5 stars (perhaps inflated by fake reviews). That is your starting reference point. The anchor. In that context, you might feel like your relatively run-of-the-mill experience deserves a four-star rating. That is almost a full star below the restaurant's average, after all, but four stars isn't all that bad, right? Even if your rating pulls their overall score down, that restaurant's rating will probably still be higher than 4.5. But if the anchor is, say, 3.5 stars, you may feel like three stars better reflects your experience. After all, your experience was unexceptional. Thus, to ensure a higher anchor score, businesses may feel compelled to get a bunch of five-star raves up on the scoreboard. The research shows that the anchoring effect works: fake and manipulated reviews have an impact on both review judgments and purchasing behaviour.

Of course, government regulators around the world are familiar with these kinds of shenanigans and have taken steps to respond. In April 2022, for instance, the U.K. made regulatory moves to make it illegal to write or post fake reviews. It was probably already illegal— as it is, technically, fraud or false advertising—so this seems more a "for emphasis" move. The U.S. Federal Trade Commission (FTC) is also not a big fan of fake and manipulated reviews. In October 2021, the FTC issued a press release to put the world on notice that it was going to crack down on fake reviews and "misleading endorsements." And it seems to be walking the talk. In February 2022, the FTC commenced lawsuits against two companies that are major fake review brokers. The companies coordinate and profit from the posting of fake customer reviews on platforms such as Amazon, eBay, Walmart, and Etsy. The FTC has also taken action against companies that have supressed negative reviews or instructed employees to write authentic-looking positive reviews for the products they sell.

While this kind of action by the U.K. government and regulators like the FTC is certainly needed and welcomed, the gargantuan scale of the problem—and the billions of dollars in play—makes such moves seem if not totally futile, then little more than symbolic. "It is very hard to police everyone, and the fake reviewers are getting better and better," Davide Proserpio tells me. And by "better and better," he means the fakers know how to ensure that the reviews look more and more authentic, thus making it difficult for either you or me or anyone, including a platform's algorithms or academic experts, to ferret them out. "The number of fake reviews is increasing all the time," Proserpio said. "This is going to be a very hard problem to solve. It is going to take a long time."

Curtis Boyd, a data scientist and the head of the Transparency Company, an initiative with the explicit goal of stopping the spread of fake reviews, tells me the same thing. "Selling fake reviews is a multi-billion-dollar business. Almost every industry is affected by it," he says. "Doctors, lawyers, preschools, everything." And like Proserpio, Boyd is not optimistic regulators can have a meaningful impact; the incentives to create and use fake reviews are too formidable. And he also agrees that the fakers are "getting better and better at making them look real."

Platforms like Google, which is the biggest source of online reviews, say they remove millions of fake posts every year. Boyd tells me his research team estimates that Google removes about 180,000 bogus reviews *a day*, which gives you a sense of the extent of the problem. But despite that impressive number, Boyd doesn't think it is making a dent. "That's just the tip of the iceberg."

Because fake reviews help everyone profit along the marketing food chain, there is little incentive to take meaningful action to remove the unreliable noise, says Boyd. He calls this the fake review cycle. It works like this: a business (a restaurant, shoe store, law office, toy manufacturer, etc.) purchases fake reviews, which results in that business selling more products or services. This, in turn, makes more money available for marketing, and often the business spends it on the platform hosting their fake reviews because it is likely where the increased sales are coming from. As a result, fake reviews become profitable for the platforms hosting them, the advertisers, the businesses creating them, and often the individuals writing them—but not you and me, the real customers. In the end, as noted in a 2021 article by Boyd in which he maps out this vicious cycle, "turning a partial blind eye to review fraud generates a win-win for big tech and their advertisers. Consumers are getting the short straw."

Let's pause here and put this reality in the context of the broader theme of this book. The information economy has been incentivized to exploit our desire for authentic, reliable, and informed opinions to the extent that those opinions are no longer authentic, reliable, or informed.

To make matters worse, many of the reviews that aren't blatant phonies are often far from truly independent or authentic. A significant portion of all reviews are influenced by or even the direct result of incentives provided by the businesses being reviewed. One 2021 industry survey found that 17 percent of consumers recall being offered a discount for a review and 6 percent were offered cash. I would argue that the resulting reviews wouldn't count as truly fake, since the reviewers aren't being paid to deceptively produce a good review. They are being incentivized to *create* one, good or bad. The concern is that the incentive nudges the rating and review's tone toward the positive. Should you perceive a review of, say, a new toothbrush as authentic and independent if the company that makes the toothbrush paid for the review? The answer, just to be clear, is no.

Research has consistently found that paying for reviews, even a small amount, increases both the number of reviews and the average rating, the latter by as much as 40 to 70 percent. But this bump comes at a cost. Studies have also found that if customers know the review has been incentivized, they trust it less than an organically produced review. The core value of the review—the honest assessment of a product or experience by a regular person, perhaps someone like you—is perceived to be compromised by the encroachment of the norms of the market. People intuitively recognize the inherent conflict of interest at play.

In the aggregate, however, it is likely still worth it for companies to incentivize reviews—which, by the way, the Federal Trade Commission says should be clearly disclosed in each individual incentivized review. Getting more people to review helps ratings (including leveraging cognitive biases like the anchoring effect) and ultimately sales since few consumers realize the big role incentives play. But you should know that that glowing review of the fancy new toothbrush might have been purchased.

Biases in the Machine

Even with authentic and honest reviews—that is, reviews that aren't fake or incentivized—there are a host of reasons we aren't often getting a balanced appraisal of quality or value. Many things that have nothing to do with the objective characteristics of a product or service can impact a reviewer's perception and posted opinion. Was a favourite song playing while the reviewer was writing the review? Did the reviewer just get in a fight with their romantic partner? Was the reviewer pissed off because of a bad internet connection? Was Nickelback playing in the background when the review was written? Was the reviewer a man or a woman? Was the weather bad?

Yep, the weather. A clever study from 2022 looked at a large dataset of online restaurant reviews and correlated the rankings with the weather at the location where and when the review was written. They found that rainy days drag down the ratings. "Reviews were lower when reviews were written while it was raining," the researchers concluded. Which also means, of course, that sunny day reviews might be sunnier than justified by the objective qualities of the product being assessed.

There are a host of biases that can greatly skew reviews. A 2021 study—with the appropriate title "Real Men Don't Buy 'Mrs. Clean'"— found that men devalue products with names that have a feminine vibe. As the authors of the study bluntly put it, "men are negatively biased against female brands." The authors speculate that this strong gender bias is due, at least in part, to the unconscious application of something called the precarious manhood principle, "whereby men feel gender role anxiety and will go to extra measures to maintain, preserve, and sustain their sense of masculinity."

Culture can also sway the tenor and conclusions of a review. Someone from, say, Germany may appreciate different characteristics in a product or service than someone from the United States. A 2021 analysis looked at over 700,000 online hotel reviews from customers from over one hundred nationalities. If you think most people are open-minded about experiencing a range of cultural perspectives, um, nope. Basically, the more significant the cultural distance between the customer and provider, the lower the average of the customer review. For most, the cultural differences translate into lower levels of satisfaction with the experience, which are then reflected in the online reviews, especially if they are anonymous. As noted by the authors of the study, this is because customers feel "less constrained and therefore feel free to give more conservative evaluations to the reviewed services." I'm speculating here, but I suspect that really means people feel more comfortable displaying their cultural prejudices.

For hotel reviews, who you are hoteling *with*, as opposed to the quality of the actual hotel, is one of the strongest predictors of the kind of online review you are likely to leave. A 2017 study looked at over 100,000 online reviews for over three hundred hotels in New York City. Those travelling as a couple left the highest ratings (average rating 8.19 out of 10) and, no surprise here, those travelling for work left the lowest (average rating 7.61). The researchers were able to rank hotel satisfaction based entirely on traveller group. Couples ranked highest, followed by friends, family, solo, and those grumpy business travellers in last place.

Brand name and price also impact reviews. All else being equal, something that costs more and is produced by a recognizable brand gets a higher review. Donald Lichtenstein, chair of the Division of Marketing at the University of Colorado tells me, "Based on our evidence, reviews are heavily influenced by brand name and price, whereas experts' ratings [like those by Consumer Reports] are not." This is no surprise. Pricing is a powerful cognitive bias and can shape how we perceive the world. Simply placing a higher price tag on an average bottle of wine, for example, causes people to like the taste of the wine more. It works in the opposite direction too. A 2005 study found that consumers who paid a discounted price for an energy drink derived less measurable benefit (that is, the likely caffeine and placebo induced ability to concentrate and solve puzzles) than consumers who purchased the exact same product at full price. This has been called the marketing placebo effect. As Professor Lichtenstein's study found, it can have a significant impact on the content of reviews.

Our opinions are also shaped by an online herd mentality. When leaving a review, we are influenced by previous reviews, a tendency known as social influence bias. A 2013 study by a team at the Hebrew University of Jerusalem explored this phenomenon by randomly manipulating online comments. Some users saw more positive responses as compared to a control group. What they found was that positive social influence—that is, seeing other positive reviews—"increased the likelihood of positive ratings by 32% and created accumulating positive herding that increased final ratings by 25% on average." A 2021 study looking at social influence bias came to a similar conclusion: "customers who are not used to writing online reviews are more prone to [social influence bias] than customers who frequently write online reviews." Of course, like the anchoring effect noted above, leveraging that herd mentality is yet another reason fake and incentivized reviews are so valuable to businesses. If they can create the impression that everyone loves something, you may feel compelled to say you love it too.

This social influence phenomenon is a big reason why the "wisdom of the crowd" appeal of online reviews is misplaced. While the phenomenon is real, as demonstrated by Galton's simple ox experiment, for it to be helpful each bit of "wisdom" must be independent—that is, not influenced by the opinion of other online reviewers. Research has consistently shown that knowledge of the views of others narrows and biases the diversity of opinions. The herding of opinions makes a crowd less and less wise.

Finally, remember that the authentic and verified online reviewer bought the damn thing or went to the hotel or spent a ton of money on a fancy meal. As a result, the reviewer is more likely to say they liked it. That's the choice supportive bias at play, also known as post-purchase rationalization. It is hard to be truly objective about stuff we've already invested in. No one wants to feel like they've made a bad decision. Five stars!

"A hole. A very, very large hole." One-star review of the Grand Canyon.

"Trees block view and there are too many gray rocks." One-star review of Yosemite National Park.

"Save yourself some money. Boil some water at home." One-star review of Yellowstone National Park.

Another major problem with online reviews? The reviewers. Who writes reviews, and why did they feel compelled to write them? The reality is that very few of us take the time to review stuff (though many more *say* they write reviews). People who do write reviews are usually at the extremes. They either love a product, service, or experience, or they hate it. Online reviews are not a random sampling of consumers. On the contrary, reviewers represent a highly biased sampling of public opinion. Almost everyone looks at star ratings and reviews, but, as Professor Maslowska says, "only a small percentage will have the intrinsic motivation to write [a review]."

A study from MIT Sloan School of Management looked at online reviews for a prominent apparel company and determined that only 1.5 percent of the customers wrote a review—that is, fifteen out of every thousand customers. While there is undoubtedly significant variation between industries and platforms (in my research I saw estimates ranging from 1 to 40 percent), the general theme remains. Reviewers do *not* represent the average consumer. They don't provide the wisdom of the crowd. They provide an average of mostly raves and rants.

The above one-star reviews of U.S. national parks highlight the problem. These negative assessments are from a project by Amber Share, an artist who used these absurd (and very real) reviews as inspiration for a unique series of illustrations of national parks. Her project—which is called Subpar Parks and includes beautiful posters that depict both an image of the relevant park and the damning review—works because we all know the reviews are ridiculous. As the artist mused in an interview with the *Washington Post*, "Was it possible that someone had visited the Grand Canyon and only seen a very, very large hole?" Sure, the person who doesn't like grey rocks probably shouldn't have gone to Yosemite, but online review systems do not filter out bad or weird or esoteric tastes. So, these kinds of polarized impressions remain and pollute the online review ecosystem. Consider this: a scientifically accurate representation of consumer experiences would require a relatively large and random sampling (i.e., not just those with extreme experiences) of consumers.

Another kind of online consumer who can distort reviews is the "super contributor." You may know one of these individuals. Reviewing things is part of their personal identity. It is what they *do*. Perhaps they have a social media presence or feel that they are an expert traveller or foodie or fashionista, and dammit, they are gonna let the world know how they feel via online reviews and social media posts. These super contributors can make up a large hunk of the reviews, and their comments become more a form of personal expression—and perhaps brand building—than a sincere assessment of the product or experience. In other words, the review is more about signalling something about them, such as wanting to be seen as an expert, than the product or experience. Because their reviews are often written in a more authoritative voice (justified or not) and with a professional feel, they can be disproportionately influential.

"My Dream Is Over . . . "

Aside from the above diatribes about unimpressive national parks, most of my analysis thus far has been about unreliable *positive* reviews. Those five star-ers. But we should also consider the impact of the less-than-genuine negative reviews. Those nasty one-star rants can have a big impact on how the public perceives a business or experience. Survey research has consistently found that over 90 percent of people say that negative reviews make them less likely to use a business, and a 2021 survey found that 94 percent of consumers say that a bad review has convinced them to avoid a business.

Targeted online negativity happens for a host of reasons, ranging from anger to politics to money. A 2016 study of Yelp restaurant reviews found that nearly a fifth are fake and that, no surprise here, economic factors often drive the decision to commit marketing fraud. As concluded by the authors of the study, "organizations are more likely to game the system when they are facing increased competition." This often means posting fake negative reviews about competitors—especially if they are in a similar geographic region. Another study used over

2.3 million reviews of almost five thousand hotels and found that, alas, posting fake reviews of competitor hotels can be a very effective strategy. They found that posting as few as fifty fake negative reviews is often sufficient to surpass a competitor in terms of online visibility. Because more visibility means more profits, the incentive to continue this practice is intense.

Fake negative reviews can also be used to hurt individuals or entities for ideological reasons. A good example of this phenomenon is when anti-vaxxers spam pro-vaccine businesses or products with negative comments.

I've personally experienced the wrath of anti-vaxxers—including receiving one-star reviews for a book that hadn't been released yet. Another book about vaccination hesitancy that I published pre-pandemic received one-star anti-vax reviews ("propaganda," "in it for the money," etc.) and a post-pandemic one-star threat that "Nuremberg is coming" (i.e., I will be executed) due to my public support of COVID vaccines, a topic that wasn't even covered in the book being reviewed. The same kind of thing happened to a TV documentary series I hosted. The one-star reviews ranted about stuff that wasn't even in the show.

For me, this one-starring strategy is certainly aggravating and likely had an impact on public perceptions of my books and show, but for a small business, it can be fatal. A local café, a few miles from my home, decided to maintain a proof of vaccination policy after the provincial government ended its COVID mandate policy. "I want to be able to feel safe myself and have my customers be able to sit down and enjoy a meal without having to worry," the owner was quoted as saying. Almost immediately, an online backlash occurred. Within days, there were dozens of one-star reviews posted about the café. Despite this intense negativity, the owner remained confident. "I think we're strong, we've pushed through, and I think we can survive and keep going," he said at the time.

Less than a month later, the café was out of business. "My dream is over," their website read.

Bottom Line: Often Wrong

So, online reviews are often (very often) fake, biased, polarized, and influenced by everything from cultural norms to herding behaviour to bad weather to hate and ideological agendas. But despite all the twisting influences, are they still, well, *accurate*? That is, do they still provide some reasonably objective truth about the quality and value of a product or service?

While this may seem a straightforward research question, it isn't. Many products have a host of subjective qualities—aesthetic appeal, taste, etc.—that make an "Is the review accurate?" analysis challenging. Is there an objective expert opinion about, say, the best colour for a beach towel? Would the expert review be more accurate than the opinion of a beach towel novice? Not really. So, comparing expert and consumer opinion on items like beach towel colour is pretty meaningless. However, for many products, such as cars, computers, phones, electronics, and household appliances, independent expert opinion is likely relevant in an assessment of quality.

A fascinating study from 2016 looked at over 1,200 products and compared consumer online reviews with assessments done by Consumer Reports, which, though far from perfect, is a commonly used measure of objective product quality. As noted by the study authors, this is because of "the impartiality and technical expertise of the [Consumer Reports] organization." The study found a significant lack of agreement between online reviews and the opinions of the experts at Consumer Reports. For example, products with higher star rating on Amazon only received a higher score from Consumer Reports 57 percent of the time. In other words, agreement between experts and consumer reviewers was only just a bit better than flipping a coin.

In addition, the researchers found that online reviews did not predict "prices in the used-product marketplace," but Consumer Reports scores did predict resale value. The researchers note "average star ratings bore essentially no relationship to used prices." This is a pretty damning conclusion, especially if you are a believer in the power of market forces to tease out the good from the bad. Put another way, online reviewers did not agree with either the experts or the marketplace.

Why the large disconnect between experts and online reviews? In addition to all the reasons mapped out above, the reviews done by experts at Consumer Reports often also involve a comparative component. As Professor Lichtenstein, one of the authors of the study, tells me, "Users [are generally] doing a single product evaluation, and Consumer Reports is doing evaluations relative to the range of products in the product class." This makes the expert report a more meaningful assessment of quality. Comparisons matter. A product might be acceptable—so a reviewer gives it a good score—but is it *better* or *worse* than a competitor's product?

Professor Lichtenstein also notes yet *another* reason online reviews can be less than ideal: timing. "[Consumer] reviews are often done right after purchase, before the reviewer has had full experience with the product," he says. Expert reviews, on the other hand, often involve a more rigorous, long-term, and systematic evaluation.

Now, the statistically minded out there might be thinking, *Yes, yes, there are many biases impacting online reviews, but if there are lots and lots of reviews—all these biases will balance out and we'll get some semblance of a valid picture of public opinion.* Alas, while compiling thousands of reviews may nudge the overall picture in the right direction, huge numbers alone won't save the day. When so many forces twist such a large percentage of the ratings, you can't fix the problem with quantity. The garbage in, garbage out statistics truism gets magnified unless the twisting forces—fraud, biases, ideologically motivated rants, posturing, etc.—are addressed on a relatively large scale. Given economic incentives to *not* address them, there are reasons to be pessimistic about meaningful progress.

Reviews of Professionals? Even Wronger

Consumer reviews of professionals, such as physicians, lawyers, dentists, psychologists, etc., provide another example of the distance between online reviews and objective quality. As with so many areas, consumer reviews of professionals are becoming increasingly influential. A 2021 survey of over one thousand Americans found that ratings and reviews were the number one factor influencing their choice of a physician, with 84 percent saying they would not see a physician with a less than four-star rating. In a 2018 survey, 95 percent of Americans and 97 percent of millennials said they found online physician reviews reliable.

These numbers are shocking when you consider that research has consistently shown that online reviews of physicians rarely have any relevance to actual clinical outcomes. A physician with a high ranking doesn't guarantee they'll be a good physician. For example, a 2020 study explored this exact question by comparing online reviews of physicians to how the patients' health issues turned out. Does having a high online rating matter? Nope. The authors conclude that "there is no clear relationship between online reviews of physicians and their patients' clinical outcomes." Another study found no correlation between online reviews and clinical outcomes for total knee replacements. As a result, the authors advise that patients should "exert caution when interpreting ratings on these websites." A 2018 study by a research team from Cedars-Sinai Medical Center compared online patient reviews with an assessment of the relevant clinical care by physician peers. Basically, they compared patients assessing experts with experts assessing other experts. They found that the online ratings "do not predict objective measures of quality of care or peer assessment of clinical performance."

There are a bunch of reasons for this well-established disconnect, but the main one, as highlighted by that last study, is this: unless you are a physician, how the hell do you know what a good clinical decision looks like? There is usually a large asymmetry in knowledge. That is kind of the point of going to see an expert. You aren't picking a beach towel or a coffee shop. You are looking for a physician to provide evidence-informed advice about your health. As my University of Alberta colleague, health economist Christopher McCabe, mused, "If consumers' assessment of the quality of health care was accurate, one would have to wonder whether medical training was necessary."

Also, the unfortunate experiences that might influence patient reviews are often either completely or somewhat out of the control of their physicians or healthcare institutions. Adverse drug reactions. Unsuccessful treatment protocols. Complications that arise despite everything being done well. In healthcare, bad stuff happens. Really bad stuff. My personal experiences with the healthcare system are almost uniformly one-star terrible. Ditto for my immediate family. But in most (but not all, a point I'll come back to) of these situations, I genuinely believe the healthcare providers were doing their best. But how do I know? I don't.

My wife is a physician. Her sister and brother are physicians. My son is a physician. My daughter is in medical school. I work in the healthcare space doing research in large interdisciplinary teams that involve clinicians and biomedical researchers. I study healthcare topics. Despite being surrounded by an abundance of healthcare knowledge, I have only a vague (and my wife would say I have zero) idea of how to evaluate the relationship between a personal clinical outcome— good or bad—and the actions and skill of a particular physician.

Some research has found, not surprisingly, that online reviews are often consistent with actual patient experiences, especially at the level of the organization. In other words, patient reviews can reflect what it is like to be a patient at, say, a local hospital. But a patient's *experience*— while certainly something that healthcare providers and institutions should always consider—may have nothing to do with the quality of the clinical care or advice a patient receives.

When I was in university, my mother had cancer. While in hospital for treatment, she started experiencing severe stomach pain. Her physician thought her discomfort was related to her underlying condition. My mother—who was still relatively young at the time—was a woman with cancer and this was her time, or so her medical team seemed to think. The attending physician was kind to my mother and me. But it was a horrific experience, especially as the pain intensified. My girlfriend, the woman who is now my wife, was in medical school at the time, and she insisted to anyone who would listen—and to those who wouldn't—that my mother's pain had nothing to do with her cancer. It was a ruptured bowel that needed to be treated immediately. *Immediately.* She was right. My mother had emergency surgery and lived for another year. She passed away peacefully at home. I was holding her hand. Had Joanne not been there to correct the physician, my mother likely would have died, perhaps within days or even hours, in a not-very-peaceful manner.

I also would have been unaware—at least at the time—of the medical error. As such, if asked, I might have given the physician a five-star review. He was compassionate, attentive, and seemed to be doing his best to provide comfort and care to my mother.

My review immediately after I found out how badly he'd screwed up? One star.

As my mother was recovering from her surgery, the physician found me in the waiting room. He took me aside and apologized for his error. I can't remember exactly what he said, but I vividly remember the intensity of the moment. He seemed crushed. Genuinely and deeply sorry. While I was still confused and angry and worried and sad and lost and to-the-bone exhausted, I was grateful for this remorse.

Still, in *that* moment, one star.

I recount this story because it underscores both the flaws in using consumer-style online reviews for complex, expert-informed interactions and the potential harm our obsession with reviews might inflict. The rise and influence of patient reviews may cause an inappropriate shift away from the ethical obligation placed on physicians and institutions to focus on the best interest of patients toward a more consumer-oriented ethos. You want a physician who will provide the best, most science-informed advice, even if that advice is tough to hear and unlikely to make you feel five-star happy. Of course, even difficult conversations about things like drug dependencies, weight management, smoking cessation, and the futility of treatments should be done in a respectful and caring manner that is responsive to the patient's values and culture. But physicians have a legal and ethical obligation to have those hard-to-hear conversations, an approach that does not always produce happy "customers." As noted by Kaci Durbin, a physician critical of the patient review system, "If a customer is willing to spend $100 on a shirt that looks terrible on him, the boutique owner does not have a moral obligation to tell him he looks awful."

Physicians also have a clear duty to tell patients when things go wrong—an essential requirement for both respecting patient autonomy and improving patient care. Again, the growing sway and ubiquity of online reviews seems unlikely to incentivize this obligation. Would a chef come out of the kitchen to tell you he dropped your chicken on the floor after you had eaten and enjoyed the meal? "Damn, that chicken was good. Unique taste."

Another reason consumer-oriented online reviews of experts can be particularly problematic is that they are even more polarized than other online reviews. A 2019 analysis of over 1.5 million reviews found that as compared to reviews for other businesses, like restaurants or hotels, physicians are 64 percent more likely to receive a five-star review, but 194 percent as likely to receive a one-star review. This makes total sense. We often engage physicians for very personal or stressful issues. When things go well, we are tremendously grateful. When things go poorly, we are tremendously frustrated and upset. So, these reviews are an even *more* biased and skewed sampling of opinion than most online reviews. (And, of course, I could go on and on about *fake*—both good and bad—physician reviews.)

No surprise, research has shown that most physicians hate online reviews. From their perspective, they increase workplace stress, are inaccurate, and hurt patient care. Some have gone so far as to successfully sue patients who have, in their opinion, defamed them online. One survey found that 90 percent worry about the potential impact of negative reviews, which is not something you want your physician thinking about when they should be focusing on having an honest conversation about your health! There is also a Change.org petition that, at the time of this writing, had been signed by nearly fifty thousand physicians asking for the "immediate withdrawal of ALL doctors and providers . . . from being reviewed on these online review sites" because, in part, they feel that physicians "should not be pressured to do things to get good reviews. We want to provide medical care not customer care."

I want to be crystal clear: how physicians and other healthcare providers treat patients matters. Patient opinions about their experiences matter. Dismissive attitudes, poor communication skills, a chronic lack of time for meaningful clinical exchanges, and gender, weight, and racial bias are just a few of the patient interaction issues that demand more attention. One illustrative bit of data: a study from 2018 found that on average physicians stopped listening and interrupted patients after eleven seconds. Yep, *eleven* seconds. Not good. Other studies tell us that poor bedside manner, as it is often called, may have a small but clinically significant impact on healthcare outcomes. There is growing recognition that working with patients and patient communities to inform health policies and priorities is an enormously worthwhile exercise. This allows for system changes that, among other things, reflect patient and community needs and values.

But meaningfully engaging with patients in a systematic and rigorous manner is *not* the same as relying on heavily biased consumer-oriented online reviews. The ubiquity and sway of online reviews creates inducements that may, paradoxically, make healthcare systems worse, especially in situations where resources are limited. Might online reviews nudge physicians and institutions to focus more on superficial features that have little to do with clinical outcomes or cause physicians to avoid tough but much needed conversations? There is no doubt that clinical care and healthcare systems should always be striving to improve, but the online review ecosystem is not a constructive path forward.

The twisted nature of professional reviews is a poignant example of how the exploitation of the intensifying market for certainty can do significant harm. People likely look at online reviews for healthcare providers and other professionals during stressful moments in their lives—exactly when we need reliable, easy to access, and objective opinions as a guide. But as the urgency and desire for authentic opinions increases, so too does the systemic pressures to distort them. I wish I could provide a less depressing conclusion beyond *don't rely on them.* Here's a slightly less cynical take: be aware of the profound limitations of these reviews and use them with caution.

Five Stars for Fake, Harmful, and Exploitive BS?

What's worse than questionable reviews for real medicine? Questionable reviews for alternative medicine BS, especially in the context of serious diseases, like cancer.

As I write this book, my colleague and research associate Marco Zenone is leading a project that analyzes the online reviews for alternative medicine cancer clinics. The results are, to be frank, infuriating. Zenone collected over one thousand reviews for thirty-nine clinics. The average review—remember, these are, allegedly, cancer patients receiving expensive and completely unproven therapies, often in another country—was 4.4 stars, which is, likely *not* coincidentally, the ideal high end of that believably good Goldilocks zone for online reviews. This includes reviews for clinics claiming to cure stage-four terminal cancer. Our research found that reviews from stage-four and terminal cancer patients were, by far, the most common. Here is just one rage-inducing example of a positive review: "My brother-in-law started his cancer treatment journey here after being diagnosed with terminal cancer. He is now cancer free from a cancer they said you couldn't cure."

Take a moment to consider how this might play out for a cancer patient or a loved one. They are scared, desperate, and looking for hope. They see *that* review. Remember, reviews that resonate with a person— from, say, someone who has also experienced the horrors of a terminal cancer diagnosis—are uniquely persuasive. How would you respond?

"If prospective patients read the reviews, which contain powerful and emotional narratives about lives being saved, it is highly convincing and may lead them to spend thousands on unnecessary and ineffective treatment," Zenone tells me when I ask him about his reaction to these reviews. "Even worse, it can offer false hope of a cure when one is unavailable and take valuable time away from loved ones while receiving ineffective treatment."

Okay, here is the science-informed reality: there is no good evidence to support any of the alternative therapies being marketed to cancer patients. On the contrary, studies have consistently shown that cancer patients who use alternative therapies to treat their cancer have *worse* outcomes. Simply put, these clinics are exploitive. While our study doesn't analyze the authenticity of the reviews, the tension between the biomedical reality (*this stuff does not work*) and the positive reviews is telling. These clinics know the power of testimonials and online reviews. They are fully aware of the impact such reviews have on desperate cancer patients. It is criminal to take large sums of money from people at what is possibly one of the worst moments, if not *the* worst moment in their life. The search engines, Google in particular, must take steps to address this mess.

Zenone agrees: "Search engines need to respond and ensure their tools, which they profit from, aren't enabling the exploitation of very ill people." Zenone, who has done a good deal of research looking at how unproven therapies are represented online, believes that search engines should consider treating reviews on medical services differently than those of restaurants, stores, and other businesses. "Inauthentic or misleading reviews for medical services have the potential for greater consequences."

Again, the higher the stakes and the more desperate the search for answers, the stronger the incentives to manipulate the authenticity of the content.

You Can't Detect Them.
Seriously, You Can't.

Me: "Ya know, online reviews are often manipulated."

Joanne: "Yeah, yeah. I know. Oh, this looks like a good one. Almost five stars."

Our twenty-year-old dishwasher had given up, and we needed a new one ASAP. I was working on *this* chapter at our kitchen counter next to my wife as she was looking at online consumer reviews. My deep dive into the world of fakery did not alter her path toward dishwasher optimization. She was going to read the reviews. (To be fair, she has patiently put up with a lifetime of my I'm-researching-this-now pontification, so the power of my persuasion is fairly muted at this point.)

I also asked many of my friends and colleagues if they used online reviews. Everyone said yes. I don't think a single person equivocated. Yes, yes, and yes. Always. And they use them for absolutely everything.

When I told them about the evidence that suggests reviews and ratings are unreliable and biased, most seemed vaguely aware of the problem but felt, for them, those stars, raves, and rants were still useful. They could find the value. Try this on your friends, and I guarantee you'll get the same response.

Research has consistently shown that even if people recognize that the circulation of bad or unreliable information is a problem, they often think it isn't a problem for *them* because *they* can spot the bad stuff. This is a well-known cognitive bias called illusory superiority. We all (yes, all of us) tend to overestimate our abilities in comparison to others. Most drivers are terrible, but I'm terrific! Most professors are bad teachers, but I'm the best! Most people get sucked in by online scams, but not me!

A 2021 study on the spread of fake news highlights the practical implications of this cognitive bias. The researchers were specifically looking at the impact of overconfidence in our assessment of misinformation. They found that most Americans recognize the problem of fake news and view the ubiquity of misinformation as a serious challenge, but three in four also overestimate their ability to tease out the credible good stuff from the bunk. To make matters worse, those with the most overconfidence in their abilities were also the ones most likely to believe and spread misinformation. The research team, which was led by professor Benjamin Lyons from the University of Utah, concluded that "overconfidence may be a crucial factor for explaining how false and low-quality information spreads via social media."

Studies have shown the majority of us realize that fake online reviews exist and that it is a problem. A survey of over one thousand Australians found that 52 percent of people suspect they have fallen for fake online reviews. Despite this awareness, almost everyone still views them as reliable (again, more so than friends, family, or experts) and essential to our consumer decisions. A study in Germany found that 86 percent of consumers consider online reviews "credible" or "very credible." And the more independent—that is, authentic and not swayed by biasing forces—a review is perceived to be, the more users trust it and are influenced by its conclusions. So, people know there are fake reviews and they *still* think reviews are reliable, even though that trust is built on valuing an independence and authenticity that most of us know isn't there. Huh?

This paradox of recognizing that fake and unreliable reviews are a problem but still viewing them as tremendously reliable can be explained by both illusory superiority and another pernicious psychological tendency: overconfidence. It's the Dunning-Kruger effect at play. Adrian Camilleri, a consumer psychologist and professor at the University of Technology Sydney, explained it in an article exploring fake reviews: "The worse you are at something, the less likely you have the competence to know how bad you are. The fact is most humans are not particularly good at distinguishing between truth and lies."

Here is the sad reality: you probably can't identify most fraudulent posts even if you think you can. Past research has found, for the general public, the odds of picking the inauthentic from the authentic is only slightly better than flipping a coin. Yes, historically, fake reviews often had red-flag characteristics that you could watch for, such as few details about the reviewer, an over-the-top headline, and little balance. (It is still worth watching for those things, by the way.) But the technology to produce fake reviews is evolving so quickly and becoming so sophisticated that it is probably safest to just assume you can't. For example, researchers from Finland and Japan used a computer program to generate fake restaurant reviews using an approach called neural machine translation; it uses artificial neural networks to make highly believable reviews. They found that even experienced, tech-savvy users couldn't detect the fake stuff. The research participants' detection rate was not statistically different from random predictions. So, no. You can't flush out those authentic, wisdom-of-the crowd nuggets.

Do the academics who research the unreliability of online reviews use online reviews?

"I do!" Ewa Maslowska tells me with a laugh, looking slightly embarrassed. I was a bit shocked by this response. She is, after all, a renowned expert on the unreliability of online reviews. She knows how bad they are. "I still look at reviews. Of course, I look at them critically and look for reviews by people who seem similar to me, taste wise. But, yes, I look at them."

Sherry He, the researcher who took a deep dive into the business of fake reviews, tells me the same thing. While she remains highly skeptical, "if it is something I really care about," she reads reviews "across multiple review platforms" and thinks "extensively about the review content."

The pull and persuasive force of online reviews coupled with the hard-wired cognitive biases that make us all think we are perceptive enough to see through the fakes keep us coming back, even when we should know better. Even when we *do* know better. I think a big reason this happens is our desperate desire for some degree of certainty. Online reviews so clearly play to our desire for clear and convenient guideposts to navigate through the storm of consumer noise. We feel such a strong need for information that is reliable and genuinely helpful that we ignore the reality that it isn't. Online reviews are an authenticity mirage in a desert filled with bunk. We can't stop ourselves from giving into the certainty illusion.

By the way, our new dishwasher is excellent. Five stars.

And the Impact of AI?

Will programs like ChatGPT make it easier to write authentic-sounding and tremendously persuasive fake reviews? Yep.

Will AI make the opinion ecosystem even more chaotic and unreliable? Yep.

Do we have a straightforward answer to the AI problem? Nope.

Should the rapid rise of this technology make you even more suspicious of online reviews? Absolutely.

A Recommended Escape Plan?

Let's pause here to reflect on the value, influence, and general unreliability of online reviews. Globally, billions of dollars are in play. Often the very existence of businesses—even entire industries—may be affected by consumer reviews. It isn't hyperbolic to say that online reviews have become a critical element of today's global consumer economy. This has resulted in the creation and growth of a massive, and lightly regulated, opinion economy. Reviews. Raves. Rants. Virtually all the incentives are aligned in a manner that promotes and facilitates the circulation of unreliable and inauthentic online reviews. To make matters worse, our own human tendency to, for example, only post polarized reviews and to be influenced by our cognitive and cultural biases adds significantly to the problem. Despite an awareness of these problems, the review economy continues to exert tremendous influence over our decisions, big and small.

Can we escape the sway of this fake authenticity? The experts I spoke to were almost uniformly pessimistic.

"I'm not sure individual consumers can do much to extract more signal from [the noise of] reviews," Bart de Langhe tells me when I ask him what advice he'd give to the public. He is a marketing researcher and professor, and he has spent years exploring the unreliability of online reviews. Despite his gloomy assessment, he does have one practical recommendation: "I think side by side comparisons of product performance in standardised environments can provide a valuable input for consumers."

Saoud Khalifah, the CEO of Fakespot, agrees with de Langhe about both the intractable complexity of the problem and that the best approach is to seek out independent expert assessments. They won't be perfect—and they are also often incentivized—but the consensus among those I talked to was that this is the most reliable strategy, especially if you go to multiple sources that do comparative analysis. "Try video reviews, other websites for opinions and reviews, along with outlets such as Consumer Reports and *Wirecutter* that do a really good job in describing products professionally," Khalifah said. Ignore the online consumer reviews and star ratings and try to focus on a range of reviews by experts, the more independent the better.

Still, some commentators, despite years of research and analysis, simply feel exasperated. They don't see a clear path forward. Professor Proserpio, one of the academics studying the size of the problem, offers this straightforward, glum, and, on the face of it, not terrifically helpful guidance: "Be very skeptical of online reviews."

But despite its obviousness and simplicity, Proserpio's advice is exactly what we need to remind ourselves to do. When authenticity becomes financially valuable, it can quickly lose its actual authenticity while simultaneously constructing, amplifying, and leveraging a veneer of the real. The power of online reviews comes from the feeling that they are authentic. Online reviews aren't sophisticated advertisements or paid endorsements, or so the review industrial complex would have us believe.

Of course, the online platforms and relevant regulators also must do more to cull the bad reviews and punish those that wilfully distort reviews. But when so much money is at stake and when the sheer volume of content is so vast, it seems highly unlikely that standard oversight approaches will work. It is a lot like trying to regulate the stock market. All of the relevant players are, at a minimum, operating at the edge—because they can, it works, and their competitors are doing the same. As a result, manipulated and unreliable reviews are the norm and are likely here to stay. We need to accept this reality and proceed accordingly.

More broadly, remember that our own cognitive biases also distort both the writing of reviews and how reviews are used by consumers. If you really want a product, the positive reviews will weigh more heavily in your assessment. If you aren't sure, the negative reviews might hold more sway. So not only are reviews unreliable, how we engage with them is also twisted by our own biases, wants, and preconceived ideas.

Part of the reason we now default to online reviews is that they seem trustworthy. They feel real. It's the opinion of people like us looking for the same kind of stuff and experiences as us. A not-a-disaster holiday. Some moving music. A washing machine that won't conk out. Reviews give the perception of clarity. The wisdom of the crowd. Five stars is better than one star or three and half. But remember that because authenticity and trustworthiness make the reviews valuable to us, they have become a massive industry, with authenticity and trustworthiness the aspects of reviews most likely to be exploited and distorted.

Opinion Polls

This portion of the book is devoted to the opinion illusion, so it seems appropriate to provide a quick critique of the classic, and much maligned, representation of public opinion: the public opinion survey. Let's keep this brief. Yes, they are often methodologically problematic. Yes, how you ask a question shapes the answer you get. Yes, size matters—a lot.

Still, surveys are not all bad. I've had the opportunity to work with some of the very best survey scholars. They are all fully aware—and seek to minimize—the inherent limitations of the research approach.

"Sound public opinion research can be a very valuable tool supporting public policy and communications," Frank Graves tells me. Graves
is a sociologist, president of EKOS Research, and a renowned survey
expert. "It needs to be conducted to the highest standards in terms of
the way samples are drawn, questions are formulated, and how the
analysis and interpretation are conducted."

When you see a survey referenced, ask yourself a few key questions:
1. How big was the survey? Bigger is better, but for a national survey
a reasonable number is around one thousand respondents. 2. Are the
results representative of the population? Randomly selecting respondents is much better than, say, an open internet poll where respondents
self-select. 3. Who did the research? For example, was it done by survey
experts or a social media influencer? 4. Are there any obvious biases
to consider? Does the sponsor have a vested interest in the results?
If available, you might also want to look at how the questions were
worded. Good surveys—and I've been involved in crafting many—
have carefully worded questions that are usually pre-tested to avoid
making them too leading.

Representations of public opinion, even those that are not methodologically robust, can also *shape* public opinion. This is one reason
that we see so many companies rely on opinion surveys to push products ("90 percent of people say they love natural, organic, non-GMO
fruit juice!") and political parties relying on iffy polls to support their
candidates. An illusory public opinion can shape actual public opinion. Even likes on a social media platform can impact public opinion.
A study for 2019 found, for example, that more likes on, say, Twitter
or Facebook impacted public opinion on the issue being shared. This
happens, the authors note, because likes "serve as a cue for societal
consensus." The study found that "exposure to likes directly affected
personal opinion. Likes next to media items changed users' opinions."
The study results were also consistent with a phenomenon called the
spiral of silence: people are less likely to share an opinion if they feel
they are in the minority. So, social media reactions, such as likes,

give people the opportunity to "derive public opinion and get hints to acceptable opinions to conform with." This can create a silencing feedback loop. As more and more people like a post—in part, because others have liked the post—it can make it less and less likely that minority voices will speak up.

Unfortunately, bad public opinion data is everywhere. "There is too much 'faux research' or just flawed research which is having a corrosive impact on the public interest," Graves says. "Sound survey research should be a mirror measuring public opinion, not a force shaping it."

The lesson here: be on the watch for poorly done polls and other metrics of opinion that seek to sway or silence you by using illusory consensus. You be you!

Taste Makers or Aggregators?

"Its framework is emaciated. [A] surprising shoddiness in composition permeates the entire album. By the third depressing hearing, it begins to sound like an immense put-on." These are just some of the damning comments from the June 1967 *New York Times* review of the newest Beatles album. Ultimately, it was concluded that "there is nothing beautiful on 'Sergeant Pepper.'" It is "ultimately fraudulent" and an "undistinguished collection of work."

Before we leave the topic of online reviews and the growing economy of opinions, let's consider the impact they have on our own opinions and perceptions of the world. Exploring things like musical tastes and critics' reviews may seem like an odd detour in a book about our chaotic information environment. But these topics highlight the powerful and often unexpected ways in which the opinions of others—and the opinion economy more broadly—shape what we like and how we see the world, even in the context of creative products and entertainment. Do positive or negative reviews—from experts or consumers—have an impact on our impression of the product, service, or experience? Do we like stuff more if the reviews are good and less if they are bad?

When critical reviews don't align with the zeitgeist, such as the above noted misfire on the Beatles' masterpiece, they can get ignored (except by the contrarians who embrace them as the hipster contrarian truth!). My guess is that many who bought *Sgt. Pepper* when it was first released in the summer of 1967 hadn't read a single review. Most people probably listened with relatively fresh ears. True, there was huge buzz and anticipation of something special. It was the Beatles, after all. And that cover! Still, unless they were hardcore music nerds and had access to reviews (no internet, remember), there weren't many who were aggregating the opinions of the world's music critics. Record buyers dropped the needle and listened.

That rarely happens anymore. Now we have instant access to not only almost all the music ever recorded but also to online reviews and services that summarize both consumer and critical opinion. Aggregated and averaged opinion is everywhere—for books, movies, video games, podcasts, plays, live performances, and recorded music. This is a big part of the growing economy of opinions. It is often pushed onto our radar via social media and news alerts. Being exposed to the "collective wisdom" about the value of a creative product can't be avoided.

There has always been a complex interconnectedness between what entertainment, especially music, represents and what we say we like. Music, almost more than any art form, is a badge of who we are. I've always believed musical taste is shaped by 70 percent iconography, 25 percent quality, and 5 percent random exposure. (Guaranteed: if four old, unhip, suburban retirees released *Sgt. Pepper* tomorrow, it wouldn't register.) There are some artists, like the Ramones, that are nearly 100 percent iconography. Others have far more of that ingredient of indisputable musical quality, such as Prince. Regardless, what the music *represents* still influences the listener's impression.

This is especially true for teenagers and young adults. A 2019 *New York Times* analysis of every popular song from 1960 to 2000 found that the music we listen to as teenagers sets our taste for life. On average, men are fourteen when their favourite song is released. Women are thirteen. (I was sixteen when my top song, "London Calling," was released—but fourteen when I first discovered the Clash, so the analysis is spot on for me.) This makes sense. Adolescence is the time when we are very much figuring out who we are. Music is a way to signal to the world the direction we are taking. As noted by the authors of a 2009 study from Cambridge University, appropriately titled "You Are What You Listen To," "the themes and images evoked by preferred styles of music may resonate with individuals because they recognize these qualities in themselves, or because they wish to embody them." The study found that among British teenagers, the stereotypes associated with each musical genre were consistently believed. For example, those who liked classical and jazz were seen—rightly or not—by the teenagers as upper class and smart, while rock fans were rated as middle class and not particularly conscientious or agreeable (ditto electronica aficionados).

As we age, our musical tastes evolve, but it remains a central tool for personal branding. While establishing identity and independence is a big theme in our youth, studies have found that as we get older the desire to project social status, intellect, and wealth "play into the increased gravitation towards 'sophisticated' music." So, more classical, jazz, and perhaps a dash of world music, please.

Studies have also demonstrated a strong correlation between ideology and how we experience music. We've known this for a long time. A classic 1974 study, for example, found that university students who identified as liberal went to more rock concerts, bought more albums, and listened to music more than their conservative peers. Admittedly, 1974 was a time—just a few years after the heyday of the hippies, the Kent State shootings, Vietnam War protests, and President Nixon's famous declaration that "if the music is square, it's because I like it square"—when the connection between popular music and politics was especially overt. But studies since then continue to find that personal identity, ideology, and musical taste are tightly intertwined. A 2010 study of over six hundred college students found that the more you think music is part of your identity, the more you enjoy rebellious music (e.g., punk). If you think of music as a way to position yourself at the core of a social group, the more you like music with a sentimental vibe. As the researchers describe it, for this latter cohort, the music you like describes you "as typical members of the group of people that like the same type of music." It satisfies a need to belong. Again, studies tell us this signalling works remarkably well. A 2009 study from the University of Edinburgh involving three hundred participants found that stated musical tastes serve as a "social 'badge' of group membership" and caused "ingroup favoritism" toward those who shared musical taste.

As ideological flags go, expressed musical taste seems to be a remarkably efficient marker of political identity. The signalling is almost as effective as, well, an actual flag. A 2020 analysis by Caroline Myers, a PhD student at Johns Hopkins, found she could identify a person's politics with 70 percent accuracy based solely on musical taste. And, yep, studies have consistently shown many of the clichés generally hold—such as the idea that conservatives often say they prefer country music.

The mix of ideology, in-group signalling, and musical taste can result in some telling tensions. Myers's study also found that an individual's stated taste often didn't align with their actual, objectively measured tastes. For example, in her study 60 percent of liberals said they listened to and liked R&B, but when tested, they weren't any more knowledgeable about the genre than any other group and they actually liked R&B songs *less* than conservatives—a finding that reinforces how projecting an image is central to our stated tastes. Liberals thought that as a liberal, they should like R&B, but many actually didn't.

To be clear, it is the iconography and symbolism that surrounds the music that matters—not necessarily the quality and sound of the actual music. Think of a band like the Rolling Stones. Much of their work was heavily influenced by country music. Songs like "Sweet Virginia" and "Country Honk" *sound* as country as anything on the most country of country radio. In some of their numbers, Mick Jagger even sings with a (kind of cringey) Southern drawl. But, as noted by the music historian and professor John Covach, most fans of the Rolling Stones "wouldn't want to hear a note of country and western music, and they consider themselves liberal."

Okay, so what does this all have to do with ratings and reviews? Everything. Today, what a song or band or genre represents is largely, if not entirely, instantaneously mediated by the aggregation of opinion in the form of online critical analysis and customer reviews. Yes, as the above Rolling Stones example highlights, iconography and in-group signalling has always mattered. But because of social media platforms and online websites that summarize opinions, there are more opportunities to become instantly aware of how music is positioned within our cultural landscape and to broadcast our tastes to the world, thus magnifying the identity badge and in-group signalling power of our musical preferences. The opinion aggregation is now so fast and efficient you can follow reviews for new music as if you're watching the rise and fall of the stock market. Musicians are expected to do their best to create viral social media posts on platforms like TikTok in coordination with the release of new material, which acts as both a marketing and identity branding exercise. In May 2022, the artist Halsey complained on TikTok about the requirement to generate a "fake viral moment" on socials about her music—and then that video went, um, viral (ten million views in just a few months), becoming the viral content the record label wanted. A win-win. Halsey builds her authenticity and identity as the artist with the viral TikTok moment ranting against viral TikTok moments.

The critics that review music are also bombarded by this information and can hardly escape its influence—thus creating an accelerating cycle of online "this is what is good or bad and what it means" taste curation. While that *New York Times* review did little to impact public opinion regarding *Sgt. Pepper*, research tells us that the musings of critics usually does have a significant impact on what we say we like. A study from the University of Redlands, for example, found that the mere exposure to a music critic's review of a song influenced whether someone felt that they liked the song. The researchers concluded that "a critic's review had a greater influence on people's opinions of a song than merely listening to samples of that song." The critical review carried more weight than the *actual song* in determining whether the person liked the song!

The algorithms that feed us streaming playlists are, in turn, shaped by the same cultural influences, which further accelerates the cycle. There is some evidence that streaming has diversified tastes and increased the fluidity of musical categories. It is now easier to find new stuff. But for the most part, streaming services feed us playlists of songs that not only fit the genre and vibe we are after but also the iconography associated with that music. Your hip indie Spotify playlist might have Phoebe Bridgers and Faye Webster and perhaps Kacey Musgraves, but never Shania Twain or LeAnn Rimes, even though an alien from Alpha Centauri couldn't tell the sonic or thematic difference. (Of course, Taylor Swift is on everyone's playlist.)

"The [streaming] algorithms are more successful when they are more social than musicological," Kelefa Sanneh tells me. He is a journalist, music critic for the *New Yorker*, and author of the 2021 book *Major Labels: A History of Popular Music in Seven Genres*. "It's not that this song *sounds* like this other song. It's that [the streaming service algorithms] have noticed that people who like that song also like this. We're talking about genres primarily as communities. These are primarily social worlds."

Who's Reviewing the Reviewers?

During a recent interview about my academic research, the journalist asked which websites I visited the most. I think she was probably expecting me to reference a fancy biomedical literature resource.

My honest answer: IMDb and Rotten Tomatoes, two popular movie review sites. The former summarizes public opinions, and the latter is best known for providing an averaging of the ratings of film critics. I love movies, and I rely heavily on reviews and commentary. While my faith in them has dissipated more than a little after researching this book, I still find myself drawn to the aggregated conclusions provided by these influential platforms. The intuitive appeal of online reviews doesn't die easily.

As with music, movie reviews—from both critics and consumers—have a substantial impact on what we watch and our stated tastes. (My wife often tells me she won't waste her time on any film that has less than 90 percent on Rotten Tomatoes. A tough customer.) While the connection between websites like Rotten Tomatoes and IMDb and box office success is complex—for example, they might have less of an impact on an action film than a prestige drama—they have become a vital part of the film and TV industry. As with online reviews in general, there are issues with fake and manipulated movie reviews. It has long been known that movie studios often seek to skew public perception by creating positive buzz for a new movie via fake social media posts, online consumer reviews, and even fake critics. In the early 2000s, Sony was fined for creating fake movie reviewers—including the fictitious David Manning of the *Ridgefield Press*—and they would attribute quotes to them for marketing purposes, like calling Rob Schneider's 2001 unwatchable comedy *The Animal* "another winner!"

But here I'd like to use movie reviews to explore another question: who are the dominant voices shaping our entertainment-consuming tastes and behaviours? What voices dominate the opinion economy? Who is deciding what entertainment is good, and what that entertainment represents to our personal identities? The answer is depressingly predictable: white men.

A 2018 study done at the University of Southern California of almost twenty thousand reviews of the one hundred highest-grossing movies—so, movies we have embraced and that have helped to shape popular culture—found 82 percent were written by white critics, 78 percent by men, and 64 percent by white men. Underrepresented female critics wrote 4 percent of the reviews. If you consider the most influential and prestigious critics, the numbers look even worse. Eighty-nine percent of the reviews were written by white "top critics."

The patterns are similar for consumer reviews. An analysis of over four thousand movies on IMDb done by the FiveThirtyEight found that only ninety-seven had more ratings from women than men. That's 2.4 percent. For most films, the consumer reviews are completely dominated by the male perspective. For 90 percent of the movies, male reviews outnumbered women by at least two to one. And for 51 percent, men outnumbered women more than five to one. A reanalysis of the ranking of movies using reviews from only women produced some interesting rejigging of the rankings. For example, men rank *The Godfather* second overall. A ranking based on reviews by women drops it to tenth. *The Godfather II* drops from third to twenty-second. *Star Wars: The Empire Strikes Back* drops from thirteenth to forty-first. I suspect if the historically male-dominated public and critical discourse around movies—which obviously influences how people rate movies— was more balanced, the gap between the rankings of men and women would be even larger as the women's rankings would not be influenced by the current, male-dominated hierarchy.

This data is a good reminder to always pause and ask yourself who is doing the reviewing, what reviews are being aggregated, and if it's really relevant to your tastes and what you find enjoyable.

Like What You Like?

The point here is not that our tastes—for music or movies or whatever—are inauthentic. Does it matter if a love of Garth Brooks or Kendrick Lamar or Arcade Fire or U.K. drill or speed metal or German opera is shaped by a desire to project a particular identity? If you are a fan, you are a fan. If the music brings you joy, it brings you joy. As Clayton Childress, a sociology professor at the University of Toronto who studies the formation of cultural preferences, tells me, "The desire to project a particular identity is definitely a big part of it, but at the same time, the configuration of tastes being projected aren't just projections. They are generally probably real too." Again, if you are a fan, you are a fan.

I also recognize musical taste is a fantastically complex phenomenon. It isn't *only* about personal identity. Culture, upbringing, exposure, friends, and many other (usually interconnected) factors are relevant. Biology seems to matter too. Research has shown that a person's cognitive styles—that is, how our brains tend to work—is relevant to musical taste. (Those who are more empathetic enjoy mellow music, while those who are more analytical prefer intense genres.)

Still, recognizing the significant role of personal identity, ideology, and in-group signalling—as mediated through the ever-expanding economy of online reviews—in the formation of our tastes can be freeing. These forces, no doubt, narrow what we experience and our opportunities for enjoyment. In a 2021 study, co-authored by Professor Childress, it was found that a higher level of education and greater childhood exposure to musical genres and artists is associated with liking *fewer* artists. This narrowing of taste happens, at least in part, because, as Childress explains, "it's important to people of higher social status for other people to know their social status." He emphasizes that in the real world it ends up being a bit circular, "in that whatever high-status people collectively like over time tends to become high status. But high-status people also want others to know that they're *one of those people* with the good taste."

Maybe you feel that these conclusions are vaguely insulting—as if I'm saying you aren't self-aware or that your tastes aren't real. But know this: the research in this section describes *me* to a tee. I'm an annoying music snob. When I was a teenager and young adult, I judged (harshly) people by their musical taste. I wore the uniform of my musical tribe (punk rock). And I still check the aggregated reviews of critics and consumers before I listen to new music.

So, I decided to try a personal musical taste experiment. For over a year, I forced myself to listen to music that I once said I loathed. I streamed '70s yacht rock. I sought out stuff I used to mock. If a song came on the radio that I used to hate, I had to listen—really listen—with an open mind. While listening, I did my best not to think about the associated iconography. I also actively sought out artists and genres I once banished to my towering pile of the uncool. If there was some rising musical trend that my gut told me I'd despise, I had to lean into that trend.

The results? How the hell did I dismiss the brilliance of Fleetwood Mac? The AC/DC hits? Fun stuff. And '70s disco? Glorious. The punk-rock me had done little more than grudgingly acknowledge the existence and popularity of this music. It was stuff other people listened to. Now I thoroughly and unironically enjoy it all. It isn't a guilty pleasure; it is a pleasure. It is important to note that despite my honest effort to remain musically agnostic, there are some once-hated songs, artists, and styles that remain firmly in the "can't stand it" file. (I'll refrain from mentioning any as I don't want to anger any readers. But I will say that I've checked out and left that mind-numbingly boring hotel.) Altering deep-rooted tastes isn't easy. As Childress notes, people do change their consuming behaviour over the course of their life, "but the basic configurations of that consumption are more locked in." Still, in total, I'd say my experiment was a success. I've increased the list of artists in my "this is great" category by about 30 to 40 percent. And more music is always good thing.

Building Bridges

It is often said that music is the universal language. This notion, attributed to an 1835 quote by poet Henry Wadsworth Longfellow, is certainly intuitively appealing and hopeful. But, as we've seen, it is mostly wrong. Not all people respond to music the same way, emotionally or neurologically. And the iconography of music is often used to divide and exclude. While some musical forms have become a bit less divisive—studies have found that fewer and fewer people say they *dislike* rap music, for example—the polarizing effect of many genres, such as country music, has increased in recent years.

We live in a fantastically divisive time—particularly in the context of politics. In many countries, including Canada, the pandemic made this situation significantly worse. A 2022 survey of Canadians found that 82 percent believed that the country has been pulled further apart. As shown throughout this book, the information ecosystem is rigged to exploit our search for signals of certainty in a manner that further polarizes discourse. Might trying to set aside the personal branding aspect of music serve as a small bridge between communities? A fascinating study from the University of Mannheim in Germany, published in 2021, explored whether finding common ground on a non-political topic—such as musical taste—might decrease the polarization on more contentious, political issues. The good news: it worked. The researchers found that discovering "incidental similarities" can lead to "increased feelings of closeness toward the source of a political message and that these feelings of closeness, in turn, predicted openness toward opposing views." In other words, building a relationship around a mutual love of, say, Garth Brooks's "Friends in Low Places" might lead to greater consensus regarding the grave injustice of wealth inequality. Okay, that is a bit of hopeful hyperbole, but you get the idea.

Given the depth and destructive force of our current levels of polarization, I know my "let's give all music a chance" proposition likely reads as naive and wishful. But, heck, if a universal recognition that the groove from Stevie Wonder's "Superstition" is absolute perfection can reduce the tension surrounding a discussion about, say, GMOs, gerrymandering, gun rights, abortion, immigration, etc., then please, more Stevie.

"Based on the results of our experiment, my intuition is that music can definitely be a bridge for polarized topics," Dr. Stefano Balietti, lead author of the above Mannheim study, tells me. Especially songs "based on some universal values of humanhood and storytelling." Or, I would add, a ridiculously funky bass line.

Of course, the point here is not only about appreciating a broad range of music as a bridge to other communities and perspectives. The sentiment is more universal. We should do our best to consider other points of view. A fascinating study from 2022 from Berkeley and Yale universities provides hope that efforts to break out of our often-too-small information environments can help to expand our perspectives, even on highly divisive issues. The researchers paid hundreds of hardcore Fox News watchers fifteen dollars an hour to watch seven hours of CNN for an entire month. Despite the fact that many of the participants were likely suspicious of the goals of the research ("you're trying to brainwash us with Anderson Cooper propaganda!"), the results were both surprising and encouraging. Watching CNN caused the Fox News fans to alter their perspectives, even on highly contentious and politically polarized issues like the COVID response in the U.S.

While this is just one study with obvious limitations (paying people to be exposed to different perspectives isn't a sustainable solution!), it is clear we need to consider ways to penetrate the citadels of certainty created by information echo chambers. The power of polarization to shape perceptions—even around things like medical advice—is remarkable. Consider the 2023 study from the University of Pittsburgh that I referenced in the introduction. In the U.S., the cable news channel a physician favours (and increasingly the most popular cable news shows, regardless of ideological leanings, are often nothing more than in-group signalling opinion forums) is more predictive of beliefs about COVID treatments than exposure to scientific research. That is both depressing and absolutely horrifying.

Big picture, the near total corruption of online reviews is an illustration of how our search for the authentic, the wisdom of the crowd, the un-filtered, and relatable and trusted advice can be hijacked and twisted by the information economy. Yes, opinions have always been manipulated, manufactured, and bought. But now their value is at a premium. They have become a key part of the world economy. And because they are so valuable, the incentive structures built into our information universe are robbing them of their meaning.

Can we do anything to fix this situation?

Conclusion: A Path Forward?

When I'm having a particularly kerfuffled and stressful moment, I weirdly think about Ernest Shackleton's epic 1914 failed Antarctica expedition. Part of me thinks, *Yes, I'm having a bad day, but at least I'm not stuck on an ice floe eating penguin.* Considered one of the greatest survival stories of all time, Shackleton and his entire team survived freezing temperatures, rowing across the Antarctic Ocean in tiny boats, and an attack by a giant leopard seal.

Another part of me thinks—and this is the very weird part—it must have been nice to have a singular, clear, and uncluttered purpose. It must have been nice to be certain about your goals and what you need to do. Shackleton didn't have to deal with hundreds of emails telling him to get a move on. Or social media posts about how he's about to fall off the side of our flat Earth. Or media polls on how most of the public thinks he's already dead. Or conflicting expert advice on ice floe etiquette. The expedition team just focused on the task of survival. And Shackleton found a path home.

I'm guessing few people muse about such extreme situations (in my version, there is ample espresso, dark chocolate, and lightly roasted almonds with just a dash of sea salt) as a way of escaping our noise-filled information ecosystem. But I bet most of you can at least relate to the sentiment.

Research has consistently found that the information chaos is stressing us out. One industry survey found that 89 percent of workers believe their environment of unrelenting communication is the most unpleasant part of their job, with 38 percent saying "email fatigue" could push them to quit their jobs. Numerous studies have found a correlation between social media use and mental health issues, such as depression and anxiety. Both doomscrolling and the constant onslaught of bleak news stories have also been linked to poor mental health. And the cacophony of conflicting recommendations and opinions not only stress us out, but they make it much more difficult for us to make critical decisions.

An interesting 2022 study from the University of Minnesota found that being subjected to conflicting health information—and, because of the fragmentation and polarization of our sources of news, information, and entertainment, we increasingly are—causes people to become less receptive to subsequent evidence-informed advice, even if that advice is unrelated to the content of the conflicting information. This is an important and distressing finding. The systemic pressures and incentives built into our information environment encourage the creation of conflict and confusion, which, in turn, undermines our receptivity to those kernels of evidence-informed truths that might make a genuine difference to both individual and public well-being and happiness. Our information environment fosters a population-level fatigue and frazzle while, at the same time, heightening the value and thus the likely exploitation and distortion of anything that might de-frazzle or create a sense of clarity.

It is no surprise that we all crave reliable and authentic guidance. Sure, we aren't being attacked by a giant leopard seal while starving on an ice floe in the Antarctic. But we are constantly bombarded by a monstrous amount of information that is, as I said at the very beginning of this book, a tangle of lies, distortions, and rage-filled rants. Finding a path out of this chaos and toward some approximation of the truth feels both urgent and near impossible. The guideposts that we look for—science, authentic opinions—have been co-opted, exploited, and degraded to the point that they are no longer helpful beacons that light a path through the darkness, but a central part of our corrupted and exploitive information ecosystem.

We need to take bold action—as individuals and a society—to address these issues. Our twisted information environment is threatening democratic institutions, social cohesion, economies, and our health and well-being. It is as if we are all prisoners stuck in a cave of twisted facts, and the shadows on the wall, our only access to the reality of the outside world, are being manipulated by the people who put us in the cave. (Yes, I just butchered Plato's cave allegory.)

Finding evidence-informed strategies to correct, counter, and reduce the impact of the inaccuracies, misinformation, and conspiracy theories is an important part of this effort, as is teaching critical thinking and media literacy. But without access to trustworthy evidence, science-informed recommendations, and genuinely authentic opinion, we have no hope of finding a degree of certainty about almost anything. Instead of uncovering a path toward the light, we are being lured—for profit, politics, and the anarchic desire for chaos—deeper into the dark.

What can we do?

The Fundamental Fix

This book started with an analysis of the ways in which the scientific process and the language of science are being corrupted by the incentives built into our information ecosystem and the knowledge production process, most notably the academic research environment. If I could wave a magic wand and fix just one thing, it would be this.

Okay, "fix the way that science is funded, done, and communicated" is a bit of a cheat for a fix-this-one-thing ask. It is a *big* ask. But if we have any hope of escaping the post-truth quagmire that we find ourselves being sucked further and further into, a strong and trustworthy empirical foundation is absolutely essential. If we continue to pollute the scientific literature with questionable scholarship and continue to incentivize hype, not only will it get more difficult to correct misinformation and maintain public trust in the scientific process, but progress in the advancement of knowledge could be jeopardized. That may sound alarmist, but there are reasons to be concerned.

A study published in 2023 in the journal *Nature* looked at data from 45 million academic papers and 3.9 million patents. The goal of the project was to explore how much truly innovative research was happening now as compared to in the past. What the researchers found was that since 1945, the production of disruptive research—such as work that is subsequently referenced by future researchers—has slowed substantially. In terms of innovative publications, the study suggests the decline is more than 90 percent.

It is important to note that this slowing of innovation and disruptive research is happening even though there are more research papers published per year now than at any time in human history; increasingly, nations around the world fund large science projects with the specific goal of producing revolutionary scientific advances. This is occurring at a time when public representations of science have never been more hyped. Headlines and social media posts and press releases and scientific abstracts are filled with declarations of promised—but seldom realized—breakthroughs and amazing and novel advances.

As I've argued throughout this book, the way we incentivize research—and the dissemination of research results—is clearly broken. And the research community knows it and feels it. For example, a 2020 study by the U.K.'s Wellcome Trust found that most researchers believe that creativity is a critically important feature of an ideal research culture, "but 75 percent of researchers believe it's currently being stifled." The constant pressure—to publish, get grants, commercialize, etc.— is taking a toll.

A change—a *fundamental* change—is needed. We must shift to research funding and support strategies that do not incentivize hype. As the authors of the above noted paper in *Nature* note, universities, governments, and funding agencies need to "forgo the focus on quantity, and more strongly reward research quality." The career of a researcher should not depend on spinning exaggerated tales of near-future benefit or on the frantic publication of poor-quality work.

Russell Funk, a professor at the University of Minnesota's Carlson School of Management and senior author of the *Nature* paper, agrees. Funk worries that existing incentive structures motivate unhelpful quantity-over-quality practices like "salami science"—that is, dividing the findings of research projects into many small publications with the central goal of creating the appearance of productivity. As Funk explains, "The easiest path to producing a large number of papers is by publishing a series of studies that build on one another (or on existing work)." This will look good on an academic resumé or annual report, and it is easier than, as Funk says, "attempting to disrupt the status quo." A 2023 international survey of the research community found that 20 percent admit to "sacrificing the quality of their publications for quantity." And that's just the percentage who are willing to explicitly admit the practice. Salami science is likely far more prevalent.

The intense publish-or-perish pressure is being exploited for profit by predatory publications—those low-quality journals with dogs and dead people for editors that promise fast and easy publication but that have little or no actual peer review. It also creates a market for the paper mills to push junk science and for the hijacked journals that look real but aren't.

How out of control can the impact of publish-or-perish pressure get? Spain's most prolific academic is a meat researcher named José Manuel Lorenzo Rodriguez. It was reported in *El País*, a leading Spanish newspaper, that Rodriguez published 176 papers in 2022. That's one paper every two days, working weekends. Are these publications high quality, and did he make meaningful contributions? I'll reserve comment.

I'm not a meat expert. Perhaps he really knows how to get a lot out of forty-eight hours. Or perhaps he is just focused on quantity, quantity, quantity. As the journalist of this news piece concluded, "This system—known as 'publish or perish'—has created monsters." Yes, it has.

Worse, this competitive publication environment invites questionable research practices. Research fraud—large or small—is never justified. One would hope that research integrity would drive all scholarly activities. But when you put academics, particularly those early in their career, under intense pressure to perform and there is one very clear metric that is used to measure that performance, trouble seems inevitable. It is no surprise that some studies have found that there is an association between publication pressure and scientific misconduct.

In 1675 Sir Isaac Newton wrote, "If I have seen further it is by standing on the shoulders of Giants." It is one of the most famous and celebrated statements in science, touching on the iterative nature of scientific inquiry, the value of scientific consensus, and how scientific progress depends on the quality of the work of those who went before. But I fear that current and future researchers don't have such a solid foundation to stand on. As our knowledge production environment becomes increasingly polluted, and as we sink in a mire of unreliable noise, the chance to see further diminishes greatly.

I'm a full-fledged, card-carrying science geek. I recognize that there are still examples of dramatic scientific progress—such as the remarkable recent advances in astronomy, vaccines, information technology, obesity drugs, computing power, and artificial intelligence. We haven't totally lost the science-informed plot. Exciting stuff is happening. But, as I hope this book has illustrated, there seems to be little doubt that we need to fix our knowledge production economy. Yes, we can and should give the public strategies to cut through the noise and useless BS that increasingly contaminates our information environment. (Don't be discouraged, dear reader! There is a path forward.) But governments, scientific institutions, and research funders must take the lead, including by facilitating a massive culture shift toward quality and impact over quantity and hype. Of course, much more needs to be done. Here are some other reforms that should be considered as a priority:

- Scientific organizations, academic publishers, and research institutions must do more to identify, delegitimize, and shut down fake academic journals, such as those created to publish harmful nonsense (e.g., anti-vaccines advocacy). I recognize that drawing a clear line between quality and crap won't be easy, but a line must be drawn somewhere.

- The retraction of bad science must happen more quickly, and it must be immediately clear—in research databases, search engine results, and on journal websites—that a paper has been retracted.

- We need to fund and reward academics for doing replication research—that is, research that confirms past work—and the publication of negative results. Currently, this kind of research isn't considered sexy or career-making, but it should be. Let's celebrate this stuff!

- As much as is practically possible, research data should be accessible to all. (This will help with replication research and public trust in the scientific process.) Let's do our best to create a culture of open, creative, and independent science!

- More work needs to be done to encourage and enforce research integrity within the research community—and this should involve making it clear how problematic it is to publish in or work with predatory or vanity publications.

- Scientists, research institutions, professional organizations, and funding agencies must take a stand against the questionable use of scientific concepts and emerging research. Let's make it a responsibility for publicly funded researchers to correct the record—or to work with others to do so—when their work or their field is misrepresented or spun in the press, on social media, or by those selling unproven products. In this era of misinformation and bunk science, cleaning up our polluted information ecosystem must become a high-priority task.

The Certainty Six

You may be wondering, *What can I do personally? How can I protect myself and my community?* Simply recognizing that the above noted reforms are urgently needed is a good start as it will prime you to critically assess the content you see. If you know there are bugs in the knowledge production system, you will be more sensitive to their impact. (Also, please advocate for change!) But here are six more evidence-informed strategies you can use:

1. Pause and recognize the information ecosystem isn't rigged for accuracy.

It is now a truism that a host of forces—including social media and search engine algorithms, the polarization and politicization of science and opinion, and old-school marketing tactics—are the enemy of accuracy. At this point, this is hardly a hot take. But a reminder to listen to your Spidey sense for accuracy is still a worthwhile and evidence-based recommendation!

I want to be clear: I'm not suggesting that you become a cynical disbeliever of everything that comes across your radar. Not only would that be a cheerless and nihilistic approach to life, but it's not the point. There is lots of reliable, engaging, and evidence-informed content out there. But many of the forces that nudge us toward believing and sharing misinformation—such as those that play to our fears, emotions, ideological leanings, and propensity to be swayed by narratives—influence us in that moment when we first see and react to a headline, meme, tweet, TikTok, etc. Research by my colleagues Gordon Pennycook and David Rand has found that simply reminding people to pause and consider accuracy can help to counteract the power of these cognitive biases. It makes us all more discerning information consumers. A study they published in 2022 found that "a simple nudge or prompt that shifts attention to accuracy increases the quality of news that people share."

I asked Rand, a professor at the Massachusetts Institute of Technology, how we can all use his research in our daily lives. His advice is refreshingly straightforward: just take a beat and "ask yourself if this is accurate before you hit share." Yes, we should do more to engage our critical thinking skills, such as fact-checking and considering the type of research being used to support a claim. But don't underestimate the power of the humble pause.

2. Watch for scienceploitation.

From alternative medicine to direct-to-consumer diagnostic tests to the beauty and diet industries to anti-vaccine advocacy, science-y language is exploited to legitimize and sell products, brands, and (frequently nefarious) agendas. This scienceploitation strategy works because it leverages both our shared understanding of the power of science as an explanatory framework and the public expectations generated by pop culture representations of emerging areas of research. Scienceploitation is used to obfuscate, impress, and sell, but never to provide actual science-informed guidance. There are several strategies that we can use to guard against this increasingly common persuasion scam.

First, be extra suspicious of claims that use hot topics. When electricity was a big new thing in the 1800s, the language of electricity was used to sell bunk. When radiation was all the rage, people were buying radioactive water as a cure-all. Now it's stem cells, regenerative medicine, genomics, nanotechnology, the microbiome, and quantum physics that are being used to make a sale.

Second, always ask yourself about the nature of the science being name-checked. Are the claims supported by actual research or just vague references to buzz words and phrases? If an explanation is provided, does it make conceptual sense or is it a science-y word salad?

Third, be especially cautious when the trappings of science are used by practitioners and industries often associated with pseudoscience, such as when quantum physics is used to support astrology. Or apple stem cells are used to market anti-aging facial creams. Or when the science of the microbiome is used by alternative medicine practitioners to sell colon cleanses or DIY fecal transplants (um, do not do this).

3. Resist the allure of science hype.

Exaggeration and overly optimistic claims of near-future benefit have become the norm for the research community. All the incentives—for research grants, academic publications, institutional press releases, pop culture portrayals, social media posts, commercialization, and the marketing of related products—push public representations of science in one direction: toward hype. There are very few moderating forces anywhere along the science and innovation pipeline. The current knowledge production ecosystem incentivizes both quantity-over-quality research advances *and* hype about those small advances. The reality is that translating exciting research from the laboratory—or even from promising clinical trials—is a fraught, uncertain, and usually unsuccessful enterprise. Science is super hard!

A good rule: if you see a science-y headline or marketing claim that sounds too good to be true, it is likely too good to be true. The cliché holds. Exciting, impactful, and rapid knowledge translation does, very infrequently, happen—the best recent example being the COVID vaccines, which were the result of a massive and coordinated global effort that built on decades of related research. When another genuine breakthrough like this happens, you'll hear about it from a range of sources—not only from a random clinic's website, a wellness influencer's social media feed, or the raves of a podcaster.

4. Take a closer look when goodness is used as a marketing strategy.

A recent study by the U.S. Department of Agriculture examined food scanner data—which is basically all food scanned when purchased at a store—for the entire country for one year. The researchers found that almost 17 percent of the food was labelled as "natural." In other words, a ridiculously high portion of all food purchased in the U.S. is labelled with a near meaningless health halo term. And (surprise!) the term is most often used on products that many would consider—rightly or not—unnatural, such as highly processed products. For example, 95.6 percent of the purchased supplements were labelled natural.

So many terms like *natural* are deployed because they operate as a shortcut to an illusory certainty. They exploit the confusion caused by our chaotic information environment by offering the appearance of a quick answer. And they play to our desire to do the right thing, for ourselves and our community. But the reality is that too often terms like *clean, locally grown, non-GMO, healthy, chemical-free*, etc., are scientifically incoherent and tremendously misleading. Don't be fooled. When it comes to products like food—where the use of health halos is likely most common—the best approach is to recognize what you are purchasing. When buying packaged products, look at the ingredients listed on the label and assume that any health-halo terms are meaningless or misleading. A safe bet is to focus on real food. Real food is real food, such as fruits, veggies, nuts, legumes, and whole grains.

I'm not saying we shouldn't be urging companies to make products safer, more sustainable, and healthier. And, of course, finding paths to virtuous goals is a very good thing. But in the current information ecosystem, the frequently marketed goodness goals are often little more than a harmful and misleading distraction.

5. Always consider the existing body of evidence.

Predatory and hijacked journals pollute the scientific literature with fake science. Retracted studies live on as zombie papers that will not die or stop influencing public perceptions. And there is a depressing amount of dodgy and straight-up fraudulent scientific research. There is so much bad science out there that navigating your way through this minefield can be tremendously difficult, especially when the bad science finds its way into pop culture.

I've spent decades considering, analyzing, and critiquing evidence on a host of biomedical and health policy topics. A significant portion of my life revolves around reading academic papers and investigating emerging science. Despite this experience, I am also finding it more difficult to separate the good stuff from the marginal and the full-on manure. While writing this book, I found studies that I planned on citing, but after double-checking, it appeared the publication skewed toward being predatory. Punt.

This is a good time to recognize a big paradox with my own work and with this book, wherein I reference hundreds of studies. (My editor will likely tell me too many!) Isn't all this literature also subject to the same twisting forces as the stuff I critique? Moreover, I'm an academic. I apply for grants. I do research. I publish papers. I interact with the media. Isn't my work—and the claims I make in this book—also a target of the same perverting pressures and incentives I argue have infected academia more broadly?

The short answer is yep. The polluting of scientific literature is likely also polluting the literature on the polluting of the scientific literature. The situation is a mess! In this book—and in my career more broadly—I've done my best (undoubtedly failing at times) to deploy the strategies I recommend throughout, especially the ones I'm about to recommend here.

First, don't fall for the single study syndrome (one study rarely changes anything), especially if that study confirms your preconceived notions or hoped-for contrarian take. This isn't to say you shouldn't get excited about an interesting new study, but always put it in the context of the broader scientific literature—particularly if it is about a complex topic involving complex systems with numerous variables (e.g., human biology, human behaviour, the impact of public health policies, the environment).

Let me offer an example. Say a study comes out tomorrow claiming climate change isn't happening. While you can bet there are individuals who would embrace this conclusion and share the bejesus out of it on social media as the gospel truth, it is highly unlikely that a single study—even one that has been done well—can reverse the huge body of evidence that points in the opposite direction.

It's also crucial to be aware of your personal biases! I'm a sucker for studies on the benefits of healthy behaviours like exercise, sleep, and strong social connections. While all those things are *undoubtedly* good for us, many of the relevant studies are small and often overhyped. I tend to get too enthusiastic about any study that reinforces the value of a healthy lifestyle. I remind myself to take a beat and look closely at the methods. You should do the same.

Second, if a study's claims seem extraordinary or contrarian, be extra careful. Check to see if it has been retracted or if it was published in a marginal or predatory publication. This can be a bit more challenging and time-consuming if you aren't familiar with academic publications, but checking to see if a breadth of other academics references the piece is a good start. This can be done by putting the study title in a research search engine (e.g., PubMed) or even Google Scholar.

And most important, always consider the body of evidence. What is the scientific consensus on the topic in question? This recommendation is key to so much of what I've covered in this book—including countering science hype, health halos, predatory publications, and the spread of misinformation. The idea here is that the scientific process—especially when it is working well—inches us closer to an objective truth.

Looking to what the body of evidence says may sound conformist, boring, and kind of overly conservative. After all, contrarian views do, sometimes, turn out to be correct. Contrarian and controversial scientific views are an important part of the scientific process. Plate tectonics and the idea that bacteria cause ulcers were both once viewed as fringe. But once these controversial views were raised—at scientific venues, it is worth noting—they were subsequently supported by data and cogent arguments. The proponents didn't ignore the evidence and rant about conspiracy theories on social media, popular podcasts, and cable news shows. When truly disruptive and scientifically valid contrarian ideas do emerge—which is a fantastically rare occurrence—they still need to be tested empirically, a process that incrementally moves them into the always evolving scientific consensus.

So, as a day-to-day guide to evaluating fantastical claims—especially in this era of misinformation—considering the body of evidence remains a crucial recommendation. Indeed, it is exactly what good scientists do. When researchers write up a study for publication, they must place the conclusions in the context of the existing literature. Yes, enjoy watching the science evolve, even those contrarian musings. But do your best to measure them against what the existing weight of evidence says on the topic.

How do we know what the body of evidence says? For some topics, I bet you already know the consensus. Smoking is bad for you. Fruits and vegetables are healthy. Exercise is good for you. Ditto sleep. Climate change is happening and is influenced by human activities. Vaccines work and have saved millions of lives. The Earth isn't flat. For other topics, the scientific consensus may not be as well known to the public but can be relatively easy to find by turning to reliable sources. GMOs are not associated with health risks. Unless you have a clinically identified deficiency or specific need, most supplements are not helpful. Homeopathy is total nonsense. And then there are the topics for which the consensus may be in flux and the science complex and evolving. Psychedelics as a therapy for mental health conditions. The use of probiotics in the prevention of disease. The potential health risks of parabens in cosmetics.

CONCLUSION: A PATH FORWARD?

It is for this latter category that independent expert advice can be most helpful. Sometimes the scientific consensus is harder to discern because, as my colleague Jonathan Jarry noted, it emerges slowly and iteratively. It can feel mundane. "It often isn't sexy," Jarry tells me. "It doesn't have the brashness of a contrarian hammer. It doesn't feel like insider knowledge or discovering the truth buried in a vault underneath a pyramid." As a result, unconfirmed but exciting scientific speculation often gets more headlines and social media traction. This can give the false impression that the science is stronger than it is in an area, which can do great harm to social policy, public discourse, and public health. Studies have found that the public often greatly underestimates the degree of scientific consensus on key topics. In part, this is because contrarian views are often overrepresented in the popular press, on social media, and by those prominent individuals (like well-known podcasters and cable news hosts) pushing the contrarian views.

Jarry, a science communication expert at McGill University, co-hosts a terrific podcast called, wait for it . . . *The Body of Evidence*. So, yes, he's pretty committed to the value of exploring the scientific consensus. On his show, he brings in renowned experts to do just that. And that is what you should try to do. Not host a podcast, but find trusted voices—good science communicators, science journalists, university resources, government websites—that aggregate the science in a responsible manner. "It is built around solid pieces of evidence all pointing in the same direction, and you will find it coming out of competent governments, credible professional organizations, and mainstream media sources. That's the consensus, in its prosaic glory," Jarry says.

Given the value of knowing the scientific consensus, I think more needs to be done—by the scientific community, universities, and research funding entities—to support science communication strategies to make it easier for the public to find. One such project, called the Institute for Ascertaining Scientific Consensus, is being developed by Durham University. The goal, as described to me by the leader of the project, professor Peter Vickers, is to "provide policymakers and the general public with easy access to data on scientific community opinion." He hopes this kind of data will "have the power to influence opinions, behaviour, and high-stakes decision-making." Perhaps most important, it might inform the public understanding of science. More, please!

6. Like what you like.

Okay, that's a simplistic recommendation. But given the degree to which public and expert opinion is twisted, biased, and straight-up manufactured, we should all be very skeptical of the growing opinion economy. A big hunk of the world economy is tethered to online reviews and commentary. The incentive to manipulate is high, *in the extreme*. And many of our hard-wired cognitive biases make even genuine posts suspect. I wish there was a simple strategy to deploy that would make it easier to find useful and authentic opinions and reviews, but this part of our information ecosystem seems terminally broken. And the rise of artificial intelligence—which can rapidly manufacture authentic-looking content—is only making the situation worse.

That said, there are a few approaches you may want to consider. Evidence suggests that independent expert reviews that involve comparative analysis are likely the most reliable. Seek those out. When it comes to reviews of subjective experiences—like art and entertainment—look for voices that reflect your tastes on a consistent basis. Also, go old school: talk to actual humans. Face to face. Your friends, family, and neighbours might know more than those biased commentators, random bots, and paid reviewers. Finally, keep an open mind and try stuff. And, yes, like what you like. Reviews be damned.

When searching for certainty, humans are drawn to the opinions of others. Despite all the research I've done on this topic, I *still* find myself looking at online reviews. Their pull is remarkable. I know they are largely unreliable and often total BS, and still I seek them out! Of course, it is our unbreakable reliance on the opinion economy that makes it such a tempting target of manipulation. So, while I bet you will continue to look at those online rants and raves, perhaps do so with a bit more caution.

The Knowledge Paradox Dark Age?

How we create, share, interact with, and respond to knowledge is a defining characteristic of human history. We've progressed (well, *largely* progressed) from relying on superstition, myths, and magic to using carefully controlled systematic methods to understand and explain our world. As a way of knowing. Yes, the process (science is hard and messy!) and relevant incentives (quantity over quality!) are far from perfect, both now and historically. But our ability to create and share research-informed explanations and recommendations—about our health, environment, and place in the universe—has never been greater. There can and should be a golden era of knowledge creation. Let's not let this opportunity slip away. Let's not let this era become known as the dawn of a new, and paradoxical, dark age—a time when our species has access to more knowledge than ever before but is systematically misinformed and deceived.

We need to recognize both the scale of the problem and the need for immediate action. It is a generational challenge that will require the deployment of a multi-pronged approach, including teaching critical thinking skills throughout the education process, recognizing the historical and socioeconomic roots of distrust with the institutions of knowledge creation, working with social media platforms, employing evidence-based strategies to counter misinformation, and empowering citizens to see through the noise.

I started this book by noting that we are adrift in a storm of information chaos and that we are tearing down the lighthouses—science, evidence-based recommendations, and authentic opinions—that could guide our path forward. Let's reverse that trend. We can and must build up and protect those lighthouses. Without them, we are truly lost. This I know, with certainty.

Acknowledgements

Despite the seriousness of many of the topics I cover in this book, it was a joy to write—in part because the core theme, how research and facts are communicated, has been a central part of my academic career for decades. I thoroughly enjoyed revisiting controversies and policy challenges that I've worked on in the past. And it allowed me to connect with and—let's be honest here—*exploit* the expertise and goodwill of many of my friends and current and past colleagues. I also had the opportunity to chat with (over the phone, in person, on Zoom, and via email, which, for the sake of efficiency, I did not distinguish in the text) and learn from many other extraordinary and interesting scholars, clinicians, scientists, and journalists.

Thank you: Ewa Maslowska, University of Illinois; David Allison, Indiana University; Gordon Pennycook, Cornell University; Amy McGuire, Baylor College of Medicine; Dylan MacKay, University of Manitoba; Davide Proserpio, University of Southern California; Stephan Lewandowsky, University of Bristol; James Hamblin, Yale University; Jonathan Jarry, McGill University; Alan Levinovitz, James Madison University; Ann Borden; Oobah Butler, London;

Saoud Khalifah, Fake Spot; Christopher McCabe, Institute of Health Economics; Sherry He, UCLA; Bart de Langhe, KU Leuven; Donald Lichtenstein, Leeds School of Business; Curtis Boyd, The Transparency Company; Susan Jelinski, University of Alberta; Clayton Childress, University of Toronto; Stefano Balietti, Mannheim University; Kelefa Sanneh, *New Yorker*; Darren Wagner, University of Alberta; Tom Spears, journalist; Mike Daube, Curtin University (and Dr. Olivia "Ollie" Doll, Subiaco College of Veterinary Science); David Moher, Ottawa Hospital Research Institute; Anna Abalkina, Freie Universität Berlin; Patricia Wells, University of Calgary; Ivan Oransky, Retraction Watch; Paul Knoepfler, University of California, Davis School of Medicine; Matthew Motta, Oklahoma State University; Mark Freeman, University of Alberta; Jessica Clark, Brock University; Manoj Lalu, University of Ottawa; Michelle Wong, Lab Muffin Beauty Science; Megan Munsie, University of Melbourne; Abby Langer, dietitian; Joe Schwarcz, McGill University; Rena Malik, urologist; Mallory DeMille; Jen Novakovich, Eco Well; Perry Romanowski, Chemists Corner; Jonathan Stea, University of Calgary; Sarah DiMuccio, Catalyst; Kate Starbird, University of Washington; John Oliffe, University of British Columbia; Stephanie Halmhofer, University of Alberta; Xiaoli Fan, University of Alberta; Ted Kyle, ConscienHealth; Bernie Garrett, University of British Columbia; Frank Graves, EKOS Research; James Tabery, University of Utah; Peter Vickers, Durham University; and anyone I forgot to mention (and I'm sure there are more than a few!).

While writing, I often drew on interdisciplinary research I did with scholars throughout the world, so I would also like to thank them—far too numerous to name, but you know who you are—for the opportunity to collaborate and co-author with you over the decades. (Yes, it has been that long.) I would like to acknowledge my wonderful colleagues at the University of Alberta, the science communication initiative ScienceUpFirst, and the co-authors of the "Homeopathy Is Pseudoscience BS" paper, including Jennifer Gunter, Jonathan Stea, Jamie Boisvenue, Robert Tuchler, Miranda van Tilburg, and

Kiki Sanford. And a special shout-out to the multi-talented Robyn Hyde-Lay. (Your magical ability to find even the most obscure research paper was essential!)

In a few spots, I've drawn on language from published commentaries in the *Globe and Mail* (an article on scienceploitation), *Men's Health* (special nod to Marty Munson for the nudge to write a piece on Tucker Carlson), and *Policy Options* ("The Problem with Personalization" and "Food Choices, the Prius, Celebrities, and My Shaved Legs"). I'm grateful for the editorial help on all those pieces.

For over a decade, my agent and friend, Chris Bucci, has provided incredible creative support and encouragement. A big thanks to my wonderful editor, Laura Dosky, for the big-picture advice and for tolerating all my random "Does this work?" emails. I feel fortunate to be part of the wonderful Penguin Random House Canada family. (Thanks to Diane Turbide for bringing me in and to Ruta Liormonas and Emily Sheppard for, well, so much!) And a big thanks to Crissy Boylan, for her remarkable editorial work.

Of course, I save my biggest cheers for my wonderful and always supportive family. Your love and understanding are no illusion—and the most authentic and valuable thing in my life.

Finally, I would also like to acknowledge the invaluable contribution of my two office mates, Lord Byron and Detective Turtles. While your frequent interruptions did little to help the creative process, your unwavering companionship got me through more than a few dark days. Meow.

References and Notes

This reference list is organized by the book's sections. I tried to strike a balance between keeping the flow of the writing and providing enough information in the text so that the relevant study could be identified in the below list. For some references, I have added a few quotes and conclusions. This reference list includes the key research I explicitly refer to, but it does not include all the material I used or that is relevant to each topic. I wanted to provide you with a sense of the significant academic research and expert commentary. I hope you find it useful and a good starting point for the further exploration of these fascinating topics, if you are keen to learn more.

Introduction: Adrift in a Storm

Barrett, P., J. Hendrix, and G. Sims. "How tech platforms fuel U.S. political polarization and what government can do about it." Brookings Institute, September 27, 2021. https://www.brookings.edu/articles/how-tech-platforms -fuel-u-s-political-polarization-and-what-government-can-do-about-it.

Explores how social media exacerbates polarization and "contributes to partisan animosity."

Bump, P. "12 Million Americans Believe Lizard People Run Our Country." *The Atlantic*, April 2, 2013. https://www.theatlantic.com/national/archive /2013/04/12-million-americans-believe-lizard-people-run-our-country/316706.

Caulfield., T. "Food Choices, the Prius, Celebrities, and My Shaved Legs." *Policy Options*, October 23, 2015. https://policyoptions.irpp.org/magazines/october-2015/food-choices-the-prius-celebrities-and-my-shaved-legs.

My review of the research surrounding the Prius effect.

Ceylan, G., I.A. Anderson, and W. Wood. "Sharing of misinformation is habitual, not just lazy or biased." *PNAS* 120, no. 4 (January 2023). https://doi.org/10.1073/pnas.2216614120.

". . . sharing of false news is part of a broader response pattern established by social media platforms."

Cibean, T. "Adults in the U.S. check their phones 352 times a day on average, 4x more often than in 2019." *Techspot*, June 5, 2022. https://www.techspot.com/news/94828-adults-us-check-their-phones-352-times-day.html.

Coletto, D. "Millions believe in conspiracy theories in Canada." Abacus Data, June 12, 2022. https://abacusdata.ca/conspiracy-theories-canada.

Source for 37% of Canadians believe great replacement theory, 13% believe "Microsoft founder Bill Gates is using microchips to track people and affect human behaviour," and another 21% are open to the idea.

Czopek, M. "The FBI didn't orchestrate Jan. 6, but a poll shows the false belief has staying power." Poynter, January 9, 2024. https://www.poynter.org/fact-checking/2024/fbi-organize-encourage-january-6-capitol-attack-insurrection.

"25% of US adults think the FBI 'organized and encouraged' the attack on the Capitol."

Desjardins, J. "How much data is generated each day?" World Economic Forum, April 17, 2019. https://www.weforum.org/agenda/2019/04/how-much-data-is-generated-each-day-cf4bddf29f.

"By 2025, it's estimated that 463 exabytes of data will be created each day."

Falconer, R. "Misinformation spurring U.S. life expectancy 'erosion,' FDA chief says." *Axios*, May 7, 2022. https://www.axios.com/2022/05/08/misinformation-us-life-expectancy-drop-fda-chief.

Heim, S., and A. Keil, "Too Much Information, Too Little Time: How the Brain Separates Important from Unimportant Things in Our Fast-Paced Media World." Frontiers for Young Minds, June 1, 2017. https://kids.frontiersin.org/articles/10.3389/frym.2017.00023.

". . . an average person living today processes as much as 74 GB in information a day."

Kennedy, B., and A. Tyson. "Americans' Trust in Scientists, Positive Views of Science Continue to Decline." Pew Research Center, November 14, 2023. https://www.pewresearch.org/science/2023/11/14/americans-trust-in -scientists-positive-views-of-science-continue-to-decline.

"73% of U.S. adults have a great deal or fair amount of confidence in scientists to act in the public's best interests."

Kim., S.-W., J.L. Lusk, and B.W. Brorsen. "'Look at Me, I'm Buying Organic': The Effects of Social Pressure on Organic Food Purchases." *Journal of Agriculture and Resource Economics* 43, no. 3 (September 2018). https://jareonline.org /articles/look-at-me-im-buying-organic-the-effects-of-social-pressure-on -organic-food-purchases.

Study found that when people are watching a purchase, consumers are more willing to pay more for organic food.

Levin, J., L. Bukowski, J. Minson, and J. Kahn. "The political polarization of COVID-19 treatments among physicians and laypeople in the United States." *PNAS* 120, no. 7 (February 2023). https://doi.org/10.1073/pnas.2216179120.

"... results highlight the extent to which political ideology is increasingly relevant for understanding beliefs."

Orth, T. "One in four Americans say they believe in astrology." YouGov, April 26, 2022. https://today.yougov.com/entertainment/articles/42292-one-four -americans-say-they-believe-astrology.

Sun, D. "90% of drugs fail clinical trials—here's one way researchers can select better drug candidates." *The Conversation*, February 12, 2023. https:// theconversation.com/90-of-drugs-fail-clinical-trials-heres-one-way -researchers-can-select-better-drug-candidates-174152.

"Only 1 out of 10 drug candidates successfully passes clinical trial testing and regulatory approval."

Thompson, S. "Many Developed Countries View Online Misinformation as 'Major Threat.'" *The New York Times*, August 31, 2022. https://www.nytimes .com/2022/08/31/technology/pew-misinformation-major-threat.html.

Survey of nineteen countries found misinformation viewed as major or minor threat.

Turner, E., and L. Rainie, "Most Americans rely on their own research to make big decisions, and that often means online searches." Pew Research Center, March 5, 2020. https://www.pewresearch.org/short-reads/2020/03/05/most -americans-rely-on-their-own-research-to-make-big-decisions-and-that-often -means-online-searches.

" . . . before making an important decision, a big majority (81%) say they rely a lot on their own research."

"2022 Survey Summary." *3M State of Science Index Survey*. 3M Forward. https:// www.3m.com/3M/en_US/3m-forward-us/2022-summary.

"Global trust in science is high and appreciation is stronger than pre-pandemic times."

"US life expectancy is at its lowest in 25 years." *BBC News*, December 22, 2022. https://www.bbc.com/news/world-us-canada-64067436.

"Americans are expected to live 76.4 years, down from a peak of 78.8 years in 2019."

Weikart, R., "The Racism of Darwin and Darwinism." *Evolution News*, February 9, 2022. https://evolutionnews.org/2022/02/the-racism-of-darwin-and -darwinism.

Yeo, A. "TikTok's search suggests misinformation almost 20 percent of the time, says report." *Mashable*, September 19, 2022. https://mashable.com/article /tiktok-misinformation-report-newsguard-abortion.

Part I: The Science Illusion

A Quantum Leap!

Gazzola, E. "Quantum physics and the modern trends in pseudoscience." In *Medical Misinformation and Social Harm in Non-Science-Based Health Practices*, edited by A. Lavorgna and A. Di Ronco. Routledge, 2019.

Nice review of the misuse of *quantum* to push bunk.

Ouellette, J. "Anti-5G 'quantum pendants' are radioactive." *Ars Technica*, December 17, 2021. https://arstechnica.com/science/2021/12/anti-5g-quantum -pendants-are-radioactive.

"The product leans on a tried and true pseudoscientific marketing gimmick: Slap the label 'quantum' on something."

Scienceploitation

Arroyo, M. "Scientific language in skin-care advertising: Persuading through opacity." *RESLA* 26 (January 2013), 197–213.

Brewer, P. "The Trappings of Science: Media Messages, Scientific Authority, and Beliefs about Paranormal Investigators." *Science Communication* 35, no. 3 (June 2013): 311–333. https://doi.org/10.1177/1075547012454.

Garrett, B., E. Mallia, and J. Anthony. "Public perceptions of Internet-based health scams, and factors that promote engagement with them." *Health and Social Care in the Community* 27, no. 5 (September 2019): e672–e686. https://doi.org /10.1111/hsc.12772.

Eriksson, G., and L. O'Hagan. "Selling 'Healthy' Radium Products with Science: A Multimodal Analysis of Marketing in Sweden, 1910–1940." *Science Communication* 43, no. 6 (December 2021): 740–767. https://doi.org/10.1177 /10755470211044111.

Good history of the market for radioactive health products.

Haard, J., M. Slater, and M. Long. "Scientese and Ambiguous Citations in the Selling of Unproven Medical Treatments." *Health Communication* 16, no. 4 (2004): 411–426. https://doi.org/10.1207/s15327027hc1604_2.

". . . effect was not moderated by science versus nonscience major, graduate versus undergraduate status."

Johnson, M. "Kid-edited journal pushes scientists for clear writing on complex topics." *Washington Post*, January 7, 2023. https://www.washingtonpost.com /science/2023/01/07/science-journal-for-kids.

Review of the journal *Frontiers for Young Minds* with reviewer quote: "I didn't understand anything that you said."

Ober, H. "Often, consumers inadvertently give too much credit to 'scientifically studied' product claims." *MedicalXpress*, July 27, 2023. https://medicalxpress .com/news/2023-07-consumers-inadvertently-credit-scientifically-product. html.

When people hear science-y terms, they "later misremember them in more definitive terms."

Peterson, E. "Does Magnetic Therapy Work?" *Live Science*, February 11, 2015. https://www.livescience.com/40174-magnetic-therapy.html.

Radium Water Advertisement, as quoted in Taylor Orci, "How We Realized Putting Radium in Everything Was Not the Answer." *The Atlantic*, March 7, 2013, and available at the Science Museum of Minnesota. https:// www.theatlantic.com/health/archive/2013/03/how-we-realized-putting -radium-in-everything-was-not-the-answer/273780/.

Shulman, H., G. Dixon, O. Bullock, and D. Amill. "The Effects of Jargon on Processing Fluency, Self-Perceptions, and Scientific Engagement." *Journal of Language and Psychology* 39, no. 5–6 (October–December 2020): 579–597. https://doi.org/10.1177/0261927X20902177.

van Mulken, M., and J. Hornikx. "The influence of scientese on ad credibility and ad liking: A cross-cultural investigation of ads for beauty products." *Information Design Journal* 19, no. 2 (January 2011): 92–102. https://doi.org /10.1075/idj.19.2.02mul.

"... ads with scientese were found to be more credible."

Wagner, D., A. Marcon, and T. Caulfield. "'Immune Boosting' in the time of COVID: Selling immunity on Instagram." *Allergy, Asthma, & Clinical Immunology* 16 (September 2020): article no. 76. https://doi.org/10.1186/s13223-020-00474-6.

High Tech Hogwash

Clark, J. "'Clever ministrations': Regenerative beauty at the fin de siècle." *Palgrave Communications* 3 (December 2017): article no. 47. https://doi.org/10.1057 /s41599-017-0029-9.

Excellent review of history of beauty products.

Erikainen, S., A. Couturier, and S. Chan. "Marketing Experimental Stem Cell Therapies in the UK: Biomedical Lifestyle Products and the Promise of Regenerative Medicine in the Digital Era." *Science as Culture* 29, no. 2 (September 2019): 219–244. https://doi.org/10.1080/09505431.2019.1656183.

"stem cell therapies have emerged as a new biomedical 'lifestyle' product that blurs the boundaries between 'science,' 'medicine,' and 'consumer culture.'"

Murdoch, B., A. Zarzeczny, and T. Caulfield. "Exploiting science? A systematic analysis of complementary and alternative medicine clinic websites' marketing of stem cell therapies." *BMJ Open* 8, no. 2 (February 2018): e019414. https://doi.org/10.1136/bmjopen-2017-019414.

Rachul, C., I. Percec, and T. Caulfield. "The Fountain of Stem Cell–Based Youth? Online Portrayals of Anti-Aging Stem Cell Technologies." *Aesthetic Surgery Journal* 35, no. 6 (August 2015): 730–736. https://doi.org/10.1093/asj/sju111.

Our study on skincare products.

It's Science!

Haack, S. "Six Signs of Scientism." *Logos and Episteme* 3, no. 1 (2012): 75–95. https://doi.org/10.5840/logos-episteme20123151.

Good review of the problem of scientism. She notes that the "honorific usage of 'science' and its cognates leads to all kinds of trouble."

Wong, M. "Scientism or 'Science-Washing' in Beauty." *Lab Muffin Beauty Science.* April 14, 2019. https://labmuffin.com/scientism-or-science-washing-in-beauty.

Science-y and Scary

Collins, J. "Interest in Gluten-Free Foods Is Hot among Gen Z Consumers and QSR Diners." CivicScience, August 16, 2022. https://civicscience.com/interest -in-gluten-free-foods-is-hot-among-gen-z-consumers-and-qsr-diners.

"38% of adults between the ages of 18 and 24 and 30% of those between 25 and 34 are interested in trying to eat gluten-free foods."

Hamel, L., L. Lopes, A. Kirzinger, G. Sparks, M. Stokes, and M. Brodie. "KFF COVID-19 Vaccine Monitor: Media and Misinformation." KFF, November 8, 2021. https://www.kff.org/coronavirus-covid-19/poll-finding/kff-covid-19 -vaccine-monitor-media-and-misinformation.

Survey outlining who believes misinformation.

King, J.A., G.G. Kaplan, and J. Godley. "Experiences of coeliac disease in a changing gluten-free landscape." *Journal of Human Nutrition and Dietetics* 32, no. 1 (February 2019): 72–79. https://doi.org/10.1111 /jhn.12597.

How the gluten-free trend is a double-edged sword for those with celiac.

Soroka, S., P. Fournier, and L. Nir. "Cross-national evidence of a negativity bias in psychophysiological reactions to news." *PNAS* 116, no. 38 (September 2019): 18888–18892. https://doi.org/10.1073/pnas.1908369116.

". . . audience-seeking news around the world to be predominantly negative."

Certainty, Fake Science, and Dunning-Kruger

Cichocka, A., M. Marchlewska, and M. Biddlestone. "Why do narcissists find conspiracy theories so appealing?" *Current Opinions in Psychology* 47 (October 2022): 101386. https://doi.org/10.1016/j.copsyc.2022.101386.

Fernbach, P., N. Light, S. Scott, Y. Inbar, and P. Rozin. "Extreme opponents of genetically modified foods know the least but think they know the most." *Nature Human Behaviour* 3, no. 3 (March 2019): 251–256. https://doi.org /10.1038/s41562-018-0520-3.

Imhoff, R., and P. Lamberty. "Too special to be duped: Need for uniqueness motivates conspiracy beliefs." *European Journal of Social Psychology* 47, no. 6 (October 2017): 724–734. https://doi.org/10.1002/ejsp.2265.

Light, N., P. Fernbach, N. Rabb, M. Geana, and S. Sloman. "Knowledge over-confidence is associated with anti-consensus views on controversial scientific issues." *Science Advances* 8, no. 29 (July 2022). https://doi.org/10.1126/sciadv .abo0038.

"... those with the highest levels of opposition have the lowest levels of objective knowledge."

Littrell, S., and J. Fugelsang. "Bullshit blind spots: The roles of miscalibration and information processing in bullshit detection." *Thinking and Reasoning* 30, no. 1 (2024): 49–78. https://doi.org/10.1080/13546783.2023.2189163.

People with a low ability to spot BS think they are better at it than others.

Pennycook, G., and J. Binnendyk. "Overconfidently Conspiratorial: Conspiracy Believers Are Dispositionally Overconfident and Massively Overestimate How Much Others Agree with Them." Preprint. *PsyArXiv* (December 2022). https://doi.org/10.31234/osf.io/d5fz2.

Galileo Was Super Science-y, Just Like Me! and The Humility Fix

Koetke, J., K. Schumann, and T. Porter. "Intellectual Humility Predicts Scrutiny of COVID-19 Misinformation." *Social Psychological and Personality Science* 13, no. 1 (January 2022): 277–284. https://doi.org/10.1177/1948550620988242.

McLaren, Z. "Everyone Wins: Vaccine Lotteries Can Cost-Effectively Increase COVID-19 Booster Vaccination Rates." *American Journal of Epidemiology* 192, no. 4 (April 2023): 510–513. https://doi.org/10.1093/aje/kwad013.

"... vaccine lotteries are likely to be more effective for booster vaccination."

Porter, T., A. Elnakouri, E. Meyers, T. Shibayama, E. Jayawickreme, and I. Grossmann. "Predictors and consequences of intellectual humility." *Nature Reviews Psychology* 1 (September 2022): 524–536. https://doi.org/10.1038/s44159-022-00081-9.

Excellent review of the nature and value of intellectual humility, including in the fight against misinformation.

Certainly Bullshit

Gligorić, V., and A. Vilotijević. "'Who said it?' How contextual information influences perceived profundity of meaningful quotes and pseudo-profound bullshit." *Applied Cognitive Psychology* 34, no. 2 (March–April 2020): 535–542. https://doi.org/10.1002/acp.3626.

Pennycook, G., J. Cheyne, N. Barr, D. Koehler, and J. Fugelsang. "On the reception and detection of pseudo-profound bullshit." *Judgment and Decision Making* 10, no. 6 (November 2015): 549–563. https://psycnet.apa.org/doi/10.1017/S1930297500006999.

The Hype Machine

Caulfield, T. "Spinning the Genome: Why Science Hype Matters." *Perspectives in Biology and Medicine* 61, no. 4 (Autumn 2018): 560–571. https://doi.org /10.1353/pbm.2018.0065.

Caulfield, T. "Stem Cell Research and Economic Promises." *The Journal of Law, Medicine, and Ethics* 38, no. 2 (Summer 2010): 303–313. https://doi.org/10.1111 /j.1748-720X.2010.00490.x.

My analysis of the over-the-top economic justification for funding stem cell research.

Chubb, J., and R. Watermeyer. "Artifice or integrity in the marketization of research impact? Investigating the moral economy of (pathways to) impact statements within research funding proposals in the UK and Australia." *Studies in Higher Education* 42, no. 12 (2017): 2360–2372. https://doi.org /10.1080/03075079.2016.1144182.

Study that involved anonymous interviews of researchers.

Fang, F., A. Bowen, and A. Casadevall. "NIH peer review percentile scores are poorly predictive of grant productivity." *eLife* 5 (2016): e13323. https://doi.org /10.7554/eLife.13323.

Percentile scores are a poor discriminator of future productivity.

Kamenova, K., and T. Caulfield. "Stem Cell Hype: Media Portrayal of Therapy Translation." *Science Translational Medicine* 7, no. 278 (March 2015): 278ps4. https://doi.org/10.1126/scitranslmed.3010496.

Li, D., and L. Agha. "Research funding. Big names or big ideas: Do peer-review panels select the best science proposals?" *Science* 348, no. 6233 (April 2015): 434–438. https://doi.org/10.1126/science.aaa0185.

Earlier analysis, contradicted by some later studies, that suggests a grant committee can, to some degree, select for productive research projects.

Li, G., L. Abbade, I. Nwosu, Y. Jin, A. Leenus, M. Maaz, M. Wang, et al. "A Scoping Review of Comparisons between Abstracts and Full Reports in Primary Biomedical Research." *BMC Medical Research Methodology* 17 (December 2017): article no. 181. https://doi.org/10.1186/s12874-017-0459-5.

This study found significant hype in abstracts.

Lindsay, B. "Doctor who offers unapproved fecal transplants in B.C. says he's a 'maverick.'" *CBC News*, June 30, 2020. https://www.cbc.ca/news/canada /british-columbia/doctor-who-offers-unapproved-fecal-transplants-in-b-c -says-he-s-a-maverick-1.5632314.

Matthews, D. "Academics 'regularly lie to get research grants.'" *Times Higher Education*, March 6, 2016. https://www.timeshighereducation.com/news /academics-regularly-lie-to-get-research-grants.

Millar, N., B. Batalo, and B. Budgell. "Trends in the Use of Promotional Language (Hype) in Abstracts of Successful National Institutes of Health Grant Applications, 1985–2020." *JAMA Network Open* 5, no. 8 (2022): e2228676. https://doi.org/10.1001/jamanetworkopen.2022.28676.

This study found increasing hype in grant applications—"the largest relative increases were for the terms *sustainable* (25157%), *actionable* (16114%), and *scalable* (13029%)."

Millar, N., B. Batalo, and B. Budgell. "Trends in the Use of Promotional Language (Hype) in National Institutes of Health Funding Opportunity Announcements, 1992–2020." *JAMA Network Open* 5, no. 11 (2022): e2243221. https://doi.org/10.1001/jamanetworkopen.2022.43221.

This study found that calls for research applications are also filled with hype.

Page, L., and A. Barnett. "Research funding is broken. Using a lottery approach could fix it." *STAT*, October 21, 2022. https://www.statnews.com/2022/10/21 /research-funding-broken-lottery-approach-could-fix-it.

Good analysis of why a different approach for funding is needed and that the current system is wasteful.

Pier, E., M. Brauer, A. Filut, A. Kaatz, J. Raclaw, M. Nathan, C. Ford, and M. Carnes. "Low agreement among reviewers evaluating the same NIH grant applications." *PNAS* 115, no. 12 (March 20, 2018): 2952–2957. https://doi.org/10.1073/pnas.1714379115.

Study found no agreement among peer reviewers.

Sumner, P., S. Vivian-Griffiths, J. Boivin, A. Williams, C. Venetis, A. Davies, J. Ogden, et al. "The Association between Exaggeration in Health Related Science News and Academic Press Releases: Retrospective Observational Study." *BMJ* 349 (2014): g7015. https://doi.org/10.1136/bmj.g7015.

"Exaggeration in news is strongly associated with exaggeration in press releases."

Sun, D. "90% of drugs fail clinical trials—here's one way researchers can select better drug candidates." *The Conversation*, February 12, 2023. https:// theconversation.com/90-of-drugs-fail-clinical-trials-heres-one-way -researchers-can-select-better-drug-candidates-174152.

Taffe, M., and N. Gilpin. "Racial inequity in grant funding from the US National Institutes of Health." *eLife* 10 (January 2021): e65697. https://doi.org/10.7554 /elife.65697.

"grant applications submitted to the National Institutes of Health in the US by African-American or Black Principal Investigators (PIs) are less likely to be funded than applications submitted by white PIs."

Youyou, W., Y. Yang, and B. Uzzi. "A discipline-wide investigation of the replicability of Psychology papers over the past two decades." *PNAS* 120, no. 6 (January 20, 2023): e2208863120. https://doi.org/10.1073/pnas.2208863120.

Study finds media coverage is negatively associated with replication success.

Catastrophizing

Caulfield, T. "Ethics Hype?" *The Hastings Center Report* 46, no. 5 (September–October 2016): 13–16. https://doi.org/10.1002/hast.612.

I outline the pressures that lead to overestimating ethical, legal, and social issues.

Caulfield T., S. Chandrasekharan, Y. Joly, and R. Cook-Deegan. "Harm, hype and evidence: ELSI research and policy guidance." *Genome Medicine* 5 (March 2013): article no. 21. https://doi.org/10.1186/gm425.

". . . seems to be informed more by speculation of harm and anecdote than by available evidence."

Investing in Science? Yes, Yes, Yes!

Bauchner, H., and F. Rivara. "The scientific communication ecosystem: The responsibility of investigators." *The Lancet* 400, no. 10360 (October 2022): 1289–1290. https://doi.org/10.1016/s0140-6736(22)01898-0.

Thorp, H. "Remember, do no harm?" *Science* 378, no. 6617 (October 21, 2022): 231. https://doi.org/10.1126/science.adf3072.

The Predator Problem

Babb, M. "Canadian academics' use of predatory journals." *Journal of the Canadian Health Libraries Association* 42, no. 3 (December 2021): 140–153. https://doi.org/10.29173%2Fjchla29579.

"The research-intensive U15 universities were found to publish more in predatory journals . . . NSERC and CIHR being top funders."

Brainard, J. "Fake scientific papers are alarmingly common." *Science* 380, no. 6645 (May 12, 2023): 568–569. https://www.science.org/content/article/fake -scientific-papers-are-alarmingly-common.

Report on study to detect predatory and fake studies.

Brandts-Longtin, O., M. Lalu, E. Adie, M. Albert, E. Almoli, F. Almoli, G. Bryson, et al. "Assessing the impact of predatory journals on policy and guidance documents: A cross-sectional study." Abstract. *BMJ Open* 12, no. 4 (April 2022): e059445. https://doi.org/10.1136/bmjopen-2021-059445.

Study co-authored by Moher and Lalu that found "hundreds of policy documents from across the globe and multiple disciplines have cited articles published by the [predatory] OMICS group."

Duc, N.M., D.V. Hiep, P.M. Thong, L. Zunic, M. Zildzic, D. Donev, S. Jankovic, I. Hozo, and I. Masic. "Predatory Open Access Journals Are Indexed in Reputable Databases: A Revisiting Issue or an Unsolved Problem." *Medical Archives* 74, no. 4 (August 2020): 318–322. https://doi.org/10.5455%2Fmedarh.2020.74.318-322.

"some fake journals have made their way into reputable databases."

Hedding, D. "Payouts push professors towards predatory journal." *Nature* 565, no. 7739 (January 15, 2019): 267. https://doi.org/10.1038/d41586-019-00120-1.

InterAcademy Partnership (IAP). *Combatting Predatory Academic Journals and Conferences* (March 2022). https://www.interacademies.org/publication/predatory-practices-report-English.

"Recent evidence puts the number of predatory journals at over 15,500."

Jacks, T. "The dodgy academic journals publishing anti-vaxxers and other 'crappy science.'" *The Sydney Morning Herald*, August 18, 2016. https://www.smh.com.au/national/the-dodgy-academic-journals-publishing-antivaxxers-and-other-crappy-science-20160817-gquu3z.html.

Jago, A. "Can It Really Be True That Half of Academic Papers Are Never Read?" *The Chronicles of Higher Education*, June 1, 2018. https://www.chronicle.com/article/can-it-really-be-true-that-half-of-academic-papers-are-never-read.

Article critiques claim and notes that 80% of citers never read the citation they're referencing. (Yes, I read the original by Simkin and Roychowdhury!)

Kennedy, K. "This Dog Sits on Seven Editorial Boards." *Atlas Obscura*, May 25, 2017. https://www.atlasobscura.com/articles/olivia-doll-predatory-journals.

Larson, A. "Covid origin conspiracies and other bogus research predatory scientific journals peddle." *NBC Think*, January 14, 2022. https://www.nbcnews.com/think/opinion/covid-origin-conspiracies-other-bogus-research-predatory-scientific-journals-peddle-ncna1287459.

Good list of bogus papers on COVID in predatory publications.

McQuarrie, F., A. Kondra, and K. Lamertz. "Do Tenure and Promotion Policies Discourage Publications in Predatory Journals?" *Journal of Scholarly Publishing* 51, no. 3 (April 2020): 165–181. https://doi.org/10.3138/jsp.51.3.01.

Study found no guidelines discouraging publication in predatory journals.

Mertkan, S., G.O. Aliusta, and N. Suphi. "Profile of authors publishing in 'predatory' journals and causal factors behind their decision: A systematic review." *Research Evaluation* 30, no. 4 (October 2021): 470–483. https://doi.org/10.1093/reseval/rvab032.

Driving forces behind predatory journals are the "evaluation policies and publication pressure that emerge from the research environment."

Meyerowitz-Katz, G. "Is Ivermectin for Covid-19 Based on Fraudulent Research? Part 3." *Medium*, September 2, 2021. https://gidmk.medium.com/is-ivermectin-for-covid-19-based-on-fraudulent-research-part-3-5066aa6819b3.

"The journal the study is published in is about as predatory as journals get."

Moher, D., L. Shamseer, K. Cobey, M. Lalu, J. Galipeau, M. Avey, N. Ahmadzai, et al. "Stop this waste of people, animals and money." *Nature* 549 (September 7, 2017): 23–25. https://doi.org/10.1038/549023a.

Oreskes, N. "Predatory Journals That Publish Shoddy Research Put People's Lives at Risk." *Scientific American*, June 1, 2022. https://www.scientificamerican.com/article/predatory-journals-that-publish-shoddy-research-put-people-rsquo-s-lives-at-risk.

Pakpoor, J. "Homeopathy is not an effective treatment for any health condition, report concludes." *BMJ* 350 (2015): h1478. https://doi.org/10.1136/bmj.h1478.

"should not rely on homeopathy as a substitute for proven, effective treatments."

Pyne, D. "The Rewards of Predatory Publications at a Small Business School." *Journal of Scholarly Publishing* 48, no. 3 (April 2017): 137–160. http://dx.doi.org/10.3138/jsp.48.3.137.

Finds that publishing in predatory journals benefits careers.

Readfearn, G. "Murky world of 'science' journals a new frontier for climate deniers." *The Guardian*, January 24, 2018. https://www.theguardian.com/environment/planet-oz/2018/jan/24/murky-world-of-science-journals-a-new-frontier-for-climate-deniers.

Remler, D. "Are 90% of academic papers really never cited? Reviewing the literature on academic citations." London School of Economics blog, April 23, 2014. https://blogs.lse.ac.uk/impactofsocialsciences/2014/04/23/academic-papers-citation-rates-remler.

"'Only' 12% of medicine articles are not cited, compared to about 82% for the humanities."

Rice, D., B. Skidmore, and K. Cobey. "Dealing with predatory journal articles captured in systematic reviews." *Systematic Reviews* 10 (June 2021): article no. 175. https://doi.org/10.1186/s13643-021-01733-2.

"We suspect our experience encountering presumed predatory journals during the conduct of a systematic review is increasingly common."

Sabel, B., E. Knaack, G. Gigerenzer, and M. Bilc. "Fake Publications in Biomedical Science: Red-flagging Method Indicates Mass Production." Preprint. *medRxiv* (October 18, 2023). https://doi.org/10.1101/2023.05.06.23289563.

Study finds "a 2020 estimate of 28.8% RFPs" [red flagged publications] and puts value of predatory industry in billions.

Sattary, L. "Publishing pressure eroding research integrity." *Chemistry World*, April 28, 2010. https://www.chemistryworld.com/news/publishing-pressure -eroding-research-integrity/3003342.article.

Shah, W., R. Ali, and A. Lashari. "De-naturalizing the 'predatory': A study of 'bogus' publications at public sector universities in Pakistan." *Accountability in Research* 31, no. 2 (2024): 80–99. https://doi.org/10.1080/08989621 .2022.2106424.

"The study shows that 69% of the sample papers were published in predatory journals."

Simkin, M., and V. Roychowdhury, "Read Before You Cite!" *Complex Systems* 14 (2003): 269–274.

Spears, T. "Blinded by scientific gobbledygook." *Ottawa Citizen*, April 21, 2014. https://ottawacitizen.com/news/local-news/blinded-by-scientific-gobbledygook.

Spears, T. "Predatory science journals pivot to video." *Ottawa Citizen*, March 14, 2019. https://ottawacitizen.com/news/local-news/predatory-science-journals -pivot-to-video.

Teixeira da Silva, J. "An Alert to COVID-19 Literature in Predatory Publishing Venues." *Journal of Academic Librarianship* 45, no. 5 (September 2020): 102187. https://doi.org/10.1016%2Fj.acalib.2020.102187.

Tomlinson, O. "Predatory publishing in medical education: A rapid scoping review." *BMC Medical Education* 24 (January 5, 2024): article no. 33. https:// doi.org/10.1186/s12909-024-05024-x.

"There remains a lack of understanding of the threat that predatory publishers pose amongst medical students."

Vervoort, D. "Money down the drain: Predatory publishing in the COVID-19 era." *Canadian Journal of Public Health* 111, no. 5 (October 2020): 665–666. https://doi.org/10.17269%2Fs41997-020-00411-5.

Orgasm Shot?

Anderson, M., S. Fonnes, and J. Rosenberg. "Time from submission to publication varied widely for biomedical journals: A systematic review." *Current Medical Research and Opinion* 37, no. 6 (June 2021): 985–993. https://doi.org/10.1080/03007995.2021.1905622.

"The mean timespan from submission to publication varied from 91 to 639 days."

Gunter, J. "The O shot is untested with a sketchy past." *The Vajenda*, May 17, 2021. https://vajenda.substack.com/p/the-o-shot-is-untested-with-a-sketchy.

Shahinyan, G., J. Weinberger, R. Shahinyan, S. Yang, J. Mills, and S. Eleswarapu. "Analysis of Direct-to-Consumer Marketing of Platelet-Rich Plasma for Erectile Dysfunction in the US." *JAMA Network Open* 5, no. 5 (May 2022): e2214187. https://doi.org/10.1001%2Fjamanetworkopen.2022.14187.

"Despite a paucity of evidence for its use, PRP injections for the treatment of ED are offered at substantial cost."

Be Enraged

Yeo-Teh, N.S.L., and B.L. Tang. "Wilfully submitting to and publishing in predatory journals—a covert form of research misconduct?" *Biochemia Medica* 31, no. 3 (October 15, 2021): 030201. https://doi.org/10.11613/BM.2021.030201.

"Wait, I Published in a Hijacked Journal?"

Bohannon, J. "How to hijack a journal." *Science*, November 19, 2015. https://www.science.org/content/article/feature-how-hijack-journal.

". . . fraudsters are snatching entire Web addresses, known as Internet domains, right out from under academic publishers, erecting fake versions of their sites."

Brainard, J. "Leading scholarly database listed hundreds of papers from 'hijacked' journals." *Science*, December 5, 2023. https://www.science.org/content/article/leading-scholarly-database-listed-hundreds-papers-hijacked-journals.

Study finds Scopus contains papers, including medical research, for sixty-seven hijacked journals.

Moussa, S. "A 'Trojan horse' in the reference lists: Citations to a hijacked journal in SSCI-indexed marketing journals." *The Journal of Academic Librarianship* 47, no. 5 (September 2021): article no. 102388. https://doi.org/10.1016 /j.acalib.2021.102388.

Retraction Watch. "The Retraction Watch Hijacked Journal Checker." https://retractionwatch.com/the-retraction-watch-hijacked-journal-checker.

This resource, started in 2022, tracks hijacked journals.

Sevunts, L. "University of Calgary journal targeted by serial 'hijacker' of scientific publications." *CBC News*, May 16, 2019. https://www.cbc.ca/news/canada /calgary/arctic-journal-university-calgary-fake-publication-scam-1.5138488.

Create Your Own Science-y Journal!

Clarke, I. "How fake science websites hijack our trust in experts to misinform and confuse." *The Conversation*, September 12, 2022. https://theconversation.com /how-fake-science-websites-hijack-our-trust-in-experts-to-misinform-and -confuse-189730.

Nice review of the issue.

Readfearn, G. "Murky world of 'science' journals a new frontier for climate deniers." *The Guardian*, January 24, 2018. https://www.theguardian.com/environment /planet-oz/2018/jan/24/murky-world-of-science-journals-a-new-frontier-for -climate-deniers.

Review of questionable, fake, and predatory publishing in climate change space.

Salzberg, S. "Fake Medical Journals Are Spreading, and They Are Filled with Bad Science." *Forbes*, January 3, 2017. https://www.forbes.com/sites/stevensalzberg /2017/01/03/fake-medical-journals-are-spreading-and-they-are-filled-with -bad-science/?sh=43d242e130c9.

Review of "fake medical journals" filled with "complete and utter nonsense."

AI . . . Sigh. It Ain't Gonna Get Any Easier

Else, H. "Abstracts written by ChatGPT fool scientists." *Nature*, January 12, 2023. https://www.nature.com/articles/d41586-023-00056-7.

Source for quotation from Oxford's Sandra Wachter.

Fazackerley, A. "AI makes plagiarism harder to detect, argue academics—in paper written by chatbot." *The Guardian*, March 19, 2023. https://www.theguardian .com/technology/2023/mar/19/ai-makes-plagiarism-harder-to-detect-argue -academics-in-paper-written-by-chatbot.

Article on the academic paper written by AI about the challenges of AI writing academic papers.

Gao, C., F. Howard, N. Markov, E. Dyer, S. Ramesh, Y. Luo, and A. Pearson. "Comparing Scientific Abstracts Generated by ChatGPT to Original Abstracts Using an Artificial Intelligence Output Detector, Plagiarism Detector, and Blinded Human Reviewers." *npj Digital Medicine* 6 (April 2023): article no. 75. https://doi.org/10.1038/s41746-023-00819-6.

Stokel-Walker, C. "ChatGPT listed as author on research papers: Many scientists disapprove." *Nature*, January 18, 2023. https://www.nature.com/articles/d41586-023-00107-z.

"At least four articles credit the AI tool as a co-author."

Zombie Science

Candal-Pedreira, C., A. Ruano-Ravina, E. Fernández, J. Ramos, I. Campos-Varela, and M. Pérez-Ríos. "Does retraction after misconduct have an impact on citations? A pre–post study." *BMJ Global Health* 5, no. 11 (November 2020): e003719. https://doi.org/10.1136/bmjgh-2020-003719.

Study finds retractions have no impact on citation rate.

Candal-Pedreira, C., J. Ross, A. Ruano-Ravina, D. Egilman, E. Fernández, and M. Pérez-Ríos. "Retracted papers originating from paper mills: Cross sectional study." *BMJ* 379, no. 8363 (December 3, 2022). https://doi.org/10.1136/bmj-2022-071517.

"Papers retracted originating from paper mills are increasing in frequency."

Coudert, F. "Correcting the Scientific Record: Retraction Practices in Chemistry and Materials Science." *Chemistry of Materials* 31, no. 10 (May 28, 2019): 3593–3598. https://doi.org/10.1021/acs.chemmater.9b00897.

"median time to retraction in this data set is 24 months."

Davidson, M. "Vaccination as a cause of autism—myths and controversies." *Dialogues in Clinical Neuroscience* 19, no. 4 (December 2017): 403–407. https://doi.org/10.31887%2FDCNS.2017.19.4%2Fmdavidson.

Good summation of Wakefield debacle.

De Cassai, A., F. Geraldini, S. De Pinto, I. Carbonari, M. Cascella, A. Boscolo, N. Sella, et al. "Inappropriate Citation of Retracted Articles in Anesthesiology and Intensive Care Medicine Publications." *Anesthesiology* 137, no. 3 (September 2022): 341–350. https://doi.org/10.1097/ALN.0000000000004302.

"89% were unaware of the retracted status . . . "

De Vrieze, J. "Landmark research integrity survey finds questionable practices are surprisingly common." *Science*, July 7, 2021. https://www.science.org/content /article/landmark-research-integrity-survey-finds-questionable-practices-are -surprisingly-common.

8% of scientists admitted to research fraud.

Deer, B. "How the case against the MMR vaccine was fixed." *BMJ* 342, no. 7788 (January 8 2011): c5347. https://doi.org/10.1136/bmj.c5347.

Ecker, U., and L. Antonio. "Can you believe it? An investigation into the impact of retraction source credibility on the continued influence effect." *Memory & Cognition* 49, no. 4 (May 2021): 631–644. https://doi.org/10.3758/s13421-020 -01129-y.

Editors. "Zombie research haunts academic literature long after its supposed demise." *The Economist*, June 26, 2021. https://www.economist.com/graphic -detail/2021/06/26/zombie-research-haunts-academic-literature-long-after-its -supposed-demise.

Eggertson, L. "Lancet retracts 12-year-old article linking autism to MMR vaccines." *CMAJ* 182, no. 4 (March 9, 2010): e199–e200. https://doi.org /10.1503%2Fcmaj.109-3179.

Else, H. "Multimillion-dollar trade in paper authorships alarms publishers." *Nature*, January 18, 2023. https://www.nature.com/articles/d41586-023-00062-9.

"sleuths have uncovered hundreds of online advertisements that offer the chance to buy authorship on research papers to be published in reputable journals."

Greenhalgh, T. "Why did the *Lancet* take so long?" *BMJ* 340, no. 7741 (February 6, 2010): c644. https://doi.org/10.1136/bmj.c644.

Analysis of the Wakefield retraction.

Guillaume, L., and P. Bath. "A content analysis of mass media sources in relation to the MMR vaccine scare." *Health Informatics Journal* 14, no. 4 (December 2008): 323–334. https://doi.org/10.1177/1460458208096654.

"The retrieval of 227 articles that reported on the MMR vaccine from five sources during the 2 month sampling period."

Heibi, I., and S. Peroni. "A qualitative and quantitative analysis of open citations to retracted articles: The Wakefield 1998 et al.'s case." *Scientometrics* 126, no. 10 (October 2021): 8433–8470. https://doi.org/10.1007/s11192-021-04097-5.

Thorough analysis of how the Wakefield study is referenced in academic papers.

Hsiao, T., and J. Schneider. "Continued use of retracted papers: Temporal trends in citations and (lack of) awareness of retractions shown in citation contexts in biomedicine." *Quantitative Science Studies* 2, no. 4 (Fall 2021): 1144–1169. https://doi.org/10.1162/qss_a_00155.

"retracted papers in biomedicine were mostly retracted within 3 years after publication and continued to be cited after retraction." Only 5.4% of post retraction references acknowledge retraction.

Hussain, A., S. Ali, M. Ahmed, and S. Hussain. "The Anti-vaccination Movement: A Regression in Modern Medicine." *Cureus* 10, no. 7 (July 2018): e2919. https://doi.org/10.7759%2Fcureus.2919.

Good review of surge of anti-vaccine movement and Wakefield's role.

Knox, D., and J. Mummolo, "A widely touted study found no evidence of racism in police shootings. It's full of errors." *The Washington Post*, July 15, 2020. https://www.washingtonpost.com/outlook/2020/07/15/police-shooting-study-retracted.

Meyerowitz-Katz, G., P. Sekhar, L. Besançon, T. Turner, and S. McDonald. "The Citation of Retracted COVID-19 Papers Is Common and Rarely Critical." Preprint. *medRxiv* (2022). https://doi.org/10.1101/2022.06.30.22277084.

"citation of retracted and withdrawn COVID-19 clinical studies is common."

Motta, M., and D. Stecula. "Quantifying the effect of Wakefield et al. (1998) on skepticism about MMR vaccine safety in the U.S." *PLoS ONE* 16, no. 8 (August 2021): e0256395. https://doi.org/10.1371/journal.pone.0256395.

"Vaccine skepticism increased following the publication of AW98."

Peng, H., D. Romero, and E. Horvát. "Dynamics of cross-platform attention to retracted papers." *PNAS* 119, no. 25 (June 14, 2022): e2119086119. https://doi.org/10.1073/pnas.2119086119.

"findings reveal the extent to which retracted papers are discussed on different online platforms."

Suelzer, E., J. Deal, K. Hanus, B. Ruggeri, R. Sieracki, and E. Witkowski. "Assessment of Citations of the Retracted Article by Wakefield et al with Fraudulent Claims of an Association between Vaccination and Autism." *JAMA Network Open* 2, no. 11 (2019): e1915552. https://doi.org/10.1001/jamanetworkopen.2019.15552.

"A significant number of authors did not document retractions of the article."

Thorp, H. "Rethinking the retraction process." *Science* 377, no. 6608 (August 18, 2022): 793. https://doi.org/10.1126/science.ade3742.

"these investigations should be a two-stage process."

II: The Goodness Illusion

Health Halos

Basker, D. "Comparison of taste quality between organically and conventionally grown fruits and vegetables." *American Journal of Alternative Agriculture* 7, no. 3 (1992): 129–136. https://doi.org/10.1017/S0889189300004641.

"No consistent preference pattern emerged."

Bernard, J., and Y. Liu. "Are beliefs stronger than taste? A field experiment on organic and local apples." *Food Quality and Preference* 61 (October 2017): 55–62. https://doi.org/10.1016/j.foodqual.2017.05.005.

"beliefs about how organic and local foods taste can play a stronger role in taste perceptions."

Bratanova, B., C. Vauclair, N. Kervyn, S. Schumann, R. Wood, and O. Klein. "Savouring morality. Moral satisfaction renders food of ethical origin subjectively tastier." *Appetite* 91 (August 1, 2015): 137–149. https://doi.org /10.1016/j.appet.2015.04.006.

"Moral satisfaction renders the taste of ethical food subjectively superior."

Budhathoki, M., A. Zølner, T. Nielsen, and H. Reinbach. "The role of production method information on sensory perception of smoked salmon—A mixed-method study from Denmark." *Food Quality Preference* 94 (December 2021): article no. 104325. https://doi.org/10.1016/j.foodqual.2021.104325.

Dasha, S., J. Olson, Ellen Langer, and M. Roy. "Presenting a sham treatment as personalised increases the placebo effect in a randomised controlled trial." *eLife* 12 (July 5, 2023): e84691. https://doi.org/10.7554/eLife.84691.

"Participants told that the machine was personalised reported more relief in pain intensity than the control group."

Harris, J., K.S. Haraghey, M. Lodolce, and N.L. Semenza. "Teaching children about good health? Halo effects in child-directed advertisements for unhealthy food." *Pediatric Obesity* 13, no. 4 (April 2018): 256–264. https://doi.org/10.1111/ijpo.12257.

"Children in the health halo condition rated the advertised nutrient-poor products as significantly healthier compared with children in other conditions."

Her, E., and S. Seo. "Health halo effects in sequential food consumption: The moderating roles of health-consciousness and attribute framing." *International Journal of Hospitality Management* 62 (April 2017): 1–10. https://psycnet.apa.org/doi/10.1016/j.ijhm.2016.11.009.

"effect of the perceived healthiness of entrées on increasing the intention for desserts."

Katz, S., A. Peterson, E. Cohen, and D. Hatsukami. "Tobacco Free Nicotine Vaping Products: A Study of Health Halo Effects Among Middle School Youth." *Journal of Health Communication* 28, no. 6 (June 3, 2023): 391–400. https://doi.org/10.1080/10810730.2023.2217431.

"the term tobacco-free nicotine triggers inaccurate nicotine content beliefs."

Klein, N., and E. O'Brien. "People use less information than they think to make up their minds." *PNAS* 115, no. 52 (December 26, 2018): 13222–13227. https://doi.org/10.1073/pnas.1805327115.

Kresova, S., D. Gutjahr, and S. Hess. "German consumer evaluations of milk in blind and nonblind tests." *Journal of Dietary Science* 105, no. 4 (April 2022): 2988–3003. https://doi.org/10.3168/jds.2021-20708.

"the taste of organic milk during the blind tasting was given a lower rating."

Toschi, T., A. Bendini, S. Barbieri, E. Valli, M.L. Cezanne, K. Buchecker, and M. Canavari. "Organic and conventional nonflavored yogurts from the Italian market: Study on sensory profiles and consumer acceptability." *Journal of the Science of Food and Agriculture* 92, no. 14 (November 2012): 2788–2795. https://doi.org/10.1002/jsfa.5666.

"the most liked conventional yogurt scored higher when labeled as organic."

The Devious Dozen

Banse, T. "Frozen Seafood Performs Better Than Fresh in OSU Taste Test." Oregon Public Broadcasting, November 7, 2019. https://www.opb.org/news/article/seafood-fish-fresh-frozen-oregon-state-taste-test.

Berry, C., and M. Romero. "The fair trade food labeling health halo: Effects of fair trade labeling on consumption and perceived healthfulness." *Food Quality and Preference* 94, no. 2 (December 2021): article no. 104321. http://dx.doi.org/10.1016/j.foodqual.2021.104321.

Caulfield, T. "The Problem with Personalized Health." *Policy Options*, December 9, 2019. https://policyoptions.irpp.org/magazines/december-2019/the-problem-with-personalized-health-information.

I draw on this piece for this section.

Deleniv, S., D. Ariely, and K. Peters. "'Natural Is Better': How the Appeal to Nature Fallacy Derails Public Health." *Behavioural Scientist*, March 8, 2021. https://behavioralscientist.org/natural-is-better-how-the-naturalistic-fallacy-derails-public-health.

Good review of the literature.

Enthoven, L., and G. Van den Broeck. "Local food systems: Reviewing two decades of research." *Agricultural Systems* 193 (October 2021): article no. 103226. https://doi.org/10.1016/j.agsy.2021.103226.

Excellent review of science that notes value of local is complex and not always beneficial.

Fan, X., M. Gómez, and P. Coles. "Willingness to Pay, Quality Perception, and Local Foods: The Case of Broccoli." *Agricultural and Resource Economics Review* 48, no. 3 (December 2019): 414–432. https://doi.org/10.1017/age .2019.21.

Fernan, C., J. Schuldt, and J. Niederdeppe. "Health Halo Effects from Product Titles and Nutrient Content Claims in the Context of 'Protein' Bars." *Health Communication* 33, no. 12 (December 2018): 1425–1433. https://doi.org /10.1080/10410236.2017.1358240.

". . . only the product title [protein] condition increased overall perceptions of product healthfulness."

Ferreira, C., F. Lopes, R. Costa, N. Komora, V. Ferreira, V. Cruz Fernandes, C. Delerue-Matos, and P. Teixeira. "Microbiological and Chemical Quality of Portuguese Lettuce—Results of a Case Study." *Foods* 9, no. 9 (September 2020): 1274. https://doi.org/10.3390/foods9091274.

Organic not found to be better.

Food and Agriculture Organization of the United Nations. "Genetically modified crops: Safety, benefits, risks and global status." FAO, 2022. https://www.fao.org /3/cb8375en/cb8375en.pdf.

"GM crops that are approved are safe."

García-Barrón, S., A. Gutiérrez-Salomón, J. Jaimez-Ordaz, and S. Villanueva -Rodríguez. "Influence of expectations on the level of liking of a local coffee in Mexico." *Journal of the Science of Food and Agriculture* 101, no. 4 (March 15, 2021): 1572–1578. https://doi.org/10.1002/jsfa.10776.

Gardner, C., J. Trepanowski, L. Del Gobbo, M. Hauser, J. Rigdon, J. Ioannidis, M. Desai, and A. King. "Effect of Low-Fat vs Low-Carbohydrate Diet on 12-Month Weight Loss in Overweight Adults and the Association with Genotype Pattern or Insulin Secretion: The DIETFITS Randomized Clinical Trial." *JAMA* 319, no. 7 (February 20, 2018): 667–679. https://doi.org/10.1001 /jama.2018.0245.

"no significant difference in weight change."

Gundala, R., and A. Singh. "What motivates consumers to buy organic foods? Results of an empirical study in the United States." *PLoS ONE* 16, no. 9 (September 10, 2021): e0257288. https://doi.org/10.1371/journal.pone.0257288.

"Healthy" by far the biggest factor.

Hallez, L., H. Vansteenbeeck, F. Boen, and T. Smits. "Persuasive packaging? The impact of packaging color and claims on young consumers' perceptions of product healthiness, sustainability and tastiness." *Appetite* 182 (March 1, 2023): article no. 106433. https://doi.org/10.1016/j.appet.2022.106433.

"cool packaging colors (i.e., green and blue) increased perceptions that food and drinks were healthy."

Holzapfel, C., C. Dawczynski, A. Henze, and M.C. Simon. "Personalized dietary recommendations for weight loss." *Ernahrungs Umschau international* 68, no. 2 (February 15, 2021): 26–35. https://doi.org/10.4455/eu.2021.008.

Iwata, K., T. Fukuchi, and K. Yoshimura. "Is the Quality of Sushi Ruined by Freezing Raw Fish and Squid? A Randomized Double-Blind Trial with Sensory Evaluation Using Discrimination Testing." *Clinical Infectious Diseases* 60, no. 9 (May 1, 2015): e43–e48. https://doi.org/10.1093/cid/civ057.

"Freezing raw fish did not ruin sushi's taste."

Kennedy, B., and C. Thigpen. "Many publics around world doubt safety of genetically modified foods." Pew Research Center, November 11, 2020. https://www.pewresearch.org/short-reads/2020/11/11/many-publics-around-world-doubt-safety-of-genetically-modified-foods.

48% say GM foods unsafe.

Kim, S., and R. Huang. "Understanding local food consumption from an ideological perspective: Locavorism, authenticity, pride, and willingness to visit." *Journal of Retailing and Consumer Services* 58 (January 2021): article no. 102330. https://doi.org/10.1016/j.jretconser.2020.102330.

Outlines the characteristics of the locavorism trend (i.e., lionization, opposition, and communalization).

Kim, Y., S. Kim, and N. Arora. "GMO Labeling Policy and Consumer Choice." *Journal of Marketing* 86, no. 3 (May 2022): 21–39. https://doi.org/10.1177/00222429211064901.

"labeling regimes reduce the market share of GM foods."

Kyle, T. "Does a Cultural Icon Need a 'Healthy' Logo?" *ConscienHealth*, January 23, 2023. https://conscienhealth.org/2023/01/does-a-cultural-icon-need-a-healthy-logo.

Lindberg, K., T. Bjørnsen, F. Vårvik, G. Paulsen, M. Joensen, M. Kristoffersen, O. Sveen, et al. "The effects of being told you are in the intervention group on training results: A pilot study." *Scientific Reports* 13 (February 3, 2023): article no. 1972. https://doi.org/10.1038/s41598-023-29141-7.

"the placebo effect may be meaningful in sports and exercise training interventions."

Lordan, R. "Dietary supplements and nutraceuticals market growth during the coronavirus pandemic—Implications for consumers and regulatory oversight." *PharmaNutrition* 18 (December 2021): article no. 100282. https://doi.org/10.1016%2Fj.phanu.2021.100282.

Huge market increase during pandemic due, in part, to a belief in immune boosting.

Lusk, J., and B. Ellison. "Who is to blame for the rise in obesity?" *Appetite* 68 (September 2013): 14–20. https://doi.org/10.1016/j.appet.2013.04.001.

"Eighty percent said individuals were primarily to blame for obesity."

Meier, B., and C. Lappas. "The Influence of Safety, Efficacy, and Medical Condition Severity on Natural versus Synthetic Drug Preference." *Medical Decision Making* 36, no. 8 (November 2016): 1011–1019. https://doi.org/10.1177/0272989x15621877.

Study demonstrated a strong preference for "natural" drugs.

National Academies of Sciences, Engineering, and Medicine. *Genetically Engineered Crops: Experiences and Prospects.* The National Academies Press, 2016. https://doi.org/10.17226/23395.

Nestle, M. "FDA's plan to define 'healthy' for food packaging: Better than the existing labeling anarchy, but do we really need it?" *STAT*, October 7, 2022. https://www.statnews.com/2022/10/07/fda-plan-define-healthy-label-food-packaging.

Nowell, C. "Is eating local produce actually better for the planet?" *The Guardian*, June 7, 2023. https://www.theguardian.com/environment/2023/jun/07/is-eating-local-better-environment.

"only 1% to 9% of food's emissions come from packaging, transport and retail."

Okada, E. "Justification Effects on Consumer Choice of Hedonic and Utilitarian Goods." *Journal of Marketing Research* 42, no. 1 (February 2005): 43–53. https://doi.org/10.1509/jmkr.42.1.43.56889.

"utilitarian alternative tends to be chosen over the hedonic alternative when the two are presented jointly."

Oselinsky, K., A. Johnson, P. Lundeberg, A. Johnson Holm, M. Mueller, and
D. Graham. "GMO Food Labels Do Not Affect College Student Food
Selection, Despite Negative Attitudes towards GMOs." *International Journal
of Environmental Research and Public Health* 18, no. 4 (February 2021): 1761.
https://doi.org/10.3390%2Fijerph18041761.

Most think a GMO label means the food is dangerous.

Palmieri, N., M. Simeone, C. Russo, and M. Perito. "Profiling young consumers'
perceptions of GMO products: A case study on Italian undergraduate
students." *International Journal of Gastronomy and Food Science* 21
(October 2020): article no. 100224. https://doi.org/10.1016/j.ijgfs.2020.100224.

Peloza, J., C. Ye, and W. Montford. "When Companies Do Good, Are Their
Products Good for You? How Corporate Social Responsibility Creates a
Health Halo." *Journal of Public Policy & Marketing* 34, no. 1 (April 2015):
19–31. https://doi.org/10.1509/jppm.13.037.

Study found that a corporate responsibility health halo can lead consumers
to overconsume calories.

Poore, J., and T. Nemecek. "Reducing food's environmental impacts through
producers and consumers." *Science* 360, no. 6392 (June 1, 2018): 987–992.
https://doi.org/10.1126/science.aaq0216.

Comprehensive analysis of food systems.

Popp, C., L. Hu, A. Kharmats, M. Curran, L. Berube, C. Wang, M. Pompeii, et al.
"Effect of a Personalized Diet to Reduce Postprandial Glycemic Response vs
a Low-fat Diet on Weight Loss in Adults with Abnormal Glucose Metabolism
and Obesity." *JAMA Network Open* 5, no. 9 (September 1, 2022): e2233760.
https://doi.org/10.1001/jamanetworkopen.2022.33760.

"Precision nutrition intervention" did not lead to more weight loss.

Purdue University. "Do GMOs Harm Health? Interview with Dr. Peter
Goldsbrough, Professor of Botany and Plant Pathology at Purdue University."
February 27, 2020. https://ag.purdue.edu/gmos/gmos-health.html.

Rachul, C., A. Marcon, B. Collins, and T. Caulfield. "COVID-19 and 'immune boosting' on the internet: A content analysis of Google search results." *BMJ Open* 10,
no. 10 (October 2020): e040989. https://doi.org/10.1136/bmjopen-2020-040989.

Our study that found a high degree of misleading claims.

Reuters. "French baguette gains place on World Cultural Heritage list to bakers'
delight." November 30, 2022. https://www.reuters.com/lifestyle/french
-baguette-makes-it-onto-world-cultural-heritage-list-2022-11-30.

UNESCO "voted to include the 'artisanal know-how and culture of baguette bread' on its list of Intangible Cultural Heritage."

Román, S., L. Sánchez-Siles, and M. Siegrist. "The importance of food naturalness for consumers: Results of a systematic review." *Trends in Food Science & Technology* 67 (September 2017): 44–57. https://doi.org/10.1016/j.tifs.2017.06.010.

"Food naturalness is very important for consumers."

Sax, J., and N. Doran. "Food Labeling and Consumer Associations with Health, Safety, and Environment." *Journal of Law, Medicine, and Ethics* 44, no. 4 (December 2016): 630–635. https://doi.org/10.1177/1073110516684805.

GMO labels consumers think product unhealthy and bad for environment.

Szczech, M., B. Kowalska, U. Smolinska, and R. Maciorowski. "Microbial quality of organic and conventional vegetables from Polish farms." *International Journal of Food Microbiology* 286, no. 9 (August 2018): 155–161. http://dx.doi.org/10.1016/j.ijfoodmicro.2018.08.018.

"significantly higher load of E. coli than from conventional farms."

Watson, E. "87% of consumers globally think non-GMO is 'healthier.' But where's the evidence?" *Food Navigator USA*, August 12, 2015. https://www.foodnavigator-usa.com/Article/2015/08/13/87-of-consumers-globally-think-non-GMO-is-healthier.

Pets Too

Albizuri, S., A. Grandal-d'Anglade, J. Maroto, M. Oliva, A. Rodíguez, N. Terrats, A. Palomo, and F.J. López-Cachero. "Dogs That Ate Plants: Changes in the Canine Diet during the Late Bronze Age and the First Iron Age in the Northeast Iberian Peninsula." *Journal of World Prehistory* 34 (2021): 75–119. https://doi.org/10.1007/s10963-021-09153-9.

Association for Pet Obesity Prevention. *2021 Surveys and Data.* https://www.petobesityprevention.org/2021.

Banton, S., A. Baynham, J. Pezzali, M. von Massow, and A. Shoveller. "Grains on the brain: A survey of dog owner purchasing habits related to grain-free dry dog foods." *PLoS ONE* 16, no. 5 (May 19, 2021): e0250806. https://doi.org/10.1371/journal.pone.0250806.

Study explores how people chose pet's food and found it's often influenced by owner's diet.

Brown, K. "More Dog Owners Are Questioning Vaccines Like Rabies after Covid." *Bloomberg*, August 28, 2023. https://www.bloomberg.com/news/articles/2023 -08-28/more-us-dog-owners-question-rabies-vaccines-amid-post-covid-anti -vaccine-wave.

Burns, K. "Banfield: Few pets allergic to food; flea, environmental allergies rise." American Veterinary Medical Association, June 27, 2018. https://www.avma.org /javma-news/2018-07-15/banfield-few-pets-allergic-food-flea-environmental -allergies-rise.

Report on Banfield Pet Hospital study.

Consumer Affairs Research Team. "Millennials prefer pets to children (Survey)." Consumer Affairs, May 17, 2022. https://www.consumeraffairs.com/pets /pets-are-family.html.

Many pet owners prefer pets to humans.

Dodd, S., N. Cave, S. Abood, A. Shoveller, J. Adolphe, and A. Verbrugghe. "An observational study of pet feeding practices and how these have changed between 2008 and 2018." *Vet Record* 186, no. 19 (June 27, 2020): 643. https://doi.org/10.1136/vr.105828.

Pets are increasingly fed homemade food.

Freeman, L., J. Stern, R. Fries, D. Adin, and J. Rush. "Diet-associated dilated cardiomyopathy in dogs: What do we know?" *Journal of the American Veterinary Medical Association* 253, 11 (December 1, 2018): 1390–1394. https://doi.org/10.2460/javma.253.11.1390.

Heinze, C. "Should you make your own pet food at home?" *Petfoodology*, Cummings School of Veterinary Medicine, July 14, 2016. https://vetnutrition .tufts.edu/2016/07/should-you-make-your-own-pet-food-at-home.

Joyner, L. "A third of pet owners prefer pets to their children, new study has found." *Country Living*, September 14, 2019. https://www.countryliving.com/uk /wildlife/pets/a29030663/pet-owners-prefer-pets-to-children.

68% said they see their pets as people.

Levin, J., A. Arluke, and L. Irvine. "Are People More Disturbed by Dog or Human Suffering?" *Animal & Society* 25, no. 1 (April 2017): 1–16. https://doi.org/10.1163/15685306-12341440.

In general, people had more empathy for puppies than for adult humans.

Mueller, R., T. Olivry, and P. Prélaud. "Critically appraised topic on adverse food reactions of companion animals (2): Common food allergen sources in dogs and cats." *BMC Veterinary Research* 12 (January 12, 2016): article no. 9. https:// doi.org/10.1186/s12917-016-0633-8.

Olivry, T., and R. Mueller. "Critically appraised topic on adverse food reactions of companion animals (5): Discrepancies between ingredients and labeling in commercial pet foods." *BMC Veterinary Research* 14 (January 22, 2018): article no. 24. https://doi.org/10.1186/s12917-018-1346-y.

"The mislabeling of pet foods appears rather common."

Olivry, T., and R. Mueller. "Critically appraised topic on adverse food reactions of companion animals (3): Prevalence of cutaneous adverse food reactions in dogs and cats." *BMC Veterinary Research* 13 (2017): article no. 51. https://doi .org/10.1186/s12917-017-0973-z.

Prevalence of food allergies between approximately 1–2% for dogs and less than 1% for cats.

Prantil, L., C. Heinze, and L. Freeman. "Comparison of carbohydrate content between grain-containing and grain-free dry cat diets and between reported and calculated carbohydrate values." *Journal of Feline Medicine and Surgery* 20, no. 4 (April 2018): 349–355. https://doi.org/10.1177/1098612X17710842.

Carbohydrate content "varied widely."

Stockman, T., A. Fascetti, and P. Kass. "Evaluation of recipes of home-prepared maintenance diets for dogs." *Journal of the American Veterinary Medical Association* 242, no. 11 (June 1, 2013): 1500–1505. https://doi.org/10.2460 /javma.242.11.1500.

Superspreader. Directed by Lora Moftah, reported by Rachel Abrams and Jan Hoffman. New York: *New York Times*, 2022.

U.S. Food and Drug Administration. "Get the Facts! Raw Pet Food Diets Can Be Dangerous to You and Your Pet." February 22, 2018. https://www.fda.gov /animal-veterinary/animal-health-literacy/get-facts-raw-pet-food-diets-can -be-dangerous-you-and-your-pet.

Clean Beauty

Cancer Research UK. "Can cosmetics cause cancer?" November 12, 2020. https://www.cancerresearchuk.org/about-cancer/causes-of-cancer/cancer -myths/cosmetics.

Concludes parabens do not cause cancer.

Dodson, R., K. Boronow, H. Susmann, J. Udesky, K. Rodgers, D. Weller, M. Woudneh, et al. "Consumer behavior and exposure to parabens, bisphenols, triclosan, dichlorophenols, and benzophenone-3: Results from a crowd-sourced biomonitoring study." *International Journal of Hygiene and*

Environmental Health 230 (September 2020): article no. 113624. https://doi
.org/10.1016/j.ijheh.2020.113624.

Found efforts to avoid certain ingredients had measurable impact.

Hujoel, P., M. Hujoel, and G. Kotsakis. "Personal oral hygiene and dental caries:
A systematic review of randomised controlled trials." *Gerodontology* 35, no. 4
(December 2018): 282–289. https://doi.org/10.1111/ger.12331.

Fluoride-free toothpaste has no health benefits.

Jones, O. "What is a paraben and why are so many products advertised as
'paraben-free'?" *The Conversation*, March 27, 2023. https://theconversation
.com/what-is-a-paraben-and-why-are-so-many-products-advertised-as
-paraben-free-198994.

"As a chemist I think parabens are well-researched, safe and necessary."

Liberman, A. "The unadulterated truth about the history of the word 'clean.'"
Oxford University Press blog, August 3, 2016. https://blog.oup.com/2016/08
/etymology-word-clean.

McDonald, J., A. Llanos, T. Morton, and A. Zota. "The Environmental Injustice
of Beauty Products: Toward Clean and Equitable Beauty." *American Journal
of Public Health* 112, no. 1 (January 2022): 50–53. https://www.ncbi.nlm.nih
.gov/pmc/articles/PMC8713635.

Notes both huge price premium of clean products and potential for
beneficial safety advocacy.

Mandell, J. "Shaky science led to a rush of 'paraben-free' beauty products.
But they might not be safer." *Washington Post*, February 15, 2022.
https://www.washingtonpost.com/wellness/2022/02/15/paraben-free
-unsafe-clean-beauty.

Nice review of parabens controversy.

Novakovich, J. "A critical look at the 'clean' beauty movement." The Eco Well
blog, September 21, 2020. https://www.theecowell.com/blog/clean
-beauty.

O'Brien, K., S. Tworoger, H. Harris, G. Anderson, C. Weinberg, B. Trabert,
A. Kaunitz, et al. "Association of Powder Use in the Genital Area with Risk of
Ovarian Cancer." *JAMA* 323, no. 1 (January 7, 2020): 49–59. https://doi.org
/10.1001/jama.2019.20079.

Petric, Z., J. Ružić, and I. Žuntar. "The controversies of parabens—an overview
nowadays." *Acta Pharmaceutica* 71, no. 1 (March 2021): 17–32. https://doi.org
/10.2478/acph-2021-0001.

"Many studies have demonstrated that parabens are non-teratogenic, non-mutagenic, non-carcinogenic and the real evidence for their toxicity in humans has not been established."

Petruzzi, D. "What clean beauty means to women?" Statista, May 2019. https://www.statista.com/statistics/1133211/perception-of-clean-beauty-among-consumers-worldwide.

58% think clean beauty means "natural."

Rivera-Núñez, Z., C. Kinkade, Y. Zhang, A. Rockson, E. Bandera, A. Llanos, and E. Barrett. "Phenols, Parabens, Phthalates and Puberty: A Systematic Review of Synthetic Chemicals Commonly Found in Personal Care Products and Girls' Pubertal Development." *Current Environmental Health Reports* 9, no. 4 (December 2022): 517–534. https://doi.org/10.1007/s40572-022-00366-4.

Review of evidence.

Rubin, C., and B. Brod. "Natural Does Not Mean Safe—The Dirt on Clean Beauty Products." *JAMA Dermatology* 155, no. 12 (December 2019): 1344–1345. https://doi.org/10.1001/jamadermatol.2019.2724.

Schwarcz, J. "Paraben Phobia Is Unjustified." McGill Office of Science and Society, March 20, 2017. https://www.mcgill.ca/oss/article/cancer-controversial-science-cosmetics-health-news-quackery-toxicity/joe-schwarczs-right-chemistry-paraben-phobia-unjustified.

"The demonization of synthetic preservatives has led not only to the glorification of less-effective natural products but to a host of 'preservative-free' ones as well."

Sicurella, S. "'Clean' Beauty Products Are a Marketing Triumph." NPR, July 12, 2021. https://www.npr.org/2021/07/12/1012666138/clean-beauty-products-are-a-marketing-triumph.

Tran, J., J. Comstock, and M. Reeder. "Natural Is Not Always Better: The Prevalence of Allergenic Ingredients in 'Clean' Beauty Products." *Dermatitis* 33, no. 3 (May–June 202): 215–219. https://doi.org/10.1097/der.0000000000000863.

Study found most "clean" products have allergenic ingredients.

U.S. Food and Drug Administration. "Parabens in Cosmetics." February 25, 2022. https://www.fda.gov/cosmetics/cosmetic-ingredients/parabens-cosmetics.

Wentzensen, N., and K. O'Brien. "Talc, body powder, and ovarian cancer: A summary of the epidemiologic evidence." *Gynecologic Oncology* 163, no. 1 (October 2021): 199–208. https://doi.org/10.1016/j.ygyno.2021.07.032.

"Genital powder use shows a weak association with ovarian cancer risk."

Who Could Be Against Safe and Sustainable?

Shackel, N. "Motte and Bailey Doctrines." Oxford University Practical Ethics, September 5, 2014. https://blog.practicalethics.ox.ac.uk/2014/09/motte-and -bailey-doctrines.

The author of the motte and bailey explains that it is really a doctrine and not a logical fallacy. I understand and agree, but since it is so commonly now called a fallacy, that is what I use.

Ancient Aliens, Wishful Thinking, and Goodness Bias

Bellos, I. "A metaresearch study revealed susceptibility of Covid-19 treatment research to white hat bias: First, do no harm." *Journal of Clinical Epidemiology* 136 (August 2021): 55–63. https://doi.org/10.1016%2Fj.jclinepi.2021.03.020.

"study raises concerns about citation bias and a predilection of reporting beneficial over harmful effects in the Covid-19 treatment research, potentially in the context of white hat bias."

Bond, S. "Pseudoarchaeology and the Racism behind Ancient Aliens." *Hyperallergic*, November 13, 2018. https://hyperallergic.com/470795 /pseudoarchaeology-and-the-racism-behind-ancient-aliens.

Cope, M., and D. Allison. "White Hat Bias: Examples of Its Presence in Obesity Research and a Call for Renewed Commitment to Faithfulness in Research Reporting." *International Journal of Obesity* 34, no. 1 (January 2010): 83–84. https://doi.org/10.1038%2Fijo.2009.239.

Paper in which term "white hat bias" was coined.

Gedin, F., S. Blomé, and M. Pontén. "Placebo Response and Media Attention in Randomized Clinical Trials Assessing Cannabis-Based Therapies for Pain." *JAMA Network Open* 5, no. 11 (November 28, 2022): e2243848. https://doi.org /10.1001/jamanetworkopen.2022.43848.

Halmhofer, S. "Did Aliens Build the Pyramids? And Other Racist Theories." *Sapiens*, October 5, 2021. https://www.sapiens.org/archaeology /pseudoarchaeology-racism.

Harrison, G. "Why Do People Keep Boarding the Chariots of the Gods?" *Psychology Today*, July 24, 2020. https://www.psychologytoday.com/intl/blog/about -thinking/202007/why-do-people-keep-boarding-the-chariots-the-gods.

Good review of survey data.

Orth, T. "A growing share of Americans believe aliens are responsible for UFOs." YouGov, October 4, 2022. https://today.yougov.com/technology/articles/43959 -more-half-americans-believe-aliens-probably-exist.

Survey data on belief in aliens.

Riekki, T., et al. "Paranormal and Religious Believers Are More Prone to Illusory Face Perception Than Skeptics and Non-believers." *Applied Cognitive Psychology* 27, no. 2 (March–April 2013): 150–155. https://doi.org/10.1002/acp.2874.

Spiritual people are more likely to see faces in patterns.

Sacco, D., M. Brown, and S. Bruton. "Grounds for Ambiguity: Justifiable Bases for Engaging in Questionable Research Practices." *Science and Engineering Ethics* 25 (October 2019): 1321–1337. https://doi.org/10.1007/s11948-018-0065-x.

Questionable research practices are viewed as more defensible when paired with justifiable goal.

Turpin, M., M. Kara-Yakoubian, A. Walker, N. Gabert, J. Fugelsang, and J. Stolz. "Bullshit Makes the Art Grow Profounder." *Judgment and Decision Making* 14, no. 6 (November 2019): 658–670. http://journal.sjdm.org/vol14.6.html.

Walker, A., M. Turpin, J. Stolz, J. Fugelsang, and D. Koehler. "Finding meaning in the clouds: Illusory pattern perception predicts receptivity to pseudo -profound bullshit." *Judgment and Decision Making* 14, no. 2 (March 2019): 109–119. https://doi.org/10.1017/S193029750000334X.

Wang, M., M. Bolland, G. Gamble, and A. Grey. "Media Coverage, Journal Press Releases and Editorials Associated with Randomized and Observational Studies in High-Impact Medical Journals: A Cohort Study." *PLoS ONE* 10, no. 12 (December 23, 2015): e0145294. https://doi.org/10.1371/journal.pone.0145294.

Quality of research has no impact on press coverage.

Zenone, M., J. Snyder, and T. Caulfield. "Crowdfunding Cannabidiol (CBD) for Cancer: Hype and Misinformation on GoFundMe." *American Journal of Public Health* 110, suppl. 3 (October 2020): s294–s299. https://doi.org /10.2105%2FAJPH.2020.305768.

Manly Men

American Psychological Association, Boys and Men Guidelines Group. *APA guidelines for psychological practice with boys and men.* August 2018. http:// www.apa.org/about/policy/psychological-practice-boys-men-guidelines.pdf.

Excellent review of connection between masculine norms and health and mental health issues.

Ellwood, B. "Multi-country study finds cultural values of collectivism and masculinity are tied to belief in conspiracy theories." *PsyPost*, May 12, 2021. https://www.psypost.org/multi-country-study-finds-cultural-values-of-collectivism-and-masculinity-are-tied-to-belief-in-conspiracy-theories.

Good summary of study on masculine norms and conspiracy theories.

Fleming, P., J. Lee, and S. Dworkin. "'Real Men Don't': Constructions of Masculinity and Inadvertent Harm in Public Health Interventions." *American Journal of Public Health* 104, no. 6 (June 2014): 1029–1035. https://doi.org/10.2105%2FAJPH.2013.301820.

Paper explores problems of reifying masculine norms in public health campaigns.

Giaccardi, S., L.M. Ward, R. Seabrook, and A. Manago. "Media Use and Men's Risk Behaviors: Examining the Role of Masculinity Ideology." *Sex Roles* 77, no. 1 (November 2017): 581–592. https://link.springer.com/article/10.1007/s11199-017-0754-y.

Media use associated with "stronger endorsement of masculinity ideology."

Heilman, B., and G. Barker. *Masculine Norms and Violence: Making the Connections*. (Promundo-US, 2018). https://www.equimundo.org/resources/masculine-norms-violence-making-connections.

Good overview of broader social implications.

Herreen, D., S. Rice, D. Currier, M. Schlichthorst, and I. Zajac. "Associations between conformity to masculine norms and depression: Age effects from a population study of Australian men." *BMC Psychology* 9 (2021): article no. 32. https://doi.org/10.1186/s40359-021-00533-6.

Horowitz, J. "Americans' views on masculinity differ by party, gender and race." Pew Research Center, January 23, 2019. https://www.pewresearch.org/short-reads/2019/01/23/americans-views-on-masculinity-differ-by-party-gender-and-race.

Iacoviello V., G. Valsecchi, J. Berent, I. Borinca, and J. Falomir-Pichastor. "Is Traditional Masculinity Still Valued?" *The Journal of Men's Studies* 30, no. 1 (March 2022): 7–27. https://doi.org/10.1177/10608265211018803.

"Participants in both experiments perceived traditional masculinity as being valued by other men."

King, T., M. Shields, V. Sojo, G. Daraganova, D. Currier, A. O'Neil, K. King, and A. Milner. "Expressions of masculinity and associations with suicidal ideation among young males." *BMC Psychiatry* 20 (2020): article no. 228. https://doi.org/10.1186/s12888-020-2475-y.

Levant, R., R. C. McDermott, and J. Barinas. "Masculinity and Compliance with Centers for Disease Control and Prevention Recommended Health Practices during the COVID-19 Pandemic." *Health Psychology* 41, no. 2 (February 2022): 94–103. https://psycnet.apa.org/doi/10.1037/hea0001119.

Traditional masculine ideology "was indirectly and inversely related to CDC adherence through conformity to playboy norms."

Lokeshwar, S., P. Patel, R. Fantus, J. Halpern, C. Chang, A. Kargi, and R. Ramasamy. "Decline in Serum Testosterone Levels among Adolescent and Young Adult Men in the USA." *European Urology Focus* 7, no. 4 (July 2021): 886–889. https://doi.org/10.1016/j.euf.2020.02.006.

McGraw, J., K. White, and R. Russell-Bennett. "Masculinity and men's health service use across four social generations: Findings from Australia's *Ten to Men* study." *SSM Population Health* 15 (September 2021): article no. 100838. https://doi.org/10.1016/j.ssmph.2021.100838.

"traditional masculinity is mostly associated with negative health behaviours."

Pavilonis, V. "Fact check: Testosterone levels have dropped in recent decades, but not by 50%." *USA Today*, May 9, 2022. https://www.usatoday.com/story/news/factcheck/2022/05/09/fact-check-testosterone-levels-lower-25-1999-2016/7381735001.

Physician notes it is "inaccurate to say that average testosterone has fallen almost 50% over the last 2 decades."

Sagar-Ouriaghli, et al. "Improving Mental Health Service Utilization Among Men: A Systematic Review." *American Journal of Men's Health* 13, no. 3 (May–June 2019): 1557988319857009. https://doi.org/10.1177/1557988319857009.

Notes potential value of content "built on positive male traits (e.g., responsibility and strength)."

Staiger, T., M. Stiawa, A.S. Mueller-Stierlin, R. Kilian, P. Beschoner, H. Gündel, T. Becker, et al. "Masculinity and Help-Seeking among Men with Depression: A Qualitative Study." *Frontiers in Psychiatry* 11 (2020): 599039. https://doi.org/10.3389%2Ffpsyt.2020.599039.

"Peer-led men-only groups may increase participants' self-esteem."

Stanaland, A., and S. Gaither. "'Be a Man': The Role of Social Pressure in Eliciting Men's Aggressive Cognition." *Personality and Social Psychology Bulletin* 47, no. 11 (November 2021): 1596–1611. https://psycnet.apa.org/doi/10.1177/0146167220984298.

"Our data align with past research showing that threatened manhood does lead to aggression."

Walther, A., T. Rice, and L. Eggenberger. "Precarious Manhood Beliefs Are Positively Associated with Erectile Dysfunction in Cisgender Men." *Archives of Sexual Behavior* 52 (October 2023): 3123–3138. https://doi.org/10.1007/s10508-023-02640-4.

"PMB are significantly associated with ED."

Warren, N., and T. Campbell. "The Sleep-Deprived Masculinity Stereotype." *Journal of the Association for Consumer Research* 6, no. 2 (April 2021): 236–249. https://doi.org/10.1086/711758.

Study found masculine norms promote less sleep.

Wong, Y., M.-H. Ho, S.-Y. Wang, and I.S.K. Miller. "Meta-analyses of the Relationship between Conformity to Masculine Norms and Mental Health-Related Outcomes." *Journal of Counseling Psychology* 64, no. 1 (January 2017): 80–93. https://doi.org/10.1037/cou0000176.

Manly Ideology?

Carrasco-Farré, C. "The fingerprints of misinformation: How deceptive content differs from reliable sources in terms of cognitive effort and appeal to emotions." *Humanities and Social Sciences Communications* 9 (2022): article no. 162. https://doi.org/10.1057/s41599-022-01174-9.

Misinformation that gets traction is negative, emotional, focused on morality, and easy to process.

Couch, A. "Jon Stewart Mocks Anti-vaccine Liberals: 'They Practice a Mindful Stupidity.'" *The Hollywood Reporter*, February 3, 2015. https://www.hollywoodreporter.com/tv/tv-news/jon-stewart-mocks-anti-vaccine-770054.

DiMuccio, S., and E. Knowles. "The political significance of fragile masculinity." *Current Opinion in Behavioral Sciences* 34 (August 2020): 25–28. https://doi.org/10.1016/j.cobeha.2019.11.010.

DiMuccio, S., and E. Knowles. "Something to Prove? Manhood Threats Increase Political Aggression among Liberal Men." *Sex Roles* 88, no. 5–6 (March 2023): 240–267. https://doi.org/10.1007/s11199-023-01349-x.

Garrett, R.K., and R. Bond. "Conservatives' susceptibility to political misperceptions." *Science Advances* 7, no. 23 (June 4, 2021): eabf1234. https://doi.org/10.1126/sciadv.abf1234.

"conservatives have lower sensitivity than liberals, performing worse at distinguishing truths and falsehoods."

González-Bailón, S., D. Lazer, P. Barberá, M. Zhang, H. Allcott, T. Brown, A. Crespo-Tenorio, et al. "Asymmetric ideological segregation in exposure to political news on Facebook." *Science* 381, no. 6656 (July 27, 2023): 392–398. https://doi.org/10.1126/science.ade7138.

"most misinformation, as identified by Meta's Third-Party Fact-Checking Program, exists within this homogeneously conservative corner, which has no equivalent on the liberal side."

Jones, J., "Democratic, Republican Confidence in Science Diverges." Gallup, July 16, 2021. https://news.gallup.com/poll/352397/democratic-republican -confidence-science-diverges.aspx.

Data on the Democratic and Republican flip.

Kaiser Family Foundation. "Unvaccinated Adults Are Now More Than Three Times as Likely to Lean Republican than Democratic." KFF News release, November 16, 2021. https://www.kff.org/coronavirus-covid-19/press-release /unvaccinated-adults-are-now-more-than-three-times-as-likely-to-lean -republican-than-democratic.

MacDonnell Mesler, R., R.B. Leary, and W. Montford. "The impact of masculinity stress on preferences and willingness-to-pay for red meat." *Appetite* 171 (April 1, 2022): 105729. https://doi.org/10.1016/j.appet.2021.105729.

"we provide convergent evidence that masculinity stress is associated with red meat preference."

McDermott, R., K. Brasil, N. Croft Borgogna, and J. Barinas. "The politics of men's and women's traditional masculinity ideology in the United States." *Psychology of Men & Masculinities* 22, no. 4 (October 2021): 627–638. http://dx.doi.org/10.1037/men0000367.

Traditional masculinity linked to conservative ideology.

Mosleh, M., and D. Rand. "Measuring exposure to misinformation from political elites on Twitter." *Nature Communications* 13 (2022): article no. 7144. https://doi.org/10.1038/s41467-022-34769-6.

Nikolov, D., A. Flammini, and F. Menczer. "Right and left, partisanship predicts (asymmetric) vulnerability to misinformation." *Misinformation Review*, February 15, 2021. https://misinforeview.hks.harvard.edu/article /right-and-left-partisanship-predicts-asymmetric-vulnerability-to -misinformation.

Those on the political extreme, especially on right, spread more misinformation.

Oliffe, J., and M. Phillips. "Men, depression and masculinities: A review and recommendations." *Journal of Men's Health* 5, no. 3 (September 2008): 194–202. https://doi.org/10.1016/j.jomh.2008.03.016.

Schermerhorn, N., T. Vescio, and K. Lewis. "Hegemonic Masculinity Predicts Support for U.S. Political Figures Accused of Sexual Assault." *Social Psychological and Personality Science* 14, no. 5 (July 2023): 475–486. https://doi.org/10.1177/19485506221077861.

Endorsement of traditional masculine norms "predicted more positive evaluations of a political figure accused of sexual violence."

Vescio, T., and N. Schermerhorn. "Hegemonic masculinity predicts 2016 and 2020 voting and candidate evaluations." *PNAS* 118, no. 2 (January 4, 2021): e2020589118. https://doi.org/10.1073/pnas.2020589118.

Masculinity strong predictor of how someone will vote.

Xia, R. "Measles outbreak grows to 107 cases, latest in Marin County." *Los Angeles Times*, January 30, 2015. https://www.latimes.com/local/lanow/la-me-ln-measles-outbreak-hits-marin-county-20150130-story.html.

A Good Story

Belluz, J. "Debunking What the Health, the buzzy new documentary that wants you to be vegan." *Vox*, July 25, 2017. https://www.vox.com/science-and-health/2017/7/25/16018658/what-the-health-documentary-review-vegan-diet.

Good review of all the inaccuracies in the popular documentary.

Bradshaw, A., D. Treise, S. Shelton, M. Cretul, A. Raisa, A. Bajalia, and D. Peek. "Propagandizing anti-vaccination: Analysis of Vaccines Revealed documentary series." *Vaccine* 38, no. 8 (February 18, 2020): 2058–2069. https://doi.org/10.1016/j.vaccine.2019.12.027.

Qualitative analysis of anti-vaccine documentary.

Dahlstrom, M. "The narrative truth about scientific misinformation." *PNAS* 118, no. 15 (April 9, 2021): e1914085117. https://doi.org/10.1073/pnas.1914085117.

Janpol, H., and R. Dilts. "Does viewing documentary films affect environmental perceptions and behaviors?" *Applied Environmental Education and Communication* 15, no. 1 (January 2016): 90–98. http://dx.doi.org/10.1080/1533015X.2016.1142197.

Kaplan, A. "Roku has allowed hundreds of thousands of installations of a channel dedicated to QAnon conspiracy theories." Media Matters for America, January 4,

2023. https://www.mediamatters.org/qanon-conspiracy-theory/roku-has
-allowed-hundreds-thousands-installations-channel-dedicated-qanon.

Males, J., and P. Van Aelst. "Did the Blue Planet set the Agenda for Plastic
Pollution?" *Environmental Communication* 15, no. 1 (2021): 40–54. https://
doi.org/10.1080/17524032.2020.1780458.

"*The Blue Planet* generated this interest in plastic pollution which was, for
both the media and political agendas, long-lasting."

Michalovich, A., and A. Hershkovitz. "Assessing YouTube science news'
credibility: The impact of web-search on the role of video, source, and user
attributes." *Public Understanding of Science* 29, no. 4 (May 2020): 376–391.
https://doi.org/10.1177/0963662520905466.

Production quality adds to the persuasive force.

Renken, E. "How Stories Connect and Persuade Us: Unleashing the Brain Power
of Narrative." NPR, April 11, 2020. https://www.npr.org/sections/health-shots
/2020/04/11/815573198/how-stories-connect-and-persuade-us-unleashing-the
-brain-power-of-narrative.

Review of fMRI studies.

Trevino, A., C. Cardinal, and C. Douglas. "Altered health knowledge and attitudes
among health sciences students following media exposure." *Nursing and Health
Sciences* 22, no. 4 (December 2020): 967–976. https://doi.org/10.1111/nhs.12754.

Study shows impact of documentaries on opinions of an informed audience.

Doing Good and the Certainty Grift

Barnwell, P., E. Fedorenko, and R. Contrada. "Healthy or not? The impact of
conflicting health-related information on attentional resources." *Journal of
Behavioural Medicine* 45, no. 2 (April 2022): 306–317. https://doi.org/10.1007
/s10865-021-00256-4.

"Participants in the conflicting health information condition made more errors."

Curry, O.S., L. Rowland, C. Van Lissa, S. Zlotowitz, J. McAlaney, and H.
Whitehouse. "Happy to help? A systematic review and meta-analysis of the
effects of performing acts of kindness on the well-being of the actor." *Journal
of Experimental Social Psychology* 76 (May 2018): 320–329. https://doi.org
/10.1016/j.jesp.2018.02.014.

Gama, F., S. Quinet de Andrade Bastos, and T. de Paula Assis. "Does being ethical
make you happier?" *Revista Argentina de Ciencias del Comportamiento* 13,
no. 2 (August 25, 2021): 59–65. https://doi.org/10.32348/1852.4206.v13.n2.27761.

"results show that jointly (globally), countries presenting the virtues proposed by Aristotle is positively correlated with happiness."

Loprinzi, P., A. Branscum, J. Hanks, and E. Smit. "Healthy Lifestyle Character- istics and Their Joint Association With Cardiovascular Disease Biomarkers in US Adults." *Mayo Clinic Proceedings* 91, no. 4 (April 2016): 432–442. https://doi.org/10.1016/j.mayocp.2016.01.009.

"Only 2.7% of all adults had all 4 healthy lifestyle characteristics."

Melamed, D., B. Simpson, and J. Abernathy. "The robustness of reciprocity: Experimental evidence that each form of reciprocity is robust to the presence of other forms of reciprocity." *Scientific Advances* 6, no. 23 (June 3, 2020): eaba0504. https://doi.org/10.1126/sciadv.aba0504.

Ohio State University that found the "basis of human reciprocity is remarkably robust."

Turner, L. "Why being kind could help you live longer." *BBC News*, November 11, 2019. https://www.bbc.com/news/world-us-canada-50266957.

Review of research on kindness and longevity.

III: The Opinion Illusion

That Earthy Taste!

Anderson, M. "88% of Consumers Trust Online Reviews as Much as Personal Recom- mendations." Search Engine Land, July 7, 2014. https://searchengineland.com/88 -consumers-trust-online-reviews-much-personal-recommendations-195803.

Caulfield, T., A.R. Marcon, B. Murdoch, J.M. Brown, S.T. Perrault, J. Jarry, J. Snyder, et al. "Health Misinformation and the Power of Narrative Messaging in the Public Sphere." *Canadian Journal of Bioethics* 2, no. 2 (2019): 52–60. https://doi.org/10.7202/1060911ar.

Our team reviews the evidence regarding the power of anecdotes, testimonials, and narratives.

Clerke, A., and E. Heerey. "The Influence of Similarity and Mimicry on Decisions to Trust." *Collabra: Psychology* 7, no. 1 (May 11, 2021): 23441. https://doi.org /10.1525/collabra.23441.

Good review of literature on trust and similarity.

DeAndrea, D., B. Van Der Heide, M. Vendemia, and M. Vang. "How People Evaluate Online Reviews." *Communication Research* 45, no. 5 (July 2018): 719–736. https://doi.org/10.1177/0093650215573862.

"the less people are confident that user-generated reviews are truly produced by third-party reviewers, the less people trust those reviews."

Hamby, A., K. Daniloski, and D. Brinberg. "How consumer reviews persuade through narratives." *Journal of Business Research* 68, no. 6 (June 2015): 1242–1250. https://doi.org/10.1016/j.jbusres.2014.11.004.

"reviews with a more story-like format" are more persuasive.

Hendricks, S. "You morally elevate people like yourself, study finds." *Big Think*, August 31, 2018. https://bigthink.com/surprising-science/the-mere-liking -effect-why-you-trust-people-who-are-like-you.

Summary of 2018 study.

Kaemingk, D. "Online reviews statistics to know in 2022." Qualtrics, October 30, 2020. https://www.qualtrics.com/blog/online-review-stats.

91% of 18-to-34-year-olds trust online reviews as much as personal recommendations.

Kim, M., and K. Kim. "The Influence of Authenticity of Online Reviews on Trust Formation." *Journal of Travel Research* 59, no. 5 (May 2020): 763–776. https://doi.org/10.1177/0047287519868307.

Lorenz, J., H. Rauhut, F. Schweitzer, and D. Helbing. "How social influence can undermine the wisdom of crowd effect." *PNAS* 108, no. 22 (May 16, 2011): 9020–9025. https://doi.org/10.1073/pnas.1008636108.

"even mild social influence can undermine the wisdom of crowd effect in simple estimation tasks."

OECD. "Understanding online consumer ratings and reviews." *OECD Digital Economy Papers*, no. 289 (OECD Publishing, 2019). https://doi.org/10.1787 /eb018587-en.

Good review of relevant data, including that 86% of consumers consider online reviews "credible" or "very credible."

Power Reviews. "New Consumer Survey of More Than 6,500 Consumers Reveals Increasing Importance of Product Reviews to Establish Trust and Drive Purchase Behavior." News release, May 20, 2021. https:// www.globenewswire.com/news-release/2021/05/20/2233533/0/en/New -Consumer-Survey-of-More-than-6-500-Consumers-Reveals-Increasing -Importance-of-Product-Reviews-to-Establish-Trust-and-Drive-Purchase -Behavior.html.

Survey found ratings and reviews most important factor in purchasing behaviour.

Sung, E., W.Y. Chung, and D. Lee. "Factors that affect consumer trust in product quality: A focus on online reviews and shopping platforms." *Humanities and Social Sciences Communications* 10 (November 1, 2023): article no. 766. https://doi.org/10.1057/s41599-023-02277-7.

"consumers prefer high star ratings, a large number of reviews, and a trustworthy shopping platform."

University of Royal Holloway London. "Study shows trustworthy people perceived to look similar to ourselves." ScienceDaily, November 7, 2013. https://www.sciencedaily.com/releases/2013/11/131107094406.htm.

The Opinion Economy

Chakraborty, U. "Perceived credibility of online hotel reviews and its impact on hotel booking intentions." *International Journal of Contemporary Hospitality Management* 31, no. 9 (August 2019): 3465–3483. http://dx.doi.org/10.1108/IJCHM-11-2018-0928.

Study found "two-sided" reviews more persuasive.

Luca, M. "Reviews, Reputation, and Revenue: The Case of Yelp.com." *Harvard Business School Working Paper*, no. 12-016. March 16, 2016. https://dx.doi.org/10.2139/ssrn.1928601.

"a one-star increase in Yelp rating leads to a 5–9 percent increase in revenue."

Maslowska, E., E. Malthouse, and S. Bernritter. "Too good to be true: The role of online reviews' features in probability to buy." *International Journal of Advertising* 36, no. 1 (2017): 142–163. https://doi.org/10.1080/02650487.2016.1195622.

If reviews are too good, sales decrease. Sweet spot is 4.2-ish stars.

Maslowska, E., C. Segijn, K.A. Vakeel, and V. Viswanathan. "How consumers attend to online reviews: An eye-tracking and network analysis approach." *International Journal of Advertising* 39, no. 2 (February 2020): 282–306. https://psycnet.apa.org/doi/10.1080/02650487.2019.1617651.

Fake It until . . . Well, Forever

Ai, J., D. Gursoy, Y. Liu, and X. Lv. "Effects of offering incentives for reviews on trust: Role of review quality and incentive source." *International Journal of Hospitality Management* 100 (January 2022): 103101. https://doi.org/10.1016/j.ijhm.2021.103101.

"customers have less trust in incentive-driven eWOM [online reviews] than in organic eWOM."

Boyd, C. "Fake Reviews and Brand Pimping: Who Wins and Who Loses." Near Media, December 29, 2021. https://www.nearmedia.co/fake-reviews-and -brand-pimping-who-wins-and-who-loses.

Overview of "fake review cycle."

Crockett, Z. "5-star phonies: Inside the fake Amazon review complex." *The Hustle*, June 30, 2020. https://thehustle.co/amazon-fake-reviews.

"Fake reviews boost many products' star ratings."

Elliott, C. "This Is Why You Should Not Trust Online Reviews." Forbes, November 21, 2018. https://www.forbes.com/sites/christopherelliott/2018/11 /21/why-you-should-not-trust-online-reviews.

Quoting Saoud Khalifah suggesting that "up to 70 percent of the reviews on Amazon are not real."

Garnefeld, I., S. Helm, and A.-K. Grötschel. "May we buy your love? Psychological effects of incentives on writing likelihood and valence of online product reviews." *Electronic Markets* 30 (December 2020): 805–820. https://doi.org/10.1007/s12525-020-00425-4.

"offering incentives indeed increases the likelihood of review writing. However, the effect on review valence is mixed." Paying people to write reviews results in positive, but not too positive, reviews.

Griffith, E. "39 percent of Online Reviews Are Totally Unreliable." *PC Mag*, November 7, 2019. https://www.pcmag.com/news/39-percent-of-online -reviews-are-totally-unreliable.

"83.4% said reviews were moderately to extremely influential on their purchases."

He, S., B. Hollenbeck, and D. Proserpio. "Exploiting Social Media for Fake Reviews: Evidence from Amazon and Facebook." *ACM SIGecom Exchanges* 19, no. 2 (November 2021): 68–74. http://dx.doi.org/10.1145/3505156.3505164.

He, S., B. Hollenbeck, and D. Proserpio. "The Market for Fake Reviews." *EC'21: Proceedings of the 22nd ACM Conference on Economics and Computation* (July 2021): 588. http://dx.doi.org/10.1145/3465456.3467589.

Marciano, J. "Fake online reviews cost $152 billion a year. Here's how e-commerce sites can stop them." World Economic Forum, August 10, 2021. https://www .weforum.org/agenda/2021/08/fake-online-reviews-are-a-152-billion-problem -heres-how-to-silence-them.

"Fake online reviews influence $791 billion of e-commerce spending annually."

Nakayama, M., and Y. Wan. "Exploratory Study on Anchoring: Fake Vote Counts in Consumer Reviews Affect Judgments of Information Quality."

Journal of Theoretical and Applied Electronic Commerce Research 12, no. 1 (January 2017): 1–20. http://dx.doi.org/10.4067/S0718-18762017000100002.

"Fake votes changed both review judgments and purchase behaviors."

Palmer, A. "Amazon sues two companies that allegedly help fill the site with fake reviews." CNBC, February 22, 2022. https://www.cnbc.com/2022/02/22 /amazon-sues-alleged-fake-reviews-brokers-appsally-rebatest.html.

Schwedel, H. "How Did a Cult Beauty Brand Get in Trouble with the FTC?" *Slate*, October 22, 2019. https://slate.com/technology/2019/10/ftc-sunday-riley -fake-reviews-federal-trade-commission.html.

Story on how company encouraged employees to leave fake reviews.

Shan, L.Y. "Fake reviews are a multibillion-dollar quicksand—here's how to avoid getting sucked in." CNBC, December 28, 2023. https://www.cnbc.com/2023/12 /29/fake-reviews-5-tips-on-how-to-spot-them.html.

"Up to 40% of these online testimonials are unreliable, according to a public interest research group, and these fake reviews are estimated to influence $152 -billion worth of online spending annually."

Woolley, K., and M. Sharif. "What Happens When Companies Pay Customers to Write Reviews?" *Harvard Business Review*, June 25, 2021. https://hbr.org/2021 /06/what-happens-when-companies-pay-customers-to-write-reviews.

Incentives can boost positivity of reviews by 40 to 70%.

Biases in the Machine

Ahn, D., H. Park, and B. Yoo. "Which group do you want to travel with? A study of rating differences among groups in online travel reviews." *Electronic Commerce Research and Applications* 25 (September–October 2017): 105–114. http://dx.doi.org/10.1016/j.elerap.2017.09.001.

Who you are travelling with impacts hotel reviews.

Anderson, E., and D. Simester. "Reviews without a Purchase: Low Ratings, Loyal Customers, and Deception." *Journal of Marketing Research* 51, no. 3 (June 2014): 249–269. https://doi.org/10.1509/jmr.13.0209.

Just 1.5% of customers write reviews.

Cicognani, S., et al. "Social influence bias in ratings: A field experiment in the hospitality sector." *Tourism Economics* 28, no. 8 (December 2022): 2197–2218. https://doi.org/10.1177/13548166211034645.

"customers who are not used to writing online reviews are more prone to [social influence bias]."

Linton, H., U. Gretzel, and S. Han. "'Super Contributor' Reviewer Behaviour."
Frontiers in Service Conference, 2017. https://www.researchgate.net
/publication/328049651_TripAdvisor_Super_Contributors_Projecting
_Professionalism.

"The influencer [super contributors] phenomenon is also present within
online reviews on TripAdvisor."

Liu, W., I. Simonson, and O. Amir. "Placebo Effects of Marketing Actions:
Consumers May Get What They Pay For." In *E - European Advances
in Consumer Research*, vol. 7, edited by K. Ekstrom and H. Brembeck.
Association for Consumer Research, 2005: 308–309.

Mariani, M., and Matarazzo, M. "Does cultural distance affect online review
ratings? Measuring international customers' satisfaction with services."
Journal of Management and Governance 25 (December 2021): 1057–1078.
https://doi.org/10.1007/s10997-020-09531-z.

Study that finds the bigger the cultural difference, the lower the review.

Merry, S. "Amber Share turned negative reviews of national parks into an
art form." *Washington Post*, May 27, 2021. https://www.washingtonpost.com
/entertainment/books/visiting-national-parks-amber-share/2021/05/26
/ecd5fabe-b9cd-11eb-a6b1-81296da0339b_story.html.

Muchnik, L., S. Aral, and S. Taylor. "Social Influence Bias: A Randomized
Experiment." *Science* 341, no. 6146 (August 9, 2013): 647–651. https://doi.org
/10.1126/science.1240466.

"social influence increased the likelihood of positive ratings by 32%."

Nielsen, M., and Zethsen, K. "'The Room Was Quite Small by American
Standards': Are Online Hotel Reviews Culture-Specific?" *Tourism Culture
and Communication* 22, no. 3 (2022): 259–273. https://doi.org/10.3727
/109830421X16345418234001.

"there are indeed differences between the German and the American
reviews."

Power of Reviews. "2014 The Power of Reviews." https://www.powerreviews.com
/wp-content/uploads/2015/08/13185402/ThePowerofReviews-Report.pdf.

"only 3–10% will write a review for that specific transaction."

Spielmann, N., S. Dobscha, and T. Lowrey. "Real Men Don't Buy 'Mrs. Clean':
Gender Bias in Gendered Brands." *Journal of the Association for Consumer
Research* 6, no. 2 (April 2021): 211–222. https://doi.org/10.1086/713188.

"men are negatively biased against female brands."

Zhang, Z., S. Qiao, H. Li, and Z. Zhang. "How rainy-day blues affect customers' evaluation behavior: Evidence from online reviews." *International Journal of Hospitality Management* 100 (January 2022): 103090. https://doi.org/10.1016/j.ijhm.2021.103090.

"reviews were lower when reviews were written while it was raining."

"My Dream Is Over . . ."

Hester, P. "26 Mind-Boggling Online Review Statistics & Facts for 2022." WebsiteBuilder, December 21, 2021. https://websitebuilder.org/blog/online-review-statistics.

94% of consumers refuse to patronize a business because of negative reviews.

Lappas, T., G. Sabnis, and G. Valkanas. "The Impact of Fake Reviews on Online Visibility: A Vulnerability Assessment of the Hotel Industry." *Information Systems Research* 27, no. 4 (December 2016): 940–961. https://www.jstor.org/stable/26652537.

Study of 2.3 million reviews.

Luca, M., and G. Zervas. "Fake It Till You Make It: Reputation, Competition, and Yelp Review Fraud." *Management Science* 62, no. 12 (December 2016): 3412–3427. https://doi.org/10.1287/mnsc.2015.2304.

Study explores what drives fake positive and negative reviews on Yelp.

ReviewTrackers. "Online Reviews Statistics and Trends: A 2022 Report by ReviewTrackers." January 9, 2022. https://www.reviewtrackers.com/reports/online-reviews-survey.

94% have avoided a business because of a bad review.

Statista. "How do online customer reviews affect your opinion of a local business?" January 28, 2022. https://www.statista.com/statistics/315751/online-review-customer-opinion.

92% of people say negative reviews make them less likely to use a business.

Bottom Line: Often Wrong

de Langhe, B., P. Fernbach, and D. Lichtenstein. "High Online User Ratings Don't Actually Mean You're Getting a Quality Product." *Harvard Business Review*, July 4, 2016. https://hbr.org/2016/07/high-online-user-ratings-dont-actually-mean-youre-getting-a-quality-product.

"average star ratings bore essentially no relationship to used prices."

de Langhe, B., P. Fernbach, and D. Lichtenstein. "Navigating by the Stars: Investigating the Actual and Perceived Validity of Online User Ratings." *Journal of Consumer Research* 42, no. 6 (April 2016): 817–833. https://doi.org /10.1093/jcr/ucv047.

Study finds large disconnect between online reviews and expert assessment of quality.

Repsold, M. "Multivariate Comparison of Experts' versus Users' Reviews Online." Joseph Wharton Scholars, January 2018.

Reviews of Professionals? Even Wronger

CBS News. "Plastic surgery provider faces federal lawsuit over allegedly posting fake reviews." December 30, 2022. https://www.cbsnews.com/news/allure -esthetic-javad-sajan-plastic-surgery-lawsuit-alleged-fake-reviews-yelp-google.

"federal lawsuit for allegedly posting fake positive reviews online and intimidating or bribing patients to remove negative reviews."

Daskivich, T., J. Houman, G. Fuller, J. Black, H. Kim, and B. Spiegel. "Online physician ratings fail to predict actual performance on measures of quality, value, and peer review." *Journal of the American Medical Informatics Association* 25, no. 4 (April 2018): 401–407. https://doi.org/10.1093/jamia /ocx083.

Online reviews do not correlate with physician peer assessments of clinical care.

Lagasse, J. "Doctors' online reviews show more polarization, have more impact than those of other industries." *Healthcare Finance*, December 20, 2019. https://www.healthcarefinancenews.com/news/doctors-online-reviews -show-more-polarization-have-more-impact-those-other-industries.

Physicians "194% more likely to receive a one-star review."

Ospina, N., K. Philips, R. Rodriguez-Gutierrez, A. Castaneda-Guarderas, M. Gionfriddo, M. Branda, and V. Montori. "Eliciting the Patient's Agenda - Secondary Analysis of Recorded Clinical Encounters." *Journal of General Internal Medicine* 34, no. 1 (January 2019): 36–40. https://doi.org/10.1007 /s11606-018-4540-5.

"the clinician interrupted the patient after a median of 11 seconds."

Placona, A., and C. Rathert. "Are Online Patient Reviews Associated with Health Care Outcomes? A Systematic Review of the Literature." *Medical Care Research and Review* 79, no. 1 (February 2022): 3–16. https://doi.org/10.1177 /10775587211014534.

Consistent correlation between online reviews and patient experiences, but not outcomes.

Press Ganey. "Consumer Experience in Healthcare Trends 2021." Press Ganey Associates. https://info.pressganey.com/e-books-research/press-ganey -consumer-experience-in-healthcare-trends-report-2021.

84% won't go to a physician with a less than four-star rating.

Saifee, D., Z. Zheng, I. Bardhan, and A. Lahiri. "Are Online Reviews of Physicians Reliable Indicators of Clinical Outcomes? A Focus on Chronic Disease Management." *Information Systems Research* 31, no. 4 (September 2020): 1037–1492. http://dx.doi.org/10.1287/isre.2020.0945.

"Contrary to popular belief, our study finds that there is no clear relationship between online reviews of physicians and their patients' clinical outcomes."

Trehan, S., J. Nguyen, R. Marx, M. Cross, T. Pan, A. Daluiski, and S. Lyman. "Online patient ratings are not correlated with total knee replacement surgeon -specific outcomes." *HSS Journal* 14, no. 2 (July 2018): 177–180. https://doi.org /10.1007/s11420-017-9600-6.

You Can't Detect Them. Seriously, You Can't.

Camilleri, A. "How to spot a fake review: You're probably worse at it than you realise." *The Conversation*, August 12, 2019. https://theconversation.com /how-to-spot-a-fake-review-youre-probably-worse-at-it-than-you-realise -121043.

Useful review of data on how much people rely on reviews and why they think they can recognize the fake ones. (About half think they're pretty good.)

Juuti, M., B. Sun, T. Mori, and N. Asokan. "Stay On-Topic: Generating Context -Specific Fake Restaurant Reviews." 32rd European Symposium on Research in Computer Security, Barcelona, Spain (September 3–7, 2018), Proceedings, Part I: 132–151. https://doi.org/10.1007/978-3-319-99073-6_7.

"fake reviews are very effective in fooling people."

Lyons, B., J. Montgomery, A. Guess, B. Nyhan, and J. Reifler. "Overconfidence in news judgments is associated with false news susceptibility." *PNAS* 118, no. 23 (May 28, 2021): e2019527118. https://doi.org/10.1073/ pnas.2019527118.

"overconfidence may be a crucial factor for explaining how false and low-quality information spreads via social media."

Opinion Polls

Market Research Society. *Using surveys and polling data in your journalism.* November 2019. https://www.mrs.org.uk/pdf/IMPRESS%2520MRS%2520 Guidance%2520FINAL1.pdf.

Good resource for the assessment of survey data.

Porten-Cheé, P., and C. Eilders. "The effects of likes on public opinion perception and personal opinion." *Communications* 45, no. 2 (March 1, 2019): 223–239. http://dx.doi.org/10.1515/commun-2019-2030.

Seeing more likes on social media shapes public opinion.

Sherman, E. "Reporter's tip sheet: How to assess a survey." The Reynold's Center for Business Journalism, January 9, 2017. https://businessjournalism.org /2017/01/survey.

"Be skeptical. Companies often publicize surveys in order to underscore and legitimize their marketing message, not to offer unbiased information."

Taste Makers or Aggregators?

Adler, S. "Music can be used to estimate political ideology to an 'accuracy of 70%,' researchers say." *ZME Science*, July 13, 2019. https://www.zmescience.com /medicine/mind-and-brain/music-can-be-used-to-estimate-political-ideology -to-an-accuracy-of-70-researchers-say.

Devenport, S., and A. North. "Predicting musical taste: Relationships with personality aspects and political orientation." *Psychology of Music* 47, no. 6 (November 2019): 834–847. https://doi.org/10.1177/0305735619864647.

"political orientation were superior predictors of musical taste in comparison to personality domains."

Fox, W., and J. Williams. "Political Orientation and Music Preferences among College Students." *Public Opinion Quarterly* 38, no. 3 (Fall 1974): 352–371. https://doi.org/10.1086/268171.

Gardikiotis, A., and A. Baltzis. "'Rock music for myself and justice to the world!': Musical identity, values, and music preferences." *Psychology of Music* 40, no. 2 (March 2012): 143–163. https://doi.org/10.1177 /0305735610386836.

Goldstein, R. "From the Archives: The Original Review of 'Sgt. Pepper's Lonely Hearts Club Band.'" *The New York Times*, June 1, 2017 (originally published June 18, 1967). https://www.nytimes.com/2017/06/01/arts/music/archives -beatles-sgt-peppers-lonely-hearts-club-band-review.html.

Johnes, M. "Consuming Popular Music: Individualism, Politics and Progressive Rock." *Cultural and Social History* 15, no. 1 (2018): 115–134. https://doi.org/10.1080/14780038.2018.1426815.

"What all this suggests is that what really matters is not so much what music is being listened to but how it is being listened to. This makes fans as important to the history of popular music as artists."

Lizardo, O., and S. Skiles. "Musical taste and patterns of symbolic exclusion in the United States 1993–2012: Generational dynamics of differentiation and continuity." *Poetics* 53 (December 2015): 9–21. https://doi.org/10.1016/j.poetic.2015.08.003.

"'symbolic exclusion': namely, the (differential) propensity of persons to express dislike for certain cultural styles" and the reality that country and folk music are becoming more polarizing.

Lonsdale, A., and A. North. "Musical Taste and Ingroup Favoritism." *Group Processes and Intergroup Relations* 12, no. 3 (May 2009): 319–327. https://doi.org/10.1177/1368430209102842.

"Those who share our musical taste are likely to be considered ingroup members, and should be subject to ingroup favoritism."

Rentfrow, P., J. McDonald, and J. Oldmeadow. "You Are What You Listen To: Young People's Stereotypes about Music Fans." *Group Processes and Intergroup Relations* 12, no. 3 (May 2009): 329–344. https://doi.org/10.1177/1368430209102845.

Silva, K., and F. Silva. "National Public Radio Music Critics Have the Power of Persuasion." *Media Psychology Review* 3, no. 1 (2010). https://mprcenter.org/review/silva-national-public-radio.

Listening to critics influences opinion of music.

University of Cambridge. "Musical ages: How our taste in music changes over a lifetime." ScienceDaily, October 15, 2013. https://www.sciencedaily.com/releases/2013/10/131015123654.htm.

"Whereas the first musical age is about asserting independence, the next appears to be more about gaining acceptance from others."

Who's Reviewing the Reviewers?

Brooks, S. "Movie Studios Build Buzz with Fake Film Tweets." Big Ideas, February 20, 2019. http://dx.doi.org/10.26153/tsw/38659.

Hickey, W. "What If Online Movie Ratings Weren't Based Almost Entirely on What Men Think?" FiveThirtyEight, March 6, 2018. https://fivethirtyeight .com/features/what-if-online-movie-ratings-werent-based-almost-entirely -on-what-men-think.

Lauzen, M. *Thumbs Down 2020: Film Critics and Gender, and Why It Matters.* SDSU Center for the Study of Women in Television and Film, 2020. https://www.nywift.org/wp-content/uploads/2021/12/2020-Thumbs -Down-Report.pdf.

"Men wrote 66% and women 34% of reviews."

Lee, C., X. Xu, and C.-C. Lin. "Using Online User-Generated Reviews to Predict Offline Box-Office Sales and Online DVD Store Sales in the O2O Era." *Journal of Theoretical and Applied Electronic Commerce Research* 14, no. 1 (2019): 68–83. https://doi.org/10.4067/S0718-18762019000100106.

"We generate forecasting equations, which can successfully predict movie box office and online DVD store sales."

Lindbergh, B., and R. Arthur. "Has Rotten Tomatoes Ever Truly Mattered?" *The Ringer*, September 4, 2020. https://www.theringer.com/movies/2020 /9/4/21422568/rotten-tomatoes-effective-on-box-office.

"Rotten Tomatoes scores are reliably correlated with box office performance, especially for certain genres."

Piçarra, N., N. Silva, T. Chambel, and P. Arriaga. "What Movie Will I Watch Today? The Role of Online Review Ratings, Reviewers' Comments, and Users' Gratification Style." *Projections* 15, no. 3 (November 2021): 24–46. http://dx.doi.org/10.3167/proj.2021.150302.

"participants reported a higher preference for the high rating movie."

USC Annenberg staff. "Study finds film critics, like filmmakers and casts, are largely white and male." USC Today, June 11, 2018. https://today.usc.edu /usc-study-finds-film-critics-like-filmmakers-are-largely-white-and-male.

Like What You Like?

Balietti, S., L. Getoor, D. Goldstein, and D. Watts. "Reducing opinion polarization: Effects of exposure to similar people with differing political views." *PNAS* 118, no. 52 (December 22, 2021): e2112552118. https://doi.org /10.1073/pnas.2112552118.

"incidental similarities may cold-start cross-cutting political arguments and increase consensus on divisive topics."

Gabbatt, A. "What happens when a group of Fox News viewers watch CNN for a month?" *The Guardian*, April 11, 2022.

Greenberg, D., S. Baron-Cohen, D. Stillwell, M. Kosinski, and P. Rentfrow. "Musical Preferences Are Linked to Cognitive Styles." *PLoS ONE* 10, no. 7 (July 22, 2015): e0131151. https://doi.org/10.1371/journal.pone.0131151.

"empathy levels are linked to preferences."

Nault, J.F., S. Baumann, C. Childress, and C. Rawlings. "The social positions of taste between and within music genres: From omnivore to snob." *European Journal of Cultural Studies* 23, no. 3 (June 2021): 717–740. https://doi.org/10.1177/13675494211006090.

"increased education associates with liking fewer musical artists across various consecration levels."

Conclusion: A Path Forward?

Ansede, M. "A researcher who publishes a study every two days reveals the darker side of science." *El País*, June 4, 2023. https://english.elpais.com/science-tech/2023-06-04/a-researcher-who-publishes-a-study-every-two-days-reveals-the-darker-side-of-science.html.

Barnwell, P., E. Fedorenko, and R. Contrada. "Healthy or not? The impact of conflicting health-related information on attentional resources." *Journal of Behavioural Medicine* 45, no. 2 (April 2022): 306–317. https://doi.org/10.1007/s10865-021-00256-4.

"Participants in the conflicting health information condition made more errors, had overall slower reaction times, and reported greater workload."

Belluz, J., "'Unprecedented!' 'Amazing!' 'Novel!': The Rise of Hype in Scientific Journals." *Vox*, December 24, 2015. https://www.vox.com/2015/12/24/10636608/hype-science-increase-bmj.

Cassidy, C. "Doomscrolling linked to poor physical and mental health, study finds." *The Guardian*, September 5, 2022. https://www.theguardian.com/society/2022/sep/06/doomscrolling-linked-to-poor-physical-and-mental-health-study-finds.

Caulfield, T., T. Bubela, J. Kimmelman, and V. Ravitsky. "Let's Do Better: Public Representations of COVID-19 Science." *FACETS* 6 (March 25, 2021): 403–423. https://doi.org/10.1139/facets-2021-0018.

Our paper exploring the ways in which the knowledge production system can be improved.

Conroy, G. "Surge in number of 'extremely productive' authors concerns scientists." *Nature* 625, no. 7993 (January 2024): 14–15. https://doi.org/10.1038/d41586-023 -03865-y.

"Some researchers publish a new paper every five days, on average. Data trackers suspect not all their manuscripts were produced through honest labour."

Ding, D., B. Nguyen, K. Gebel, A. Bauman, and L. Bero. "Duplicate and salami publication: A prevalence study of journal policies." *International Journal of Epidemiology* 49, no. 1 (February 2020): 281–288. https://doi.org/10.1093 /ije/dyz187.

"only 13% included policies on both duplicate and salami publication."

Dworkin, J., and J. Elliott. "Strengthen science by funding living evidence synthesis." *STAT*, March 27, 2023. https://www.statnews.com/2023/03/27 /strengthen-science-by-funding-living-evidence-synthesis.

Economist editors. "There is a worrying amount of fraud in medical research" *The Economist*, February 22, 2023. https://www.economist.com/science-and -technology/2023/02/22/there-is-a-worrying-amount-of-fraud-in-medical -research.

Forrester, N. "Fed up and burnt out: 'quiet quitting' hits academia." *Nature*, March 3, 2023. https://www.nature.com/articles/d41586-023-00633-w.

Grove, J. "'Institute for scientific facts' aims to smash fake news." Times Higher Education, January 10, 2023. https://www.timeshighereducation.com/news /institute-scientific-facts-aims-smash-fake-news.

"We need a way to access scientific opinion on a large scale and internationally."

Holtfreter, K., M. Reisig, T. Pratt, and R. Mays. "The perceived causes of research misconduct among faculty members in the natural, social, and applied sciences." *Studies in Higher Education* 45, no. 11 (2020): 2162–2174. http://dx.doi.org/10.1080/03075079.2019.1593352.

"professional strains and stressors (e.g., pressure to secure external funds and publish in top-tier journals) are most widely perceived to cause misconduct."

Horta, H., and H. Li. "Nothing but publishing: The overriding goal of PhD students in mainland China, Hong Kong, and Macau." *Studies in Higher Education* 48, no. 2 (2023): 263–282. https://doi.org/10.1080/03075079 .2022.2131764.

Huff, C. "Media overload is hurting our mental health. Here are ways to manage headline stress." *Monitor on Psychology* 53, no. 8 (November 2022): 20. https://www.apa.org/monitor/2022/11/strain-media-overload.

Recent review on some of the relevant evidence.

Kozlov, M. "'Disruptive' science has declined—and no one knows why." *Nature*, January 4, 2023. https://www.nature.com/articles/d41586-022-04577-5.

Kuchler, F., M. Sweitzer, and C. Chelius. "The Prevalence of the 'Natural' Claim on Food Product Packaging." Economic brief, no. EB-35. U.S. Department of Agriculture, Economic Research Service, May 2023. https://doi.org/10.32747/2023.8023700.ers.

"16.9 percent of all items purchased (unit sales) were for foods labeled natural."

Malički, M., I. Aalbersberg, L. Bouter, A. Mulligan, and G. ter Riet. "Transparency in conducting and reporting research: A survey of authors, reviewers, and editors across scholarly disciplines." *PLoS ONE* 18, no. 3 (March 8, 2023): e0270054. https://doi.org/10.1371%2Fjournal.pone.0270054.

"20% of respondents admitted sacrificing the quality of their publications for quantity."

Nagler, R., R. Vogel, S. Gollust, M. Yzer, and A. Rothman. "Effects of Prior Exposure to Conflicting Health Information on Responses to Subsequent Unrelated Health Messages: Results from a Population-Based Longitudinal Experiment." *Annals of Behavioral Medicine* 56, no. 5 (May 18, 2022): 498–511. https://doi.org/10.1093/abm/kaab069.

Study found a "generalized backlash toward health recommendations and research elicited by prior exposure to conflicting information."

Park, M., E. Leahey, and R. Funk. "Papers and patents are becoming less disruptive over time." *Nature* 613 (January 5, 2023): 138–144. https://doi.org/10.1038/s41586-022-05543-x.

"For papers, the decrease between 1945 and 2010 ranges from 91.9%."

Pennycook, D., and D. Rand. "Accuracy prompts are a replicable and generalizable approach for reducing the spread of misinformation." *Nature Communications* 13 (2022): article no. 2333. https://doi.org/10.1038/s41467-022-30073-5.

Pennycook, D., and D. Rand. "Nudging Social Media toward Accuracy." *Annals of the American Academy of Political and Social Science* 700, no. 1 (2022): 152–164. https://psycnet.apa.org/doi/10.1177/00027162221092342.

Segal, E. "Survey Finds Email Fatigue Could Lead 38% of Workers to Quit Their Jobs." *Forbes*, April 21, 2021. https://www.forbes.com/sites/edwardsegal/2021/04/21/survey-finds-email-fatigue-could-lead-38-of-workers-to-quit-their-jobs.

Schneider, J., N. Woods, R. Proescholdt, and the RISRS Team. "Reducing the Inadvertent Spread of Retracted Science." *Research Integrity and Peer Review* 7 (September 19, 2022): article no. 6. https://doi.org/10.1186/s41073 -022-00125-x.

"Develop a systematic cross-industry approach to ensure the public availability of consistent, standardized, interoperable, and timely information about retractions."

Steffensen, D., C. Mcallister, P. Perrewé, and G. Wang. "'You've Got Mail': A Daily Investigation of Email Demands on Job Tension and Work-Family Conflict." *Journal of Business and Psychology* 37, no. 2 (April 2022): 1–14. https://link .springer.com/article/10.1007/s10869-021-09748-1.

"email can have negative consequences on the job that can spill over into the home."

Tijdink, J., R. Verbeke, and Y. Smulders. "Publication pressure and scientific misconduct in medical scientists." *Journal of Empirical Research on Human Research Ethics* 9, no. 5 (December 2014): 64–71. http://dx.doi.org/10.1177 /1556264614552421.

"significantly associated with a composite scientific misconduct severity score."

University College London. "Social media 'trust' or 'distrust' buttons could reduce spread of misinformation." PhysOrg, June 6, 2023.

"Incentivizing accuracy cut in half the reach of false posts."

Wellcome Trust. *What researchers think about the culture they work in.* January 15, 2020. https://wellcome.org/reports/what-researchers-think -about-research-culture.

Index